How to Identify, Expose & Correct Liberal Media Bias

By Brent H. Baker

with the assistance of
Tim Graham and Steve Kaminski

Media Research Center ■ Alexandria, Virginia

Media Research Center
113 South West Street, Second floor
Alexandria, Virginia 22314

Copyright © 1994 by the Media Research Center

ISBN 0-9627348-2-9

Printed in the United States of America
First Edition, January 1994
Second Edition, November 1996

**MEDIA
RESEARCH
CENTER**®
*Bringing political
balance to the media*

http://www.mediaresearch.org

Table of Contents

About the Media Research Center

Founded in 1987, the Media Research Center (MRC) is dedicated to bringing political balance to the nation's news and entertainment media. The news media must provide equal weight to both sides of an issue, offer the best arguments forwarded by both sides, and give the public the fullest and fairest sense of political debates so that it can decide which side makes the more persuasive case. The MRC works to bring balance by identifying, exposing and correcting media bias.

To identify media bias, MRC staff members comb daily through the nation's most influential newspapers and news magazines. Summaries of all network TV stories are entered into the MRC Media Tracking System, a comprehensive computerized filing system. The MRC is the only organization with a complete tape library of network news and interview shows.

The result of the MRC's work is a mountain of evidence to support charges of bias. The key to the MRC's effectiveness is the ability to prove bias by using scientific studies and, especially, word-for-word quotes from the media. Facts, not rhetoric, prove bias.

To distribute findings to the media, the Washington political community, radio talk show hosts, newspaper columnists, the the public and MRC members, the MRC publishes newsletters, books and special reports. The MRC also maintains a web site and sends alerts via e-mail.

Newsletters:

■ *MediaWatch*, a monthly that reviews news coverage of political and current events by the television networks, major newspapers and three newsweeklies.

■ *MediaNomics*, produced by the MRC's Free Market Project, scrutinizes what the media tell viewers and readers about free enterprise in both entertainment shows and news programs.

■ *Notable Quotables*, published every other week, highlights bias by simply quoting media figures, letting their own words demonstrate their bias. At year end, a panel of 50 media experts selects quotes for the annual *Awards for the Year's Worst Reporting*.

■ *Flash*, the MRC's member's report, keeps members up to date with all of the MRC's activities, special reports and projects to combat liberal media bias. Members get discounts on all MRC publications. To become a member for $20 annually, call 800-MRC-1423.

Books:

■ *And That's the Way It Isn't: A Reference Guide to Media Bias.* In 1990 the MRC published this book containing reprints, summaries and excerpts of 45 scientific studies that prove the media's liberal slant.

■ *Pattern of Deception: The Media's Role in the Clinton Presidency*, a 270-page book by the MRC's Tim Graham published in 1996. It assembles a mountain of evidence proving the national media, especially the television networks, protected and defended Bill Clinton both as a candidate and as President, and promoted his liberal policies, from health care to gun control to the budget battles.

■ *Family Guide to Prime Time Television.* This annual analysis of television shows published by the MRC's Parents Television Council, provides a comprehensive study of prime time fare. The guide offers a brief background and summary of every series' themes, with an evaluation of each show on the basis of suitability for young viewers.

Internet:

■ Web site. In 1996 the MRC created a Web site with text of all of our newsletters and special reports as well as information on how to become a member of the MRC and buy MRC publications. The Web site address: http://www.mediaresearch.org

■ MRC CyberAlert e-mail messages. Whenever bias warrants, the MRC sends an MRC CyberAlert message detailing the tilted coverage. To receive MRC CyberAlerts, send your e-mail address to us at: mrc@mediaresearch.org

The MRC produces a twice-weekly column by MRC Chairman L. Brent Bozell III which is distributed by the Creators Syndicate to newspapers across the country. Special articles from the MRC have appeared in *The Wall Street Journal, Chicago Tribune*, the Cleveland *Plain Dealer, Los Angeles Times* as well as *National Review* magazine.

MRC spokesmen regularly appear on radio talk shows and have appeared on numerous network television programs. The MRC also provides editors and producers with information on conservative positions, suggesting conservative spokesmen to balance liberal views.

But while the MRC has developed a successful system to document, analyze and publicize evidence of liberal bias by the national outlets, the MRC does not cover local markets. Yet most Americans spend as much, if not more, time watching, listening to and reading news from local media outlets. So fighting media bias must begin at home. That's the purpose of this book -- to explain what you, too, can do.

Acknowledgments

The work of many made this book possible. The MRC's team of news media analysts who watch hours of television news everyday, not to mention reading newspapers and magazines, first identified as biased the examples of bias detailed in Chapter One.

These analysts, Andy Gabron, Mark Honig, Kristin Johnson and Mark Rogers, also suggested improvements to make the writing clearer. A special note of thanks goes to Tom Johnson, the MRC's in-house stylistic expert who carefully reviewed each page, though any remaining errors are my responsibility.

In writing the Identify chapter, I largely followed the advice and suggestions of Tim Graham, Associate Editor of *MediaWatch*. He also helped me find the right words to define and describe different types of bias. In addition, most of the studies cited in the Expose chapter were originally researched and written by him.

For the Correct chapter I relied heavily on Steve Kaminski, a MRC news analyst, who researched and wrote a first draft of the chapter. Steve also helped me typeset and layout this book on our desktop publishing system. Many of the ideas and most of the advice for the Correct chapter came from Greg Mueller, a public relations expert and President of Creative Response Concepts. With the assistance of Clay Waters, David Muska put together the list of addresses and names for the appendices.

I also consulted several people to make sure I got my facts straight, specifically: Curt Herge of Herge, Sparks and Christopher reviewed the legal issues discussed in the Expose chapter; Mark Schultz of Special Systems Inc. and Reba Morris of Complete Software Support both provided details on computer equipment; and Mark Thompson of ABR Associates made sure my descriptions of postal permits and rates in the Expose chapter were accurate.

Over the past year I have repeatedly turned to Kathy Ruff for assistance in handling hundreds of administrative details. This book wouldn't have been possible without the work of the MRC's fundraising team led by Richard Kimble, who is assisted by Larry Gourlay.

Others who play an important role in ensuring the MRC runs smoothly each day are Sandy Crawford, head of the entertainment division; Tim Lamer, who runs the MRC's Free Market Project; and Leif Noren, who tracks where all the money goes and oversees subscription acquisition.

Susan Hankoff-Estrella of Cactus Design developed the design ideas for both the interior and cover of this book. Vivian Daniels of Book-Crafters coordinated its printing at the Fredericksburg, Virginia plant.

Great thanks must go to those who have helped guide the MRC on its successful path to becoming an authoritative research and publishing operation: First and foremost, L. Brent Bozell III, Chairman of the Board of Directors, as well as the other Board members -- Burt Pines, William Rusher, Harold Simmons, Leon Weil and Curtin Winsor.

And finally, none of the MRC's work could occur without the contributions of the MRC's financial supporters across the country.

-- Brent H. Baker
January, 1994

Notes on the 2nd Edition

The importance of the Internet has grown dramatically since the first edition was printed in early 1994, so for this edition I've added sections on Web sites and using e-mail. In addition, Web addreses for conservative groups and publications have been added in the appendix.

In the first edition the list in the appendix of news media addresses included the names of editors, bureau chiefs and producers. At many media outlets these postions change frequently, which made this list out of date shortly after its printing. So, for this edition we've dropped the list of specific names and kept the street addresses while adding Web addresses.

Since the first edition, Clay Waters, Jim Forbes, Geoffrey Dickens and Eugene Eliasen have all come aboard as media analysts. Their daily analysis and research are the fuel that drives the MRC. I'm also indebted to MRC intern Joe Alfonsi for helping me track down the Web addresses and otherwise update the appendices. Kathy Ruff, now the MRC's Marketing Director, coordinated the printing of this edition.

The examples cited to illustrate how to identify, expose and correct news bias remain the same as in the 1994 edition of this book. Please remember, however, that while the topics the media distort change with time, the principles and methods suggested to counter the problem remain just as valid.

-- Brent H. Baker
November, 1996

Foreword
"What Can *I* Do?"

When MRC representatives appear on radio talk programs and answer questions from listeners, a frequent question is: How do I fight media bias in my home town? How does an average citizen work for balanced and fair news coverage in the local or state media?

That's what this book is about: taking matters into your own hands.

This book has three major emphases:

■ Identifying bias. What does bias look like? In what forms does bias appear and how do you identify each type? What is the difference between fair, balanced reporting and unfair, biased reporting? What methods can you use to compare and contrast coverage of similar events days or months apart to see if the reporting on one was biased?

■ Exposing bias. How do you prove that bias exists, either to the general public or to the offending journalist himself? How do you distribute evidence of media bias to opinion leaders in your community as well as to favorably disposed talk show hosts and columnists? How do you create a filing system or computer database to track instances of bias? What methodologies should you follow to complete an irrefutable study of media bias? How do you enlist others in your community to join with you to form a group or foundation to combat bias? What equipment will you need to publish a newsletter and to whom should you send it?

■ Correcting bias. How do you deal with the biased journalist -- and how do you get him to consider your arguments? What positive steps can you take to ensure that your views get exposure in the media? How do you write a press release and organize a press conference? How do you bring together conservatives and business leaders with members of the local media? And, if all else fails, how do you use advertiser pressure to correct bias at a particular media outlet?

We'll give you examples of biased reporting, and tell you the difference between unfavorable news and unfair news. We'll explain how you can prove that bias exists so that the guilty reporter or editor might recognize and acknowledge his error. We'll show you how to work with journalists to ensure fair coverage. And we'll give you suggestions for what to do if bias persists despite your efforts to expose and correct it. In addition, appendices at the back of this book direct you to conservative information sources: descriptions and addresses for all major conservative research institutes and foundations, as well as addresses and subscription prices for conservative magazines.

The Media Research Center has refined a sophisticated research and analysis system to document media bias on the national level. In this book we have explained our system and methods to you. This is a how-to manual. We hope that you will use it to help combat bias in the news media where you live, and we hope hundreds of others will do the same in cities and towns across America. Perhaps someday the media will treat conservatives and conservative issues fairly, but until then each of us must do our part.

As you read through this book you'll understand why we put things in the sequence we did. Following this sequence will assure you of the best results, as each step provides the necessary foundation for the next. But you don't have to carry out every step before you can complete a subsequent one. In the second chapter, for instance, you'll learn how to start a newsletter and in the third chapter how to organize a conference on media bias. But you certainly can put together a conference without having first created a newsletter.

As a good citizen, you have an obligation to work to ensure that your side is well-represented in the public debate. You have a duty to fight bias in the news. By following the suggestions in this book -- by providing a conservative contact with the media in your home town -- you can help correct media bias from the grass roots up.

We hope this book will help make you become part of the solution.

-- *L. Brent Bozell III*
Chairman, Media Research Center
December, 1993

Introduction
How the Media See the World

Thomas Jefferson once said that he would prefer newspapers without government to a government without newspapers. Our nation's founders were eager to protect the freedom of the press because they wanted the media to be one of the checks on the excesses of government.

Today the media often promote the excesses of government. The leading newsmagazine in the United States, *Time*, has endorsed a dollar-a-gallon increase in the gas tax, tightening fuel-economy regulations on U.S. automakers, and strict government regulation of industry.

Reporters often blame the lack of enough regulation for a problem. In late 1991, for instance, the *Today* show aired a report about flammable sleepwear. "Why is government abdicating its responsibility on this?" Bryant Gumbel asked the reporter. "Is this another holdover from the Reagan years and the cutbacks?" A nine-part 1991 *Philadelphia Inquirer* series on the 1980s, titled "America: What Went Wrong," carried this headline for part five: "The High Cost of Deregulation: Joblessness, Bankruptcy, Debt."

During the 1992 campaign, ABC's "American Agenda" took aim at Vice President Dan Quayle's Competitiveness Council which was created to reduce burdensome federal regulations. The Quayle council had eight staffers trying to review regulations proposed by federal regulatory agencies with a total of 120,000 employees. But reporter Ned Potter portrayed the Council as the greater threat to the public welfare: "Officials say the Council does more than get specific regulations changed. They say its very presence makes regulators flinch. For example, [EPA] chief William Reilly has lost several battles over the Clean Air Act. And senior EPA officials, who asked us not to use their names, said the effect of the Quayle council on their day-to-day work has been devastating. One official said the council 'intimidates the overall process.' Another said the council 'has a chilling effect. So much that whole areas of environmental protection are dropped because you know the council will not let them through.'"

In story after story, the media blame America's problems on federal spending and taxes that are too low, and praise politicians who favor more of both. In the Spring of 1993, Gumbel asserted: "The nation's cities have been in trouble for a long time, suffering from a variety of problems. Faced with declining levels of assistance from Washington over the last twelve years, long-standing urban problems have been aggravated." About the same time, President Clinton proposed the largest tax increase in American history. *CBS This Morning* co-host Harry Smith said Clinton deserved credit "for at least passing a budget that takes the deficit seriously for the first time."

NBC's Garrick Utley crystallized the mindset of many reporters in an October 1991 *Nightly News* commentary: "American tax rates today are, relatively speaking, low. Repeat, low. About half the top rate in the rest of the industrialized world. Our sales taxes are equally low. Fact: the United States is still a tax bargain, believe it or not."

Indeed, when Bruce Babbitt dropped out of the 1988 race, Peter Jennings ruminated: "When he entered the race nearly a year ago he had the courage to say that as President he would probably have to raise taxes. And he never recovered from his courage." Two years later when President Bush decided to break his pledge and raise taxes, many in the media were gleeful. "Bush never should have voiced his pledge, he should have never made it the focus of his campaign, and he should have backed off it long before he did. But in budget deliberations, as in other walks of life, better late than never," wrote *Time* Senior Writer George Church.

When was the last time you saw a news story that blamed social or economic problems on high taxes, too much regulation, too much welfare, or too much centralized control in Washington? For that matter, when was the last time you saw a story that blamed our problems on the decline of religion and moral values, on judges who were too lenient, or on any policy identified with "liberalism"?

Instead, liberal social policies are praised. When New York City School Chancellor Joseph Fernandez was forced from office by parental outrage over condom distribution and teaching elementary students about homosexuality, ABC's *World News Tonight* honored him as "Person of the Week." Fernandez had approved a curriculum guide which told teachers that "classes should include references to lesbians/gay people in all curricular areas" and encouraged them to teach first graders to "respect" and "appreciate" homosexuals through "creative play, books, visitors..." Jennings told viewers that Fernandez "has certainly helped us understand better what a challenge improving education and understanding really are. Which is why he makes a difference."

When a conservative looks at the major national media, he often sees:

● traditional values mocked;

● prominent and favorable coverage for liberal and radical leaders, while conservatives are ignored or ridiculed;

● conservatives who oppose racial preferences as a reversal of the Civil Rights Act of 1964 lumped with bigots and ex-Nazis like David Duke;

● conservative politicians associated with a "sleaze factor" (no matter what the offense, guilty or innocent), while pursuing liberal scandals is deplored as fighting an "ethics war";

● statistically dubious coverage of the economy based on the reports of liberal, soak-the-rich groups;

● tax cuts, not increases in spending that often far exceed the inflation rate, blamed for budget deficits;

● liberal groups consistently praised and glorified, including pro-abortion activists, environmental extremists and senior citizen groups fighting for untrammeled growth in entitlement spending. Reporters not only praise these groups, they help burnish their credibility by refusing to describe them as liberal.

The news media tend to reflect a certain mindset, a view of the world that differs from the view of most Americans. Because it reflects one viewpoint rather than exploring two or more, it can be (and often is) wrong about the historical impact of current events.

The news media predicted that the Reagan-Kemp tax cuts would cause enormous inflation and reduce government revenue. ABC News White House correspondent Brit Hume recalled in a 1991 *Washington Times* profile: "That was regarded by reporters I knew on Capitol Hill as being out there along with the Bermuda Triangle and getting a telephone call from Elvis." But instead of causing inflation and shrinking federal revenue, Reagan broke the back of inflation and tax revenues grew.

The news media also told us that most of the people behind the Iron Curtain supported their countries' communist governments. CNN Moscow Bureau Chief Stuart Loory wrote a letter to *The Wall Street Journal* in 1983 asserting: "If suddenly, a true, two-party or multi-party system were to be formed in the Soviet Union, the Communist Party would still win in a real free election."

News media bias rarely stems from a conscious effort to misinform the public. Rather, it is rooted in the fact that most of the key decision-makers in the media are liberal, have little contact with conservatives, and make little effort to understand the conservative viewpoint. Journalists can truthfully plead ignorance of conservative opinion and of the facts that support conservative positions, but that is no excuse. It's like saying: I didn't know the gun was loaded.

The now-famous 1980 Lichter-Rothman study of journalists at the top newspapers and TV networks found that, in four presidential elections from 1964 to 1976, support for the Democratic Party ticket never fell below 80 percent.

At the start of the 1992 campaign, then *New Republic* Editor Hendrik Hertzberg traveled to New Hampshire before that state's primary. He discovered little had changed from Lichter's earlier findings:

> "The group of people I'll call The Press -- by which I mean several dozen political journalists of my acquaintance, many of whom the Buchanan Administration may someday round up on suspicion of having Democratic or even liberal sympathies -- was of one mind as the season's first primary campaign shuddered toward its finish. I asked each of them, one after another, this question: If you were a New Hampshire Democrat, whom would you vote for? The answer was always the same; and the answer was always Clinton. In this group, in my experience, such unanimity is unprecedented....
>
> "Almost none is due to calculations about Clinton being 'electable'....and none at all is due to belief in Clinton's denials in the Flowers business, because no one believes these denials. No, the real reason members of The Press like Clinton is simple, and surprisingly uncynical: they think he would make a very good, perhaps a great, President. Several told me they were convinced that Clinton is the most talented presidential candidate they have ever encountered, JFK included."

The American Society of Newspaper Editors completed a study in 1989 of 1,200 newsroom employees at 72 newspapers. Sixty-two percent identified themselves as "liberal/Democrat" or leaning in that direction, while only 22 percent identified themselves as "conservative/Republican" or leaning that way.

Conservative critics have won the first round in the debate over media bias: By the late 1980s many reporters began to concede that they are primarily liberal. But they argue that a reporter's personal opinions do not matter because, as a professional journalist, he will report what he sees without letting his opinions affect his judgment. During the 1992 campaign, for instance, *Newsweek* reporter Jonathan Alter asserted on CNN's *Crossfire*: "I think one would be lying to say that most reporters are not more liberal than most Americans. You're quite right about that. But they will go for a good story before an ideological story 99 times out of 100."

A few years ago then *New Republic* Senior Editor Fred Barnes wrote:

"In trying to scotch the idea of liberal bias in news coverage, defenders of the press rely on precisely the sort of argument they would reject if made by others. The argument...goes like this: even if most journalists are liberal, their professionalism prevents this from influencing their stories. Now, what if a judicial nominee said he was a racist but that this wouldn't affect his view on civil rights cases?...Who'd buy such an argument? Not the press."

In fact, every reporter's stories are influenced by how he views the world. Being a journalist is not like being a surveillance camera at a bank, faithfully recording every scene for future playback. Journalists make subjective decisions every minute of their professional lives; they must choose what to cover and what not to cover, who is credible and who is not, which quote to use in a story and which one not to use, and even who is a hero and who is a villain.

The public now faces a homogeneous media that share a liberal outlook on the news. Most national news originates from a small list of sources: *The New York Times, The Washington Post*, the *Los Angeles Times, The Wall Street Journal*, Associated Press and other wire services, the three broadcast networks, and CNN.

These are the main sources for the rest of the country, even for "conservative" newspapers. Consider the case of *The Dallas Morning News*. Because of the positions on its editorial page, the *News* is considered "conservative" -- yet much of its national news comes straight from the New York Times News Service or the Los Angeles Times-Washington Post News Service, both of which distribute stories from those papers to newsrooms across the country.

Many large newspapers are owned by a single large newspaper company, such as Knight-Ridder, which owns dozens of newspapers, including *The Philadelphia Inquirer, Miami Herald, San Jose Mercury News* and *Detroit Free Press*. Gannett and Newhouse are two other large multi-newspaper owners, commonly called "chains." These companies operate large Washington bureaus that offer news stories from a perspective often little different than *The Washington Post* or *New York Times*.

Most non-group-owned newspapers can't afford a Washington bureau, so for news from Washington they rely entirely on the national news services and wires. Even those that do have a Washington bureau, still rely heavily upon the news services. They have one or two reporters in the nation's capital to follow hometown politicians, but the paper turns to the wires for all the national and international developments.

Often, though, the influence is indirect. Every morning network producers, reporters, and wire service editors read *The New York Times* and *The Washington Post* and decide what is important. Every night, newspaper editors watch the network newscasts to help them figure out what the country is watching. Once one of the top media organizations decides a story is worth reporting, the others often follow in lockstep.

The pattern extends to local broadcast markets. Radio and television station assignment editors and news writers monitor the Associated Press Broadcast Service all day long. When the television station news department holds its morning meeting to determine what national news they want to make time for on that night's news, what influences them? The local paper they just read and the morning network show they just watched. And the local paper may very well have run the New York Times News Service story on the budget battle in the U.S. Senate.

Still, not all bias comes from the top down. Bias is often a problem even at the level of a small-town weekly newspaper or a tiny AM radio station, and even on stories that are purely local.

When a journalist covers a mayor, a state senator, or a governor, he usually forms an opinion of that officeholder (if he didn't already have one). That sort of bias is just as likely at the state or local level than at the national level, because a local or state-level journalist quickly develops a working relationship -- whether friendly or antagonistic -- with an officeholder. If the journalist either likes the politician strongly or dislikes him strongly, that bias can be reflected in his reporting.

Journalists are only human. Who can blame them for having a strong opinion about someone they cover? The term "conspiracy" is not a correct description for what happens in the media; journalists don't meet secretly to plot how to slant the news. But often, everyday pack journalism results in an unconscious collusion that taints news coverage and allows a fair hearing to only one side of the debate. When that happens, the truth suffers.

On the hopeful side, there are as many conservative as liberal syndicated newspaper columnists. Similarly, while plenty of radio talk show hosts are liberal, some of the most successful, most notably Rush Limbaugh, are conservative. Why? Because so many Americans are tired of the bias they get on the newspaper's front page that they flip to the op-ed page for the perspective offered by a conservative columnist. So many people are turned off by Dan Rather's slanted re-cap of the day's news that they turn on a radio talk show for another point of view.

Does this mean the major newspapers and networks are becoming irrelevant, so there's no point in fighting media bias? No, columnists and talk show hosts offer opinion and analysis. The major national news outlets are still the most influential news sources for the vast majority of people, especially for those who do not follow politics closely. They still set the agenda and sway political campaigns. Until their bias is identified, exposed, and corrected, conservatives will continue to face an uneven playing field, a surface tilted to the left by the dominant media outlets.

But the rise of conservative columnists and talk show hosts does show that a significant number of Americans share your frustration with the biased media. That means you won't be talking to an empty room. Follow the instructions in this book, and you'll soon come across plenty of fellow citizens who are as upset with the media as are you. You'll learn how to channel this frustration into positive group action and how to use talk show hosts and columnists to tell the public about bias.

First, however, you must learn how to identify and prove that a story or overall coverage of an issue is biased. That's the subject of Chapter One.

IDENTIFY

It is not easy to define bias. As Justice Potter Stewart once said of pornography, "I know it when I see it," yet the law requires some sort of definition. To be effective in the fight against bias, you must have a reasonably clear idea of what to look for. There are certain patterns, both on-the-job and off-the-job, that often occur among liberal journalists.

A successful monitor of media bias must recognize a crucial point: that off-the-job behavior (say, wearing a "Clinton for President" button) may warn of potential bias, but it is not evidence of bias unless bias appears in a journalist's work. For example, Jeff Greenfield of ABC News has a liberal background as a former aide to John Lindsay and Robert Kennedy, yet he usually gives fair treatment to conservative leaders and ideas. NBC's Tim Russert, who once worked for liberal New York Governor Mario Cuomo, often challenges guests on *Meet the Press* with questions a conservative might ask. In fact, their political experience often means that they have a better understanding of conservative positions than many of their colleagues.

Many liberal journalists are dedicated enough to their profession to see both sides of a given issue, and you would only alienate them by falsely accusing them of bias. You should consider a journalist's off-the-job liberalism as a warning sign of bias, but your critique will be effective only if you can prove that bias shows up in his news stories as well.

In this chapter you will learn:

■ How to determine the personal views of reporters

■ What types of bias reporters regularly commit

■ How to analyze stories and reporting patterns to determine if they are biased

Section One:
Determining a Journalist's Political Viewpoint

By "off-the-job liberalism," we refer to behavior in which a journalist expresses his affiliation with or personal support for liberal politicians, groups, and causes. There are three ways to determine a journalist's personal political views: 1) The revolving door; 2) Self-identification; 3) Surveying reporters.

❶ **The revolving door between liberal politicians or organizations and the media.**

When a journalist switches jobs to work for a politician, political group or campaign, or when someone working for a politician or a campaign moves into a media job, he or she has gone through the "revolving door." Most of the time when members of the media elite go to work in politics, their candidates or causes are liberal or Democratic. Conversely, the vast majority of former political activists currently working in the media have professional ties to liberals and Democrats. MRC keeps track of these connections, and the total as of late 1993 stood at 275 liberals/Democrats compared to 75 conservatives/Republicans.

Some of those who passed through the "Revolving Door" are well-known or hold powerful positions, such as CNN President Tom Johnson, who used to work for Lyndon Johnson and *NBC Nightly News* Executive Producer Jeff Gralnick, who was once George McGovern's Press Secretary. Others are less well-known and less powerful, but they still are part of the news process. Clara Bingham, for instance, covered the White House for *Newsweek* during the Bush Administration. Previously, she had served as Press Secretary in Tennessee for the 1988 Dukakis presidential campaign. *Time* magazine assigned Margaret Carlson to cover First Lady Hillary Rodham Clinton, but few readers realized that Carlson held a Carter Administration job -- Special Assistant to the Chairman of the Consumer Product Safety Commission.

Some people go the other way. Just after President Clinton took office, several important members of the Washington press corps who had spent their careers in journalism, accepted jobs in his administration. ABC News Washington correspondent Kathleen deLaski joined the Defense Department as chief public affairs officer. Strobe Talbott, Washington Bureau Chief for *Time* magazine for several years, became an Ambassador-at-Large to the republics of the former Soviet Union. NBC News correspondent Carl Stern, who covered the Supreme Court and Justice Department for 26 years, jumped to the Justice Department as Director of Public Affairs under Attorney General Janet Reno.

Some go back and forth. Douglas Bennet worked for a couple of Democratic senators and then became Director of the Agency for International Development (AID) under President Carter. After Carter's loss, Bennet assumed the presidency of National Public Radio. But as soon as the Democrats regained the White House, Bennet was back in politics. Clinton named him Assistant Secretary of State for intergovernmental organizations.

At the local level, reporters regularly move from covering the mayor or state senator to serving on his staff or handling press relations for his campaign. A small controversy erupted in Boston in 1993 when a *Boston Globe* education reporter accepted a job under a man she had been covering: the chairman of the Boston School Committee. A couple of years before, San Francisco Mayor Frank Jordan hired a *Sacramento Bee* reporter as his Press Secretary. In fact, almost every Governor and Mayor has at least one media veteran in a top staff position.

Similarly, virtually every Senator and U.S. Representative employs former reporters in his or her Capitol Hill office. Most commonly, a Congressman will choose a Press Secretary from the staff of a newspaper in his district. Sometimes, they select a TV reporter. Shortly after his 1990 election, freshman Senator Paul Wellstone chose a Minneapolis television reporter as Press Secretary.

You should be interested in the past political connections of anyone with control over how the news is covered by a particular station, newspaper or magazine. That means reporters, editors, news directors and producers are all of interest, but the fact that an advertising salesman for a television station used to work for an elected official is not relevant.

Tracking these moves at the local level requires keeping records of what you learn about journalists, and sometimes a little detective work. If you think a reporter has a left-wing agenda, check to see if he is listed in such books as Who's Who in American Politics or a old Congressional Staff Directory. Did he ever live in Washington, D.C., and if so, for whom did he work? At your local library, check the computerized InfoTrac, the *Reader's Guide to Periodical Literature*, and other indexes for the by-line of local journalists. Magazines usually give a one sentence description of the author. If you find an article from a few years earlier, you'll learn what job he had at that time, or he might be identified as a "former legislative assistant to Senator Smith."

If you know a lawyer, see if you can arrange to use the law firm's Lexis/Nexis computer. The Nexis part of the service is a huge on-line database that includes every sentence of several dozen newspapers, magazines and wire services going back five to ten years. It's operated by Mead Data Central in Dayton, Ohio. Nexis is expensive -- about $30 an hour and $15 per search -- but it's well worth it. You can enter the name of a person, say John Jones, and the Nexis computer will find every mention of him. You may find that five years earlier *The Washington Post* and *Houston Chronicle* quoted John Jones in his capacity as communication director for a Democratic Congressman.

One caution: the more common the name, the more mentions you will find of different people with the same name. The John Jones working at your local CBS affiliate may not be the same John Jones who worked for the Democratic Congressman. So, unless you find an article that says "John Jones resigned today from Congressman Brown's office to join WMRC-TV as a political producer," be cautious. Call the particular person, his boss, or the media outlet's public relations representative to confirm the information. If they are not cooperative, try calling the Congressman's office to ask if they know where John Jones is now working.

Nexis Searching Tips:

✔ With a common name, you may find dozens of irrelevant mentions -- because someone by that name is or was on a high school sports team or serves as spokesman for a police department. To cut down on the number of stories found, make use of an important Nexis feature. Nexis lets you look for all instances when a name appears within so many words of another word or name. So, if you know John Jones now works for WMRC-TV and you think he might have once worked for Senator Mark Smith, search for John Jones "within 50 words of WMRC or Smith."

In Nexis computer terminology, that search would be entered as "John Jones w/50 WMRC or Smith." Usually when someone changes jobs a newspaper article will mention his past positions, so at the very least this search will call up all stories from when WMRC-TV hired Jones two years ago. If he did once toil for Senator Smith, you'll get those stories too. If not, then you're back to scanning through every story mentioning that name.

✔ On the other hand, if you search for "John Jones" and a newspaper article identified him as "John S. Jones," then your search will not find that story. So, use the "within" feature to initially search for "Jones within two words of John." If you scan through the stories Nexis finds, and you see a reference to John Jones that you are trying to track down with a middle initial of "S" then you can do another search, such as "John Jones or John S. Jones w/50 WMRC or Smith." Also follow this principle if you're not sure of the first name; e.g. David vs. Dave or Robert vs. Bob. Search for "Jones w/2 Robert or Bob."

✔ If you are trying to find the employment history of a woman, remember her name may have changed upon marriage. The Barbara Martin-Jones of today was obviously Barbara Martin at one time. If she goes by Barbara Jones today and you know she is married, look carefully at the very oldest articles you find to see any mention of her maiden name.

In addition to Nexis, several other companies operate database systems. Dow Jones, the company that publishes *The Wall Street Journal*, runs the Dow Jones Retrieval Service. The Knight-Ridder newspaper chain owns a service called Dialog which includes the content of all major Knight-Ridder newspapers. Both offer a mixture of other publications, but are not as complete as Nexis.

And don't forget the most obvious source for information on a journalist: the newspaper or broadcast station where he works. If the person holds an on-air or important off-air position at a television station, or is a high-ranking newspaper editor, there is a good chance they will provide you with a biography if you simply ask for it. But don't assume the biography is complete. Sometimes they don't mention political jobs, so make sure there are no gaps in their listed employment history.

Another valuable source: the knowledge and memory of those plugged-in to the political establishment for years. Talk to a politically connected lawyer you might know, a current or retired elected official, or even the barber near the county courthouse or city hall. Ask them if they know of any reporters who once worked for a politician or in a campaign; or of any current political aides who once toiled as journalists.

The best way to track the revolving door process is to make it an ongoing concern. Carefully read all articles about someone mulling over running for a particular office, as well as stories about their actual announcement. These stories will usually identify the potential or actual candidate's top aides, or at least quote a "spokesman." See if any are described as "a former reporter," "media veteran," or if you simply recognize the name as a former member of the media.

Virtually every daily newspaper of any substantial size run political gossip columns. Often they go by names like "Political Notes," "Capital Notes," "From Under the State House Dome" or "Pols and Politics." Most also carry a "People" or "Names and Faces in the News" type column which may focus on celebrity news, but also often includes news about local celebrities and who attended last night's charity party.

On the television page most newspapers devote a regular space to news from the local stations, often the topic of the latest 6pm news series, but sometimes you'll learn of the comings and goings of television station staffers. Read all of these sections to see who has joined the mayor's staff or been promoted to news director. If you live in a big city, check the gossip and people pages of your city magazine; i.e.: *Chicago, Boston, Seattle, Atlanta,* etc.

Cut out any articles that mention the names of those who joined the staff of a politician and put them in a file. Months or years later you may recognize their name when you see that they've become the NBC affiliate's political producer. The same goes for mentions of off-air television or radio station news department staffers. Since you won't be as familiar with these names as you will be with those of the on-air stars, saving them will help you recognize them later.

❷ Self-identification.

When they believe they are addressing a like-minded audience, or when they let down their guard during an interview, journalists often admit their liberal tendencies. At a 1988 banquet sponsored by Norman Lear's People for the American Way, Walter Cronkite declared that "I know liberalism isn't dead in this country. It simply has, temporarily we hope, lost its voice....We know that unilateral action in Grenada and Tripoli was wrong. We know that Star Wars means uncontrollable escalation of the arms race. We know that no one should tell a woman she has to bear an unwanted child....God Almighty, we've got to shout these truths in which we believe from the rooftops."

Jane Pauley once admitted to *USA Today* that "I'm a Jesse [Jackson] fan." In a *Playboy* magazine interview Bryant Gumbel said that if Mario Cuomo ran for President he "would certainly get my vote." Tom Brokaw, in a friendly interview with the left-wing magazine *Mother Jones*, said Ronald Reagan's values were "Pretty simplistic. Pretty old-fashioned. And I don't think they have much application to what's currently wrong or troubling a lot of people....he's lived in this fantasy land for so long." Brokaw also said, "I thought from the outset that his 'supply side' [theory] was a disaster. I knew of no one who felt that it was going to work, outside of zealots." During the 1992 Democratic convention, Bill Moyers, of CBS and PBS fame, declared: "It's worth dying prematurely so you can hear somebody else do your eulogy if that somebody is Mario Cuomo."

Always be on the lookout for these kinds of admissions. You never know where they will appear. In a July 1993 interview in *Good House-keeping*, hardly a news-oriented magazine, UPI White House reporter Helen Thomas praised Jimmy Carter, but of Ronald Reagan she remarked: "To my mind, a President should care about all people, and he didn't, which is why I will always feel Reagan lacked soul."

Read all profiles and interviews with members of the local media that appear in area newspapers and magazines. That means you should start getting your city/regional magazine (*Los Angeles*, *Down East*, *Texas Monthly*, etc.), plus any alternative paper that might exist (*The Phoenix* in Boston, *LA Weekly* in Los Angeles, *City Paper* in Baltimore and Washington, *The Twin Cities Reader* in Minneapolis-St. Paul, *New Times* in Phoenix and the *Riverfront Times* in St Louis, etc.).

Watch and record your local *McLaughlin Group* type show whenever a news person is a panelist. Eleanor Clift regularly issues liberal pronouncements on *The McLaughlin Group*, as does Sam Donaldson on *This Week with David Brinkley*. Don't overlook cable shows. A growing list of metro areas now have a local 24 hour a day cable news channel (Long Island's News Channel 12, the Orange County News Channel, New England Cable News, NewsChannel 8 in Washington D.C., etc.) Most fill time with daily or weekend talk/interview shows.

Don't ignore former reporters. Documenting their liberal views will help to show the ideology of those employed by a particular media outlet. And former reporters often go back into journalism at a later date. If one does, you'll have an illuminating quote or two to pull out.

If the Kiwanis Club or Chamber of Commerce is having a reporter or newspaper editor speak, go to hear the address. Check to see if a videotape of the address or panel discussion will be shown by your local cable access channel. Ask if the sponsor will be able to provide an audio tape. (At a big convention, often audio tapes will be sold for a relatively small fee at a booth set up by a convention services company.) If all else fails, you can bring a small tape recorder and record the event yourself. As long as no one specifically asks you to not do any recording, there is nothing wrong with making a tape. Of course, the smaller and less obtrusive the recorder the better.

If a media figure will address a liberal group, try to attend. If it's a public event, such as an environmental group's press conference announcing a new effort to get an environmental curriculum into junior high schools, you shouldn't have any problem getting into the room.

On the national level, the MRC caught this from ABC News reporter George Strait introducing Democratic Secretary of Health and Human Services Donna Shalala at a National Minority AIDS Council announcement ceremony shown by C-SPAN:

> "She [Shalala] restores a tradition of excellence at the Department of Health and Human Services. That agency has been headed by some of America's truly great human beings: Joe Califano, Pat Harris, and now Donna Shalala. She is an academic who is connected with the real needs of people. When it comes to being an effective advocate for those who have no voice, she has few equals, perhaps only one -- the other half of the dynamic duo here in Washington, that is the duo of Donna Shalala and Hillary Rodham Clinton."

If it's a fundraiser for major donors, you'll have to rely on media reports or information provided by the group in question. The quote from Walter Cronkite at the beginning of this section appeared in *Newsweek*. The liberal group might place a partial transcript in their newsletter or in a post-event letter to supporters. To get these materials, donate money to the major local liberal groups. A gift of $20 or $25 should get you on their mailing list. Of course, you'll have to do this well in advance.

When a reporter makes a comment that betrays his true prejudices, in whatever forum, make a record of it. Keep the tape or photocopy the article. You never know how it might be useful later in proving his prejudice. This is perfect material for an article in the newsletter you'll learn how to create in the next chapter. In producing *Notable Quotables*, the MRC has found these kinds of quotes provide some of our most persuasive material.

❸ **Surveying Reporters.**

Members of the media elite identify themselves as liberals and Democrats far more often than other Americans. On almost all political issues, members of the media are far to the left of other Americans.

A 1982 study of reporters at the nation's 50 largest papers found that, of those who voted in 1980, only one-quarter voted for Ronald Reagan.

A 1990 study of 50 editors, columnists, and reporters at *The Washington Post* found that, of those who lived in areas where voter registration is by party, only one was registered as a Republican, and the lone "Republican" said he and his wife split in party registration so they could get campaign literature from both sides.

In late 1992 a survey of 1,400 journalists working at newspapers of all sizes across the country found 44 percent consider themselves Democrats, up from 38 percent in 1983 and 35 percent in 1971. In contrast, the Freedom Forum-sponsored poll by Indiana University professors David Weaver and G. Cleveland Wilhoit found the number of Republican reporters fell from 25 percent in 1971 to 16 percent in 1992. Compared to the general population, that makes journalists five to ten percentage points more likely to be Democrats and 10 to 15 points less likely to be Republicans.

Those who saw the results of a late 1995 poll of 139 Washington bureau chiefs and congressional reporters could have forecast the media's pro-Clinton and anti-Dole tilt in the 1996 campaign. The Roper Center survey taken for the Freedom Forum determined that 89 percent voted for Bill Clinton in 1992, but just seven percent for George Bush. That's a 12-to-1 ratio for an election in which fewer than half of the electorate pulled the lever for Clinton.

To document the views and backgrounds of those staffing your local media outlets, you may want to consider conducting a survey of journalists' attitudes and opinions. Ask an academic such as a political science or journalism professor to conduct a scientific survey of the political attitudes of local journalists. Utilizing the services of college students, he may be able to conduct such a survey at no cost to you, as part of his normal research activities. (In the next chapter, you'll learn how to set up a group or foundation to combat bias. If at that point you have sufficient financial resources, you can hire a polling firm to do the survey. To find such a firm, talk to the campaign managers for political candidates.)

These surveys are conducted in the same way as opinion surveys of any group. A random sample is selected from the members of the group being studied, which should include reporters, editors, producers, publishers, etc.

When Professor S. Robert Lichter and his colleagues released their first-of-its-kind survey of the media elite in 1981, they probably had no idea that they would transform the debate over media bias. But when some of their earliest studies showed that members of the "media elite" (key personnel at the nation's top media outlets) voted overwhelmingly for George McGovern and Jimmy Carter, 90 percent favored abortion, 80 percent believed in affirmative action programs, and most thought the U.S. caused Third World poverty, charges of liberal media bias began to be taken seriously for the first time.

They asked questions like the following, which in some cases are paraphrased:

● Who did you vote for in 1972 -- Nixon or McGovern? ...in 1976, Ford or Carter?

● Do you consider yourself liberal, moderate, or conservative?

● Do you consider yourself a Democrat, a Republican, or an independent?

Regarding the following statements, do you agree, agree strongly, disagree, or disagree strongly, or do you have no opinion?

● The government should require "affirmative action" quotas for the hiring of women and minorities.

● A woman has a right to an abortion.

● Less regulation of business would serve the national interest.

● The U.S. exploits the Third World, causing poverty.

● Voluntary prayer should be allowed in public schools.

● There should be stricter controls on the private ownership of handguns.

On a scale of zero to 100, with zero meaning "very unfavorable" and 100 meaning "very favorable," rate the following persons:

● Ronald Reagan

● Margaret Thatcher

● Fidel Castro

● The Sandinistas

Which of the following would you consider a reliable source for information on welfare reform?

● Liberals

● Conservatives

● Federal regulatory agencies

● State and local officials

• When you need information on [an issue], whom do you turn to as an "expert"?

Of course, you should update these questions and adapt them to your local political scene. Ask for whom they voted in some recent elections and/or whether they have a favorable or unfavorable opinion of local officials. Don't ask about an upcoming election, just past ones. Inquire about their views of current issues, but again, not something being currently debated. That will trigger a journalist's instinctive "I'm an impartial observer" or "I don't comment upon a topic I'm covering" reaction. Instead, ask about issues in more general terms. Ask "Do you believe the rich pay too much or too little in taxes?" not "Do you favor or oppose Governor Smith's proposal to raise income taxes on the wealthy to provide more education aid to poorer communities?"

Ask "Is parental opposition to increased sex education in schools given too much or too little weight by school officials?" not "Do you favor or oppose the school superintendent's wish to distribute condoms to high schoolers?"

You can also ask about national and international topics, since those will serve just as well to discover their general political orientation.

Two important notes. First, some reporters may not be willing to take part in a poll about their personal political views. Since several national surveys have demonstrated the media are full of liberals, a journalist may suspect that the survey is meant to prove the same once again. So he may not wish to help you prove a point he does not want proven. But you'll never know if this is a problem until you try.

Second, surveys and polls must remain confidential. You can't call a reporter, tell him you are conducting a survey, take down his answers and then write about how "John Smith" responded. A scientific survey is conducted by making random calls to a certain percentage of people. The survey taker should not know the name of the person he is polling. In this case, a potential sample group would be narrowed to the staff of certain media outlets.

To determine the demographics of those surveyed (income, title, type of employer, etc) such questions would be included. Then you could say that "In a survey of 78 members of the Smithtown metro area media, 22 percent employed by radio stations, 55 percent by newspapers and 33 percent by television stations, 68 percent opposed...." And, "The poll, which included eight TV news producers and five on-air reporters, found...."

Section Two:

Types of Bias: Descriptions and Examples of Each

Sometimes liberal bias reflects a conscious choice by the reporter or editor. Sometimes it stems from mere laziness; it can take a lot of work to produce balanced news stories on a consistent basis. And a reporter under deadline pressure may just not understand the conservative viewpoint well enough to explain it in his story. So if the conservative expert he called doesn't call back in time, that perspective won't make it into the story.

But none of these are valid excuses. A reporter's job is to present a balanced story. (Of course, the reporter who tries but fails because he's just so rushed and can't get a conservative to comment deserves more understanding from you than the reporter who never bothers to call a conservative and regularly writes or broadcasts biased stories.)

As you read, listen and watch news stories you probably already notice stories that you think are biased. To see if they really are biased, you need to determine if the story falls into at least one of several forms in which bias occurs:

- Bias by commission
- Bias by omission
- Bias by story selection
- Bias by placement
- Bias by the selection of sources
- Bias by spin
- Bias by labeling
- Bias by policy endorsement or condemnation

The following pages provide descriptions and actual examples to illustrate each type of bias. Most come from national news outlets, so read them to gain an understanding of bias that can guide you as you read, watch and listen to local news sources.

Bias by commission:

A pattern of passing along assumptions or errors that tend to support a left-wing or liberal view.

This is the most common form of bias. Within the space or time limit constraining them, reporters are supposed to provide roughly equal time to presenting the best arguments of both sides of an issue. If liberals say "A" and conservatives "B," then the story should summarize both perspectives. For example, liberals cite government statistics to show that during the 1980s the rich got tax breaks while the middle class and poor paid more taxes. Conservatives, on the other hand, contend federal figures demonstrate that the rich paid more of federal tax receipts as everyone else paid less. Who's correct? A properly done story would recite the figures and analysis behind both views, so that a news consumer could make up his own mind about which perspective makes more sense.

If the reporter presents only one perspective or passes along only the "facts" espoused by liberals without any acknowledgement that conservatives disagree, then he has committed bias by commission.

Some examples of "facts" espoused by liberals and passed on by the media that conservatives know don't stand up to scrutiny: that the Reagan and Bush Administrations cut funding for social programs (when in fact social spending rose dramatically in both administrations); that the rich grew richer and the poor grew poorer during the Reagan years (when all income groups grew richer); and that there are three million homeless people in the United States (when every reputable study places the number well under one million). Still, that doesn't dissuade reporters. Just after Christmas 1992, on the *CBS Evening News*, reporter John Roberts found "more than three million homeless in America."

In May 1993, CBS reporter Terence Smith charged: "In 1989, after nearly a decade of federal cutbacks for immunizations, the previously successful measles vaccination program broke down." A quick check by the MRC with the Centers for Disease Control revealed that spending actually rose from $32 million in 1980 to $186 million in 1990, and then up to $257 million in 1992. Some "cutbacks."

On both the local and national level reporters regularly refer to "cuts" when in fact the program was not cut -- its rate of increase was reduced. If a conservative legislator proposes increasing welfare spending 5 percent instead of the planned 7 percent, (while inflation is predicted to hold at 4 percent), that's a one percent real increase. But reporters often call it a "cut."

Why? As explained in a *Washington Post* opinion piece by James Glassman, because the federal government and many states calculate "budget cuts from an imaginary number called the baseline." The baseline is figured by factoring in population increase and other "technical" measures. A program could cost $50 billion one year while baseline adjustments mean it will take $53 billion the next year to reach the same percent of the population. So if the budget for that program jumps from $50 to $52 billion, politicians will consider that a $1 billion "cut."

The summer of 1993 debate over Clinton's budget also showed how reporters, by choosing the interpretation of one side, commit bias by commission. At the time, Republicans claimed the plan had far more taxes than spending cuts while Democrats insisted the ratio was one-to-one. Some reporters endorsed the Democratic view. A *USA Today* reporter asserted Clinton's plan had "slightly more spending cuts than tax increases." A CNN anchor reported "the economic package now in the Senate reduces the federal deficit by more than $500 billion dollars with spending cuts and $249 billion in tax increases," meaning a one-to-one ratio.

In a balanced story, the reporters would have said something like: "Democrats claim the deficit package consists of an equal amount of spending cuts and tax increases, while Republicans argue many of the cuts are phony so that there are three dollars in tax hikes for every one dollar in real cuts." By portraying one view as the correct one, the reporters committed bias by commission.

A few months before the Clinton Administration released its health care reform plan, ABC's *World News Tonight* aired a piece summarizing the "managed care" option favored by Hillary Clinton. At one point, reporter Bob Zelnick asserted: "Unlike Mrs. Clinton's plan, under single-payer, employers would no longer have to provide coverage for their employees. There would be no need for private insurance companies, a change studies show could save between 35 and 70 billion dollars a year in paperwork and other administrative costs."

Note that Zelnick didn't say "studies from liberal groups" or "studies from those favoring additional government regulation." He said "studies show," as if their conclusions were beyond dispute. If Zelnick had followed that statement with the conservative view, saying "But other studies from those who think too much government regulation is already a problem show that a single-payer system will cost billions more for increased bureaucratic red tape," then he would have done a balanced story.

➡ Documenting bias by commission often requires research. Unfortunately, while reputable books and studies include citations or footnotes, the media (especially television reporters) often ask you simply to believe them. So when reporters cite a specific group or study, try to get a copy of the original report. Most of the time you'll recognize bias by commission because the reporter will have presented only the liberal slant on an issue you know has another side. If you're not sure, find an expert in the field, and ask him if a story's statistics ring true. The offices of conservative state legislators are excellent sources to consult on any issue facing state lawmakers. If they don't know, try a conservative group that specializes in the area in question, or a conservative-leaning professor at a local college.

Bias by omission:

Ignoring facts that tend to disprove liberal or left-wing claims, or that support conservative beliefs.

To catch this kind of bias you'll have to be knowledgeable about the particular subject. If you know the various points of view on an issue, then you'll recognize when one side is left out. Bias by omission can occur either within a story, or over the long term as a particular news outlet reports one set of events, but not another.

At an early 1992 media conference, CBS reporter Betsy Aaron warned about bias by omission: "The largest opinion is what we leave out. I mean, it sounds simplistic, but I always say worry about what you're not seeing. What you are seeing you can really criticize because you're smart and you have opinions. But if we don't tell you anything, and we leave whole areas uncovered, that's the danger."

An example of bias by omission within a story at both the local and national level can be found in pieces on education spending. The reporter will refer to the need for increased spending to improve test scores, but omit any mention of the fact that many school systems that spend less get better student test scores than those which spend more.

"The White House balks at any federal bailout of poor school districts," reporter Fred Briggs claimed on *NBC Nightly News* one evening during the Bush Administration. "It says it's up to the states, to the districts to do it. Critics say that's passing the buck." Holyoke, Massachusetts needs a tax increase, he reported. "Voters in Holyoke are being asked to raise taxes today, something they refused to do twice in the past year....It's one of the poorest school districts in the state."

What did Briggs omit? "School administrators stubbornly maintained special programs for poverty-stricken and disruptive students while cutting back programs for the majority of children," wrote *Wall Street Journal* reporter William Bulkeley in a story about the same time. "Some voters are angry at school administrators they consider uncommunicative and wasteful." In addition, in the Heritage Foundation's quarterly magazine *Policy Review*, writer Patricia Summerside spotlighted South Dakota, ranked 51st in teacher salary and 43rd in spending per pupil: "South Dakota's 1988 ACT scores rank fifth among the 28 states that take the test. Its high school graduation rate ranks second."

Looking to liberal politicians as role models while ignoring the successes of those who implemented conservative policies is also fairly common. Shortly after President Clinton took office, *NBC Nightly News* anchor Tom Brokaw introduced a report on governors "who have raised taxes, cut programs, and yet politically survived." Reporter Bob Herbert referred to "tough economic medicine," including tax hikes by New Jersey Governor Jim Florio, Connecticut Governor Lowell Weicker and California Governor Pete Wilson. Preceding soundbites from Weicker, Wilson, Florio, and Florida Governor Lawton Chiles on the merits of taxation, he insisted "the governors say Clinton should stick to his guns."

Herbert omitted any mention of governors who balanced budgets by cutting spending, not raising taxes, such as John Engler of Michigan and Bill Weld of Massachusetts.

Shortly after gays in the military became a hot news story, coverage of crime committed against and by gays showed how bias by omission can skew public perception. Specifically, when U.S. Navy Airman Terry Helvey confessed to beating fellow sailor Allen Schindler to death, the case received national coverage. A heterosexual had killed a gay man in the middle of the gays in the military debate. All the networks, except NBC, reported Helvey's confession. A few days later, all four networks reported Helvey's life sentence. The major print icons followed suit. *The Washington Post* carried two stories and *The New York Times* ran four consecutive stories.

But where were the media when the violence was committed by gay soldiers? Several weeks later the *Times* carried a thorough story on the sentencing of two Navy homosexuals in Jacksonville, Florida. In separate incidents, the convicted gays had raped shipmates. The *Post* covered both cases in a brief blurb on June 9. The networks, however, ignored the story so those relying upon television for their news never heard about the gay rapes.

When South African revolutionary Nelson Mandela visited America in June 1990, the MRC found that none of the networks mentioned his communist past. None reported that he welcomed to his New York City platform three of the four Puerto Rican terrorists who shot and wounded five U.S. Congressmen in 1954. When Mandela went to Cuba to celebrate the anniversary of the Cuban Revolution with Fidel Castro in July 1991, the networks did no story.

➡ To find instances of bias by omission, keep abreast of the conservative perspective on current issues. See if that perspective is included in stories on a particular event or policy. If it's not, you may have uncovered bias by omission.

Bias by story selection:

A pattern of highlighting news stories that coincide with the agenda of the Left while ignoring stories that coincide with the agenda of the Right.

IDENTIFY

Bias by story selection often occurs when a media outlet decides to do a story on a study released by a liberal group, but ignores studies on the same or similar topics released by conservative groups. During the 1980s newspapers and television stations regularly highlighted studies showing how the rich got tax breaks in the '80s as this or that social problem was caused or exacerbated by "Reagan era budget cuts."

Numerous studies from conservative think tanks, such as the Heritage Foundation and the Cato Institute, showed how the rich paid more taxes, social spending was not cut, and social problems were worsened by a breakdown in values. But those conservative studies were rarely, if ever, reported. In other instances, non-ideological research institutes released studies that supported a conservative contention. The American Association of Fund Raising Counsel, for example, found charitable giving by individuals grew dramatically in the '80s. But when a liberal group issues a study showing how the rich made out or advocating more spending to solve a supposed problem, many in the media consider it newsworthy.

"Everyone knows the rich got richer in the 1980s. Now a new study shows how dramatic the change was," Dan Rather began a brief *CBS Evening News* story a week before the 1992 election. "According to the Economic Policy Institute (EPI), more than half of America's new wealth went to the richest one-half of one percent of families," explained Rather. The next morning on NBC's *Today* show, Margaret Larson promoted the same study, referring to the "non-partisan Economic Policy Institute" whose "independent study" revealed that during the 1980s "the top one-half of one percent of this nation's families received 55 percent of the total increase in wealth. The concentration of wealth is seen as the most extreme since 1929." But EPI is hardly independent. It was founded by Clinton Labor Secretary Robert Reich and Jeff Faux, a former aide to Michael Dukakis.

In fact, the national media are sometimes more impressed with (and less skeptical of) reports by liberal interest groups than government reports. Marianna Spicer-Brooks, Executive Producer of CBS' *Face the Nation*, told a MRC analyst that "studies" from the liberal Children's Defense Fund, which aren't original research, but reworked data from government agencies like the Census Bureau, are more reliable than the Census Bureau itself. She asserted: "This is my own peculiar feeling about the Census Bureau. It has proved itself to be unreliable on a number of various issues, but the Children's Defense Fund has made it their business to check out the statistics. They're specialized."

Here's the complete transcript of a June 1993 story read by anchor Tom Brokaw on *NBC Nightly News*: "Hunger in America. There are some startling facts tonight. A study conducted by the Center on Hunger, Poverty, and Nutrition Research at Tufts University claims 12 million American children are malnourished. This problem is nation-wide, but it is most serious in the American South." A brief story, but one prompted solely by a press release from a liberal group. In fact, close examination of the Tufts report by the MRC found that 12 million were not "malnourished," but hungry sometime during the year.

Claims from liberal environmental groups are given similar credibility. *New York Times* Science Editor Nicholas Wade has conceded that the media often serve as a "passive conduit" for environmental critics. Asked to explain why the media do so many stories on environmental threats that scientists consider minor, Wade told a *Washington Post* reporter: "Often we're just doing our duty in following the activism of environmentalists, who make an issue of radon in houses or abandoned Superfund sites. Then it gets taken up in Congress and we have to cover it."

Contrast the media's treatment of ethical charges against Ed Meese when he was Attorney General and Jim Wright when he was Speaker of the House (and second-in-line for the presidency). The MRC compared the number of stories about Meese in January and February 1988 and stories about Wright between January 1987 and February 1988. The media covered charges against Meese in 17 times as many stories in just one-seventh the time. The nightly newscasts on ABC, NBC, and CBS carried 26 reports of charges against Meese in just two months, compared to zero stories about Wright in 14 months.

As it turned out, none of the charges against Meese were sustained, while the charges against Wright drove him from office in disgrace. Anti-Meese charges were considered news, regardless of whether the charges were justified, but accusations against Wright (mostly by Congressman Newt Gingrich of Georgia) were ignored month after month -- until the liberal group Common Cause joined in the criticism.

When White House Chief of Staff John Sununu was investigated by *The Washington Post* for his extensive government travel habits, the *Post* devoted 27 stories to the supposed scandal. But at the same time,

House Armed Services Committee Chairman Les Aspin had also flown in a lot of government planes, including a flight back from a ski vacation in Colorado. The *Post* did no story on Aspin.

Often, charges made by conservatives are (at least initially) written off as the product of paranoia. Charges made by the Left -- that the Korean airliner shot down by the Soviets in 1983 was on a spy mission, or that the Reagan campaign negotiated to delay the release of the Iranian hostages in 1980 -- are taken seriously, regardless of the strength of the evidence.

Look at how the three networks' responded to the "October Surprise" theory, which suggested that the Reagan campaign bargained with the Iranians to delay the hostage release until after the 1980 election. The networks did 27 evening news stories on the theory in 1991. But when major exposés in *Newsweek* and *The New Republic* challenged the dubious sources behind the theory, the network evening news shows did nothing. (By early 1993, Senate and House reports had thoroughly discredited the October Surprise theory, but the networks failed to look at how they had been used.)

➥ Like bias by omission, to identify bias by story selection you'll need to know the conservative and liberal issue agenda -- the events of concern to the two sides of the political scene. See how much coverage conservative issues get compared to issues on the liberal agenda. If a liberal group puts out a study proving a liberal point, look at how much coverage it got compared to a conservative study issued a few days or weeks earlier. If charges of impropriety are leveled at two politicians of approximately equal power, one liberal and one conservative, compare the amount of coverage given to each.

Bias by placement:

A pattern of placing news stories so as to downplay information supportive of conservative views.

Does a story appear across the top half of the front page, or is it buried back with the obituaries and the horoscopes? News editors exercise great discretion in their placement of stories. The news they consider most important and/or most likely to sell papers goes "above the fold" on the front page, where it can be read as the newspaper sits on the rack. Less important stories go on the bottom half of the first page, on the first page of other sections of the paper, on page two or three, and so on.

Bias by placement can occur with television or radio news -- making a story the lead versus running it 25 minutes into an hour-long newscast. But, it's a lot easier to identify this kind of bias in a newspaper where placing a story on page one versus on the bottom of an inside page makes for a dramatic contrast.

There are limitations on a newspaper editor's discretion, of course. He must fit stories together in an attractive way and place stories around advertising, a job that is like assembling a giant jigsaw puzzle. He must use graphic elements such as charts, graphs, and photos effectively. But as a general rule story placement is a measure of how important the editor considers the story.

In the spring of 1993 *The Washington Post* ran a front page story focusing on a Fairfax County, Virginia Republican Party roast where Oliver North imitated a homosexual calling the White House, complete with lisp. The story focused on how the incident showed Republican "insensitivity" toward a minority group. Condemnation quickly followed, much of it from Virginia Governor Doug Wilder, a Democrat. Yet two months later, *Post* staff writer Donald Baker reported that Wilder donned his own lisp. Responding to a reporter's question concerning his future marital plans, "the Governor [Wilder] feigned a lisp and a limp wrist in replying, 'Oh Don, you shouldn't have.'" While North made Page 1, the *Post* revealed the Wilder incident at the end of Baker's story on page 7 of the Metro section.

One of the most obvious expressions of bias by placement came in *The Washington Post's* coverage of 1989 and 1990 abortion rallies. *Post* ombudsman Richard Harwood took his own paper to task, noting the NOW pro-abortion rally the year before dominated the front page, generating a dozen stories taking up 15 columns of space. But the equally large 1990 pro-life rally received two stories in the Metro section.

Another form of bias by placement is the placement of facts *within* a story. Again, this is a kind of bias that occurs much more in print than broadcast media. A television or radio story lasts anywhere from a few seconds to two minutes, and so only has time for one or two brief soundbites from each side. It really doesn't matter where in the story the two sides are presented, just as long as they are given equal time and weight.

Newspaper stories are usually written in a "pyramid" style -- that is, the most important facts are supposed to appear early in the story, with each paragraph a little less important than the previous paragraph. Newspapers use that style for two reasons: (a) so that editors, editing a story to fit the available space, can cut from the bottom up, and (b) so that the average reader will get the most important facts. Editors know that, the farther down you go in a news story, the fewer readers you have.

Studies have shown that, in the case of the average newspaper reader and the average news story, most people read only the headline. Some read just the first paragraph, some just the first two paragraphs, and some read just to the bottom of the column and don't bother to read the continuation. Very few people read the average story all the way through to the end, especially if it is continued to another section of the paper.

When the liberals at People for the American Way released a report questioning the travel habits of Supreme Court nominee Clarence Thomas, *The Boston Globe* put the story on its front page, but didn't mention People for the American Way until the eighth paragraph, after the story had jumped from page 1 to page 17.

Robert Rector, a poverty expert at the conservative Heritage Foundation in Washington, laughs at his regular "slot" in *Washington Post* news stories on studies released by liberal groups. Rector regularly appears in one of the last paragraphs, which the *Post* then considers balanced. "The income gap between rich and poor widened in the 1980s," began *Washington Post* reporter Spencer Rich in a 1991 news story on the latest study by the Center for Budget and Policy Priorities (CBPP). Rich included several quotes from CBPP chief Robert Greenstein, but he waited until the second-to-last paragraph before letting Rector point out that the source for the CBPP figures, the Congressional Budget Office (CBO), doesn't include $130 billion in non-cash government benefits in its calculations.

In a 1993 story, *Boston Globe* reporter Peter Gosselin explored the possibility that overspending by the federal government is not what caused the huge deficit. The third paragraph of Gosselin's article read: "'On the vast expanse of the domestic budget,' former Reagan budget director, David A. Stockman wrote recently, 'overspending is an absolute myth.'" The next five paragraphs summarized Stockman's arguments, explaining his "myth" that Congress has been "beefing up already bloated bureaucracies, handing out pork-barrel projects, and distributing government benefits as if they were candy."

In the 12th and 13th paragraphs, Gosselin quoted Brookings Institution economist Henry Aaron, who insisted that the public doesn't "have any awareness at all of the fact that most of government has shrunk as a share of GDP."

Not until the 17th paragraph did Gosselin turn to a conservative expert: "'He must have drunk too much Beltway water when he was here,' Scott Hodge, an analyst with the Heritage Foundation, quipped of Stockman. 'There are plenty of plans around' for balancing the budget without tax hikes, said Hodge. And there are, among them a proposal by Heritage for cutting government spending by more than $600 billion during the next five years."

➡ To locate examples of bias by placement, observe where a newspaper places political stories. Compare the placement of a story that makes a liberal point or makes a conservative look bad to a story on a similar topic that makes a liberal look bad. Whenever you read a story, see how far into story the conservative viewpoint first appears. In a fair and balanced story, the reporter would quote or summarize the liberal and conservative view at about the same place in the story. If not, you've found bias by placement.

Bias by the selection of sources:

Including more sources in a story who support one view over another. This bias can also be seen when a reporter uses such phrases as "experts believe," "observers say," or "most people think."

When a reporter says "most experts believe...," he often means, "I believe..." Quoting an expert by name does not necessarily add to the credibility of a story, because the reporter may choose any "expert" he wants. The same goes for the use of politicians or "man on the street" interviews.

Experts in news stories are like expert witnesses in trials. If you know whether the defense or the prosecution called a particular expert witness to the stand, you know which way the witness will testify. And when a news story only presents one side, it is obviously the side the reporter supports.

Stephen Hess of the Brookings Institution is one of the most quoted experts in Washington, or in television terminology, "talking heads." So he knows how journalists often go looking for quotes to fit their favorite argument into a news story. Hess wrote in *The Washington Post*: "If I don't respond appropriately, they say they'll get back to me. Which means they won't. This is a big city and someone else is sure to have the magic words they are looking for...TV news is increasingly dishonest in that increasingly its stories are gatherings of quotes or other material to fit a hypothesis."

Who qualifies as an "expert" depends on the story. Obviously, someone identified on-screen as a "budget analyst," "terrorism expert," or who has the name of a specific research institute under his name is being used as an expert. But in a story on education, in addition to citing an "education analyst," a reporter may quote a teacher, PTA leader or principal. In the context of the story, these people are all experts -- the reporter is citing them because of their knowledge of the topic.

Besides "experts," the two most often cited sources are politicians and "man on the street" quotes or soundbites from those portrayed as representative of the community. "Man on the street" quotes allow a reporter to load a story with non-expert testimony that supports one point of view. This happens most often with television news stories. In 1990 the MRC found that CBS reporter Ray Brady not only selected pessimistic economists, but followed the same pattern in choosing non-experts. Of 41 soundbites from such "man on the street" interviews, 74 percent were negative, 8 percent were positive, and 18 percent were ambiguous. Not one of the "average people" aired in 1989 or 1990 said something positive. One woman told Brady: "We eat at coffee shops, the few that are left. Most of them have gone out of business."

When the Pope visited Denver in the summer of 1993, the CBS *Evening News* examined how the Pope would "find much of his American flock gone astray, disagreeing with and violating fundamental Church teaching." In addition to having an imbalance of experts, one soundbite from an Archbishop versus four from those opposed to Church teaching (a liberal Catholic newspaper editor, a liberal Catholic scholar and a nun favoring female priests), all eight soundbites of average Catholics were critical of the Church. A teenage girl said: "You know, the Church says, abstain, abstain, abstain, but that doesn't fit our society today."

On the January 22, 1990 *CBS Evening News*, anchor Dan Rather introduced a story on the latest events in the Soviet Union with the sentence: "Bruce Morton sampled the debate in this country." But Morton's sampling ranged from left to left: Ellen Mickiewicz of the Jimmy Carter Center, Ed Hewett of the Brookings Institution, William Hyland of the liberal-leaning journal *Foreign Affairs*, and CBS consultant Stephen Cohen.

In September 1990, *The Washington Post* reported on the Census Bureau's annual measurement of poverty. *Post* reporters Spencer Rich and Barbara Vobejda wrote: "Economists across the political spectrum said yesterday the current economic picture could mean an even greater rise in poverty." The *Post* followed this with two economists: Henry Aaron of the Brookings Institution and Isabel Sawhill of the Urban Institute, two indistinguishable liberals.

As U.S. troops were moving into Somalia in late 1992, ABC's Kathleen deLaski took the opportunity to look at hunger in America. Her story began with video of a food bank and soundbites from Jesse Jackson and Arsenio Hall decrying the hunger problem. "Some food aid groups are calling for more spending at home, particularly after a recent study showed that the numbers of undernourished swelled by 50 percent in the last decade," deLaski declared leading into a soundbite from Robert Fersh of the Food Research & Action Center (FRAC). deLaski failed to identify FRAC as a liberal spending advocacy group or to provide a conservative's perspective.

A December 1991 *Washington Post* headline declared: "Economists Advise Against Rushing to Cut Taxes." Staff writer Eric Pianin reported how "prominent economists and financial experts" were against tax cuts.

Who were some of the economists and "financial experts" the *Post* quoted? The story highlighted liberal icon John Kenneth Galbraith who advised more federal spending "regardless of the impact on the deficit." Every expert quoted was liberal: Robert Reischauer, director of the Congressional Budget Office, which Pianin failed to identify as Democrat-controlled; Eugene Steuerle of the Urban Institute; George Korpius, Vice President of the AFL-CIO; Roy Ash and Dean Phypers from the liberal Committee for Economic Development; then-House Budget Committee Chairman Leon Panetta (D-California); and an aide to Ways and Means Committee Chairman Dan Rostenkowski (D-Illinois).

➡ To find bias by use of experts or sources, stay alert to the affiliations and political perspective of those quoted as experts or authorities in news stories. Not all stories will include experts, but in those that do, make sure about an equal number of conservatives and liberals are quoted. If a story quotes non-experts, such as those portrayed as average citizens, check to be sure that about an equal number come from both sides of the issue in question. Also check to see if a reporter's generalization about how "economists across the political spectrum" or "most health care specialists" is supported by subsequently cited experts. If they are all or overwhelmingly from one side of the political spectrum, then you've come across bias by use of sources.

Bias by spin:

Emphasizing aspects of a policy favorable to liberals without noting aspects favorable to conservatives; putting out the liberal interpretation of what an event means while giving little or no time or space to explaining the conservative interpretation.

Party spokesmen who talk with reporters after a presidential debate, seeking to convince them that their candidate won, are called "spin doctors." One expert on the news media, Professor Michael Robinson, explains "spin involves tone, the part of the reporting that extends beyond hard news;" it's a reporter's "subjective comments about objective facts."

You can see the effect of spin on what a news consumer takes away from a story by comparing how two journalists report the same or similar event. Six months into his presidency, a *Washington Post*-ABC News poll surveyed the public's view of President Clinton. Referring to the identical poll, the *Post* and ABC provided two very contrasting spins. On *Nightline*, anchor Chris Wallace intoned: "He's sounding tougher. He's acting friendlier to the press. And the polls show his long downward slide is ending," as an on-screen bar graph cited the ABC-*Washington Post* poll. The next morning, *The Washington Post* headline read: "Disapproval of Clinton's Performance Reaches New High in *Post*-ABC Poll."

Which was right and which was wrong? Both. Neither. Each chose to emphasize a different aspect of the poll. The poll asked whether people "approved" or "disapproved" of Clinton's performance and found a slight increase in Clinton's approval rating since a previous poll. That's what *Nightline* reported. The poll also found Clinton's "disapproval" level at the highest point for any President since World War II. That's what the *Post* chose to emphasize.

Our favorite example of spin control comes from CBS economics correspondent Ray Brady, the networks' Prince of Darkness when it comes to negative news on the economy. On October 12, 1989, home prices were down. That's great news for buyers, but not for sellers, so Brady focused on the sellers: "In the past, the American dream of owning your own home always had a sequel -- live in it, then sell it at a huge profit...So another dream has faded." Five months later, on March 16, 1990, home prices were rising, so the conclusion switched to the buyers: "So they keep looking. Thousands of young couples like the Wares, looking for that first house, looking for what used to be called the American dream."

During the '92 campaign, *NBC Nightly News* looked at the effectiveness of campaigning in small towns. The network offered two very contrasting views. "There's a huge pool of economic anger in these small towns, and Clinton is trying to exploit it...In the heart of America, Clinton is finding the hurt of America," reporter John Dancy found.

In the very next story, reporter Tom Pettit asserted: "Quayle also likes working obscure small towns in the South...The Quayle campaign stop begins to resemble Disney World's Main Street -- the crowds predominantly white, but Quayle officials say he has been in many ghetto areas, but says he hasn't been there recently because there aren't many Republican votes there....No urban decay, no problem...Why is Quayle avoiding big cities?" Historian Michael Beschloss answered: "The strategy is keep him away from places he can do harm." After which, Pettit concluded: "Right now, he is presenting his vision to the America of the past -- small town America."

NBC gave viewers the Democratic spin on Clinton's small town campaigning, but instead of providing the Republican spin on Quayle's travels, they put the Democratic spin on it too.

Also look to see if the spin makes one side's ideological perspective look better than another. Legal reporters reflect liberal spin when they assert that only liberal judges are interested in defending "individual rights." When liberal Supreme Court justices William Brennan and Thurgood Marshall resigned, reporters repeatedly warned that the conservative Court would repeal civil liberties. CNN's Candy Crowley intoned: "Also at risk in a court without Brennan: the limits of individual freedom."

Following Marshall's resignation, CBS reporter Bruce Morton crystallized the liberal spin: "The new court is very different from the old Warren Court and its philosophy is likely to rule for the next 25 years. The Warren Court stressed concern for individuals and individuals' rights...The Rehnquist Court is much more concerned with the rights of government, the state, authority. Government can tell the difference between good and evil in this philosophy and should encourage the one and forbid the other."

After Byron White resigned in 1993, *Washington Post* reporter Joan Biskupic wrote: "Replacing White, a conservative, with a liberal voice would give Clinton a chance to loosen the conservative hold on the bench. That could move the court toward a broader interpretation of individual rights and away from a preference for governmental authority." Conservatives, of course, contend that supporting property rights against environmental regulation and emphasizing the rights of crime victims, represent a defense of individual rights. By adopting the liberal view of what constitutes individual or civil "rights," a reporter is relaying the liberal spin.

➡ So, check the spin on a story. If liberal politicians are offering one interpretation of an event or policy, and conservatives another, see which one a news story matches. Many news stories do not reflect a particular spin. Others summarize the spin put on an event by both sides. But if a story reflects one to the exclusion of the other, then you've found "bias by spin."

Bias by labeling:

Attaching a label to conservatives but not to liberals; using more extreme labeling for conservatives than for liberals; identifying a liberal person or group as an "expert" or as independent.

The power to label politicians, activists and groups is one of the media's most subtle and potent powers. The paleontologist Stephen Jay Gould may be a Marxist, but he makes a valid point: that labels tell you as much about the person applying the labels as they tell about the subject being labeled. Gould wrote, "Taxonomy [the science of classification] is often regarded as the dullest of subjects, fit only for mindless ordering and sometimes denigrated within science as 'stamp collecting'....If systems of classification were neutral hat racks for hanging the facts of the world, this disdain might be justified. But classifications both direct and reflect our thinking. The way we [put things in] order represents the way we think." In other words, classifications, or labels, matter.

Terms like "right-wing" are used to describe hard-line communists and staunch capitalists, Israeli Zionists and Soviet anti-Semites, apartheid-loving bigots and Clarence Thomas supporters. And liberals complain about conservatives being "simplistic."

Meg Greenfield, editorial page editor of *The Washington Post*, noted that "every time there is a confrontation somewhere in the world, we manage to dub the good guys liberals and the bad guys conservatives and pretty soon that is the common currency." Indeed, that thinking was shown by a 1992 *Los Angeles Times in Education* election kit for teachers which offered these definitions:

"Conservative: An individual or policy that opposes change in political and social matters."

"Liberal: An individual or policy that favors change in political and social matters. It can also imply tolerance and open-mindedness."

Bias by labeling comes in two forms. First, the tagging of conservative politicians and groups with extreme labels while leaving liberal politicians and groups unlabeled or with more mild labels. Responsible conservatives are sometimes stigmatized as "far right," "ultra-conservative," or "right-wing extremists," while radicals, even Marxists, are called "progressives," "liberals," or "moderates." In other cases, conservative groups are identified as conservative, while liberal groups are described in neutral terms such as "womens group" or "civil rights group," or favorable terms such as "children's rights supporters," "free-speech activists," or "clean-air advocates."

In stories about Supreme Court Justice Byron White's retirement and President Clinton's nomination of Ruth Bader Ginsburg to fill his slot, CBS News correspondent Rita Braver displayed a penchant for labeling judicial conservatives as "far right" or "ultra-conservative" while soft-pedaling the ideology of liberals. Of White's departure, she asserted his "leaving will mean that the voting power of the far right will be greatly undercut." Braver declared Ginsburg is "considered a moderate to liberal, but today she cited this guideline to judging from ultra-conservative Chief Justice William Rehnquist." A few days later, Braver remarked: "You've got to remember this is an extremely conservative Supreme Court, so [Ginsburg's] not really going to be terribly liberal."

Comparing the 1992 Democratic and Republican conventions, the MRC discovered quite a disparity: While the Democrats gathered in New York City were dubbed moderate more often than liberal by a margin of 51 to 38, Republicans in Houston were described with various conservative labels over moderate ones by a margin of 9-to-1. In total, viewers heard 118 conservative labels vs. 13 moderate ones. No Democrat in New York was ever described as "far left" or "hard left," not even Tom Harkin or Jesse Jackson. But in Houston, on five occasions each, CBS and CNN used "hard right" and/or "far right" to describe Republicans.

In the first night of the Republican convention coverage ABC issued 19 "conservative" labels. Peter Jennings mused it was "very much conservatives' night. A very conservative opening prayer" and later noted that Dan Quayle "is very much preferred by the Republican right." At another point, Cokie Roberts found "an extremely conservative convention." Later in the week, Jennings asserted that the convention had "been colored by the party's most conservative elements."

Dan Rather claimed it was Pat Buchanan's job "to set a frame of reference around a moral majority right, heavily influenced party." To reporter Bob Schieffer the delegates represented "a very, very conservative group of Republicans." In total, Republicans got tagged 18 times, five of those "hard right" or "far right." Dan Rather twice described Pat Buchanan's speech as "hard right." On the last night, August 20, Connie Chung called Dan Quayle's speech "far right" and asked Pat Robertson: "Has the party gone far right enough for you?"

In four days of Democratic coverage, CNN attached 22 labels to Democrats, but at no time did CNN label any Democrat "far left." When the GOP gathered, CNN issued 49 ideological labels, five of them "far right." In fact, in the first night from Houston CNN used 25 labels, three more than all week from New York. On Monday from the Republican meeting Candy Crowley announced: "As for what Buchanan has to say, this is really an appeal to the far right." Co-anchor Catherine Crier asked analyst William Schneider whether "the Republicans made concessions to the far right in hopes that the rest of the Republican Party isn't watching." On the last night, Charles Bierbauer recalled Buchanan's speech as being "heavy-handed conservative" and Frank Sesno labeled Buchanan and Bill Bennett as "very hard, far right conservatives."

Numerous other studies have found a wide disparity in how liberal and conservative groups are labeled. Consider the two major women's political organizations in the United States -- the conservative Concerned Women for America and the liberal National Organization for Women. By all measures, NOW is at least as far to the left as CWA is to the right. But an MRC study of three newspapers (*Los Angeles Times, New York Times, Washington Post*) and the three news magazines showed that NOW was labeled liberal in only 10 of 421 newspaper stories (or 2.4 percent of the time) in 1987 and 1988. CWA, with three times the membership of NOW, was only mentioned in 61 stories in the same time period, but was labeled conservative 25 times (41 percent).

Senator Edward Kennedy (D-Massachusetts), consistently rated by various groups as one of the three or four most liberal U.S. Senators, rarely receives an ideological label in news stories, while Senator Jesse Helms (R-North Carolina) is often referred to as "conservative," "right-wing," or "far-right." During the 1990 campaign, an article in *Time* called Helms an "ultra-right conservative," but described his liberal opponent, Harvey Gantt, simply as "former Charlotte Mayor."

The same pattern holds true for comparisons of the conservative Heritage Foundation (labeled in 59 percent of major newspaper stories) and the liberal Brookings Institution (just one percent), the conservative Family Research Council (45 percent) and the liberal Children's Defense Fund (under 4 percent), and other similar pairings. The conservative organization or individual is regularly labeled, but the liberal counterpart is not. Why? Because the national media see liberal groups as "us" and conservative groups as "them."

The second kind of bias by labeling occurs when a reporter not only fails to identify a liberal as a liberal, but describes the person or group with positive labels, such as "an expert" or "independent consumer group." In so doing, the reporter imparts an air of authority that the source does not deserve. If the "expert" is properly called a "conservative" or a "liberal" the news consumer can take that ideological slant into account when evaluating the accuracy of an assertion.

CNN provided a good illustration of misleading labeling during the 1993 debate over health care policy. In one story, reporter John Holliman included two interviews: "health care expert" Bob Brandon of Citizen Action, and Ron Pollack of Families USA, which Holliman identified as a "consumer group." In reality, both men represent groups pushing a Canadian-style system of socialized health care that outlaws insurance companies. So both should have been labeled "liberal."

People for the American Way (PAW) is a left-wing group which sees the "religious right" as its enemy and fought Robert Bork's Supreme Court nomination. But a 1992 Associated Press story described PAW as "a 300,000-member, nonpartisan constitutional-liberties organization."

Another version of this comes out in coverage of the abortion battle. Reporters will label those wanting abortion kept legal with their preferred label, "pro-choice" or "pro-abortion rights." But they usually will not describe those on the other side by their preferred label, "pro-life."

The Washington Post Deskbook on Style suggests: "The terms 'right-to-life' and 'pro-life' are used by advocates in the abortion controversy to buttress their arguments. They should generally be used as part of an organization's title and in quotations, but not as descriptive adjectives in the text. Use 'abortion-rights advocates' for those who support freedom of choice in the matter, 'antiabortion' for those who oppose it."

➤ When looking for bias by labeling, remember that not all labeling is biased or wrong. A story calling Senator Helms "conservative" is accurate; as is a reporter's reference to Pat Buchanan as "the conservative co-host of CNN's *Crossfire*." But any story labeling conservatives should also label liberals. So, the story should read: "Pat Buchanan serves as the conservative co-host of CNN's *Crossfire*, sparring across the table each night with the liberal Michael Kinsley."

Bias by labeling is present when the story labels the conservative, but not the liberal; when the story uses more extreme-sounding labels for the conservative than the liberal ("ultra-conservative," "far right," and "hard right" but just "liberal" instead of "far left" and "hard left"); and when the story misleadingly identifies a liberal official or group as an "expert" or "independent watchdog organization."

Bias by policy recommendation or condemnation:

When a reporter goes beyond reporting and endorses the liberal view of which policies should be enacted, or affirms the liberal criticism of current or past policies.

As described earlier, when reporters list possible solutions to society's problems, the solutions often follow the agenda of the Left ("raise taxes," "cut defense," "have taxpayers pay for abortions," "issue more government regulations"). And when reporters review past policies, their evaluations follow a liberal script ("Reaganomics made the rich richer and the poor poorer," "slashes in social spending caused increased infant mortality and homelessness," "the lack of an energy policy has made the U.S. dependent on foreign oil," "too much defense spending has driven us into bankruptcy").

Most news stories simply relate a sequence of events, but when a story mixes reporting with specific recommendations for government policy, that's bias by policy recommendation. When a reporter conclusively declares that a past or current policy has failed, that's bias by policy condemnation. Taken together, this bias occurs whenever a reporter, without any attribution, offers a definitive policy evaluation.

Time magazine regularly includes specific policy recommendations in the middle of stories. *Time*'s "Planet of the Year" story at the end of 1988 included -- as examples of the actions government "must" take to avoid ecological catastrophe -- a wish list of liberal ideas. *Time* has recommended raising the tax on gasoline at least 25 times in the last four years. On August 8, 1990, Detroit reporter S.C. Gwynne asked for the biggest tax hike: "The most effective solution, many experts say, would be a combination of market incentives and somewhat higher fuel-efficiency standards. A stiff gasoline tax of $1 per gal. would encourage consumers to choose more economical autos."

Time called for a gas tax hike four times in the first seven issues of 1993. In the January 25 edition, columnist Andrew Tobias wrote: "As for gasoline -- which costs about $3.75 per gal. throughout Europe -- Ross Perot was right. Phase in a 50-cent tax over five years, and you raise $50 billion a year." The February 1 issue included Senior Writer Eugene Linden's idea that the U.S. "might follow [Norway's] example and implement a carbon tax, which encourages efficiency and the use of cleaner fuels." In the February 15 issue, John Greenwald called the gas tax "an ideal target" that makes "good economic and ecological sense."

On the bias by policy condemnation side, in the January 6, 1992 issue, *Time* staff writers labeled Bush Chief of Staff John Sununu's resignation the year's "Best" environmental news. The article called Sununu "notorious for his hostility to environmentalists and their agenda," and claimed, "If it was good for the earth but bad for business, Sununu's opposition generally persuaded the President."

Time listed the White House wetlands policy as one of the "Worst" environmental events, calling it "all wet....during his presidential campaign, George Bush promised 'no net loss of wetlands.' But under pressure from business, his administration proposed a new definition of a wetland that would open at least [30 million acres] of off-limits land to development." *Time* failed to explain why it's such a great idea to violate the Bill of Rights, which prohibits the government's taking of property without compensation.

A year later, a new administration was about to assume office and *Time*'s year-in-review evaluation turned optimistic, praising the Clinton team. Under "best environmental news," *Time* listed: "1. Al Gore's Election: Only a year ago, environmentalists were resigned to spending four more years as voices crying in the wilderness. The anti-ecology Bush-Quayle Administration looked tough to beat, and among the Democrats who weren't going to try was Al Gore, author of the environmental manifesto *Earth in the Balance*. Now that he will head Clinton's green team, look for efforts to boost energy efficiency, preserve wetlands and reduce global warming."

But *Time* is not the only news outlet to at least occasionally abandon any pretense of objectivity and delve into issue advocacy. For several years ABC's *World News Tonight* has run a nightly series of reports called the "American Agenda." These are essentially essays in which reporters highlight various proposals for solving the nation's problems. While some reports have publicized creative private solutions to social problems, often the reports endorse the same old government "solutions."

In 1991, ABC reporter Carole Simpson promoted the programs of France's socialist prime minister, Francois Mitterand, as more efficient and caring than the United States: "When you see how France cares for its children, you can't help but wonder why the United States won't do the same for our children. Americans continue to study and debate what to do about poor children, but the French decided long ago. Their system of social welfare is based on the belief that investing in the children of France is investing in the future of France."

A good interviewer will play "devil's advocate," making the person being interviewed respond to the arguments of their opponents. But when an interviewer endorses a viewpoint, then they've committed bias by policy recommendation. During a 1993 *Today* show interview with a criminologist about how to curb teen violence, Bryant Gumbel asserted: "So in the absence of the obvious solution in this country, of better gun control. Obvious. What kind of practical things do you suggest could be done of an immediate nature?"

A couple of months before the 1992 election, *The Washington Post* offered readers a three-part series on why the deficit grew dramatically in the previous decade. The cause cited by reporter Steven Mufson: While Congress had a role, it was mostly Reagan's tax cuts. Recalling how tax cuts were supposed to increase revenue, Mufson countered: "The idea was, in the words of Harvard University economics professor Benjamin Friedman, 'a fairy tale.'" Mufson argued that tax receipts fell in 1983, and in 1984 "barely crept back to the levels of 1982." But he failed to note that from 1984 to 1989 receipts grew an average of eight percent a year, almost twice the inflation rate, while spending mushroomed faster.

Tax hikes were Mufson's recommended solution: "Though the nation's fiscal imbalance has rarely reached such a critical point, the failure of lawmakers to impose taxes in an attempt to curry favor with voters is a problem as old as the republic." Leading into a final paragraph long quote from the first Treasury Secretary, Mufson wrote, "More than 200 years ago...Alexander Hamilton appealed for Americans to recognize the need for taxes. Two centuries later, the plea retains its note of urgency."

Though President Bush abandoned Reagan's economic policies, the *Los Angeles Times* blamed supply-side policies for Bush's 1992 defeat. In a "news analysis" five days after the election, business reporter James Risen declared: "Ultimately, Reaganomics was a failure. It produced big political dividends for the Republicans, and it may have contributed to rapid economic growth during the 1980s. But it was, at its core, a governing philosophy based on a deeply flawed economic notion: that tax cuts, especially large tax cuts for the rich, would not worsen the government's budget deficit. Ironically, it was the illogic of that theory that helped bring down President George Bush -- even though it seems clear that Bush never fully believed in the theory himself."

➡ Bias by policy recommendation/condemnation should jump out at you, but be careful. A story or sidebar which includes recommendations is biased if it endorses one view over another or urges one particular policy. If a story, however, lists various options or summarizes the policies advocated by both liberals and conservatives, then it does not reflect bias by policy recommendation. Similarly, if it explains why liberals and conservatives feel the policies espoused by the other have been failures, then the story does not exhibit bias by policy condemnation. Bias by policy recommendation or condemnation occurs when the reporter endorses one side's policy recommendation or one side's policy condemnation.

The examples we have listed are from the national media, but the same principles apply to local media. It is up to you to examine the media in your area and determine the extent to which labeling and other types of bias appear. Once you have acquainted yourself with the above examples, you should find it easy to spot local bias.

Many stories will reflect more than one kind of bias. The story which displays bias by commission may have an imbalance of experts, so it also shows bias by selection of sources. It may also exhibit bias by labeling. A story which is biased by spin may also reflect bias by omission. To illustrate, remember the story on the Economic Policy Institute study supposedly proving that the rich gobbled up most of the increase in wealth in the '80s? The *Today* show's coverage of the study from a liberal group exhibited bias by story selection. But NBC's coverage also showed bias by labeling. Anchor Margaret Larson called the liberal EPI "non-partisan" and referred to its "new independent study."

What Isn't Bias

You may come across stories that you believe fit one of these eight definitions of bias. But, they still may not qualify as examples which you should criticize. With some narrow exceptions explained later in this section, you want to identify bias that occurs in news stories and which favors the liberal view over the conservative perspective.

What isn't bias falls into three broad categories:

■ Editorials or opinion columns

■ Stories or statements that make the conservative side look bad, but are accurate

■ Non-policy stories on a specific event that don't have to be balanced

❶ Newspaper, radio and television station editorials are supposed to take a point of view. The same goes for columns which appear on the op-ed page and commentaries on television news shows. Don't equate a front page news story with an editorial. They are very different items. You should stick to analyzing news stories. They are supposed to be unbiased presentations of the news. When they are biased, the reporter is not doing his job. Editorial and column writers, in contrast, are supposed to take a point of view. They are under no obligation to be fair or balanced.

The only exception: If you are interested in showing that a newspaper's editorials are consistently liberal, or advocate liberal policies more often than conservative ones. Similarly, you can analyze the columnists run by your local paper if you want to prove that contrary to the paper's claim or public perception, they do not balance out. But don't ever cite an editorial or column as evidence of how a newspaper's coverage was biased. *The Daily Herald*'s coverage of the school bond referendum was biased if its news stories were unbalanced, not if it ran one-sided editorials.

Reporters frequently appear on roundtables or interview shows to discuss their take on current events. On the national level, this occurs on everything from the end of show discussion on NBC's *Meet the Press* to C-SPAN's weekly *Journalists' Roundtable*. As described in the "self-identification" section on page 15, liberal comments during these appearances betray a reporter's political view. But they do not prove the reporter's stories on the particular issue were biased. You can cite these comments as evidence of the liberal views held by reporters employed by a media outlet. But do not cite a journalist's opinion of the school bond referendum as evidence of biased coverage in his newspaper or on his radio or TV station. If you charge a reporter with producing biased stories based upon his off-the-job comments, but then can't show bias in his stories, you'll only have hurt your cause. You will have inadvertently demonstrated that the reporter can separate his personal feelings from his professional duties.

❷ Just because a news story portrays a conservative in a negative light does not necessarily make it biased. If a conservative politician is mired in a corruption probe, mentioning this in a news story is hardly a sign of bias. Refer back to the definition of bias by story selection. If a newspaper runs more stories on a conservative in ethics trouble than a liberal holding an equal or more powerful post, then that is bias. But the very fact that a story includes a negative reference to the conservative politician, does not make it biased.

You must step back from your activist conservative standpoint and look at things from a reporter's perspective. A story might say that a conservative leader "turns people off with his constant negativity and has lost State House supporters because he regularly storms out of meetings when his statistics are challenged." Before assuming the story is biased, ask yourself, "Is it true?" If it is, and you cite it as an example of bias, you'll only hurt your credibility.

During Reagan's White House years conservative media critics had no shortage of biased stories to analyze. The MRC critiqued many policy stories and documented inconsistencies as to which Washington scandals received media attention. Toward the end of the Reagan Administration, correspondents occasionally pointed out how the President dozed off in a meeting. Yes, these stories detracted from Reagan's image and, therefore, hurt his effectiveness when he worked for conservative policies. And yes, at least some were produced by liberal reporters out to damage Reagan. But the MRC did not criticize those stories because they were true. We avoided the problem by sticking to stories, or the parts of stories, dealing with attacks on Reagan's policies and ideas.

❸ News stories dealing with policies should always present both the liberal and conservative perspective. The same rule does not go for stories on events, however, where there are not two sides to explain. A story reciting how the Governor met with a Boy Scout troop in the morning, gave a lunch address to welfare advocates, travelled to the western part of the state in the afternoon to meet with teachers before attending a fundraising dinner, does not need to include comments from the opposition party.

Similarly, if a liberal or conservative group organizes a roast to a local politician or celebrity, the news story does not need to include critical views of the group's political agenda. It can simply describe how so many people gathered at a certain hotel and heard some politicians say x about y.

If the story on the Governor's day includes comments from him on why the state should impose a surtax to pay for higher teacher salaries, then the reporter should include an opposition view. If a liberal group's event gets covered while a conservative one a few months before went unmentioned, then that's bias by story selection.

But do not assume that just because a story does not include conservative views, soundbites or comments that it's biased. After all, if a conservative organization celebrates the tenth anniversary of its founding by holding a roast to honor a state senator, there's no need for a reporter to include negative comments from liberal activists. The reporter has met his journalistic obligations if the story summarizes the events of the evening.

Campaign coverage is a bit more complicated. Obviously, a news outlet is obligated to provide balanced coverage with approximately equal time and space given to the Democratic and Republican Party candidates. (In the primary, a news organization may not realistically be able to cover more than a few candidates and so will have to make a judgment as to which ones have a legitimate chance of winning.) Newspapers, magazines and radio stations should offer balanced coverage of issues raised by the candidates.

There is, however, one exception to the balance rule: A story describing a candidate's activities. To better explain, let's assume there's a two-candidate race for Chairman of the school committee. If a news outlet runs one story a day on the race then that story should note the latest campaign events, endorsements or policy pronouncements of both candidates. If, however, the news outlet decides to run separate stories on each candidate, then they do not need to incorporate the views of the opponent. If one candidate launches an attack against the other, then the reporter must allow the opponent's camp to respond to that charge but, as long as another story is dedicated to covering the opponent, the reporter does not need to include a reaction to every policy pronouncement.

When observing campaign coverage, focus on the overall coverage offered by a media outlet. Taken as a whole, it should offer the reader, listener or viewer a balanced picture of the disputed issues and views of the candidates involved in the race.

Section Three:
Identifying & Documenting Bias in News Stories

To demonstrate how to detect bias in a news story, take a look at a few examples of biased network news stories. Here's an ABC *World News Tonight* story from May 3, 1992, days after the Los Angeles riots:

Forrest Sawyer: "The death toll in the Los Angeles rioting rose to forty-six today, and that makes it the nation's bloodiest civil unrest in seventy-five years. Now that the smoke is clearing, L.A. residents are arguing over who is to blame. As Tom Foreman reports, many say that blame goes all the way to the top."

Tom Foreman: "As the clean-up continues, the federal government is being swept into the circle of blame, for failing to address inner-city problems, and leaving poor people in despair."

Rep. Maxine Waters: "Absolutely desperate, absolutely angry, and justifiably so. Nothing is working for them. The systems aren't working."

Foreman: "In recent years, as federal funding for social services has fallen, many have disappeared. Gone are programs for job training, health care, child care, and housing."

Bruce Johnson, L.A. resident: "A lot of black people don't have no jobs or nothing else you know."

Foreman: "Bruce Johnson once worked at a federally funded job. The funding dried up. He has been without steady work since. His wife Pat was getting a federally funded education. That's over too."

Pat Johnson: "I think the government stinks. You want me to be honest, I think it stinks. Like I say, they promise you everything, it give us nothing, you know."

Foreman: "Some people believe the President has not recognized any social motive for the violence."

President George Bush, May 1, 1992: "It's not a message of protest. It's been the brutality of a mob. Pure and simple."

Foreman: "People here say the President should listen."

Woman on street: "Who's going to listen? I bet they listen now. They listen now, won't they. If this is where you have to get their attention, damn it, get it. Any way you can."

Foreman: "Increasingly, people are saying that all of the violence had very little to do with Rodney King. Instead it was the desperate call of a community fighting for change. Tom Foreman, ABC News, Los Angeles."

Foreman's story reflected bias by spin; bias by selection of sources; and bias by commission. Foreman's spin on what caused the riots (the federal government failed to address inner-city problems and that the riots were a "desperate call of a community fighting for change"), matched the liberal spin at the time. Conservatives believed the individuals who committed the violent acts were responsible, not societal pressures.

Except for a George Bush soundbite, which Foreman used to back his thesis that Bush "doesn't get it," the other four soundbites supported the liberal view on what caused the riots. Bias by commission came in Foreman's declaration as a fact beyond dispute that "federal funding for social services has fallen, many have disappeared. Gone are programs for job training, health care, child care, and housing." That's a ludicrous assertion, since federal funding for virtually every social program grew faster than inflation during the 1980s.

Here's a March 23, 1992 *CBS Evening News* story:

Connie Chung: "A new snapshot today of the health and well-being of children in this country. For a growing number of them, it's not a pretty picture. Eric Engberg reports on the young face of poverty in America."

Eric Engberg: "The way America treats its children from newborns to teens has deteriorated to danger levels according to a study out today. This premature baby, born to a cocaine-using mother in a Washington hospital, weighed one pound, ten ounces at birth. Such underweight births, often a precursor to serious health problems, are on the rise across the country."

Dr. Victor Nelson, Greater SE Community Hospital: "Here over the last few years, we have doubled this to almost fifteen percent."

Engberg: "Other yardsticks for measuring child well-being compiled by the child advocacy group Kids Count point to trouble. While the death rate for infants has declined, the teen years have gotten more dangerous. Violent teen deaths climbed eleven percent in five years. Reason: soaring rates for murder and suicide. More children are having children; there were 76,000 more babies born to single teens in 1989 than in 1980. The number of children living in single-parent families has grown by two million in the decade. The study found one in five children was poor, an increase of twenty-two percent during the eighties."

Douglas Nelson, Annie E. Casey Foundation: "And if we don't turn these numbers around in the decade, we, I mean every American regardless of age or their family status, we're going to be in deep trouble."

Engberg: "As child poverty has grown, social workers have encountered more homeless children."

Marlys Wilson, social service worker: "They forget how to laugh, they just sit, they cry a lot. We have a lot of kids that cry. They've lost a sense of trust."

Engberg: "Americans are very aware that something is wrong in the way children are treated. A poll released with today's survey found that adults, by a margin of two to one, think today's kids have it worse than their parents did. Eric Engberg, CBS News, Washington."

Engberg's story demonstrated five types of bias. First, bias by story selection. A liberal organization released a study with a liberal theme and CBS considered it newsworthy. Second, bias by labeling. The Annie E. Casey Foundation and the Center for the Study of Social Policy, are liberal advocacy groups. Engberg failed to properly identify them. Third, bias by commission. Without citing any statistical source, Engberg insisted "social workers have encountered more homeless children." He also cited, without any balancing counterpoint, the Casey Foundation's claim that child poverty increased 22 percent in the 1980s. In fact, even the Children's Defense Fund, a left-wing lobby for increased welfare dependency, calculated that the percentage of children in poverty declined from 22.3 percent in 1983 to 19.6 percent in 1989.

Fourth, bias by omission. In building a case for how the welfare of children deteriorated in the '80s, Engberg excluded critics like Heritage Foundation analyst Robert Rector, who told *The New York Times* the report was "pure mental rubbish" that "ignores $150 billion in welfare; so it doesn't look at the children's standard-of-living conditions." Census Bureau statistics don't consider substantial non-cash welfare benefits such as housing assistance and Medicaid. The exclusion of critics like Rector brings us to Engberg's bias by selection of sources. All three espoused the same point of view.

Your turn

Now it's your turn. Read through the next two transcripts and try to figure out the kind of bias they reflect. See page 285 at the end of the book for the answers.

Story A, an October 16, 1990 *CBS Evening News* story:

Dan Rather: "Elected officials from President Bush on down are now trying to tap into and deflect voter outrage over the national debt and tax mess. At stake for the public in the final budget deal: whose taxes will go up and whose benefits will get chopped. For some perspective and context on the public's perception of a raw deal in the making, correspondent Richard Threlkeld is here tonight with the first of looks we'll be taking at the tax tangle and who pays. Richard?"

Threlkeld: "Dan, taxpayers always get mad when taxes go up, but what really gets taxpayers mad is when they suspect they've been paying more than their fair share. For a long time they accepted the conventional wisdom that if you cut taxes for the rich, the benefits would trickle down to everybody. But all the latest polls now show that most taxpayers have finally come to suspect otherwise."

Man on street: "I don't think the rich people pay what's equivalent to their wealth. I think that the poor people are taxed more and they make less."

Threlkeld: "And there's some evidence to prove their suspicions. Largely because of tax changes in the '80s, the income of the richest five percent of Americans has gone up by almost 50 percent while their tax rate's gone down about 10 percent [on-screen visual: Income Up 45%; Taxes down 10%]. Meantime, the income of the poorest 10 percent has gone down 10 percent and their tax rate has gone up by more than a fourth [on-screen visual: Income Down 10%; Taxes Up 28%]. While Congress was vainly trying to balance the new budget, millions of taxpayers were having the same problem balancing their budgets and finally figured out why: taxes."

Kevin Phillips, 'Republican Political Analyst': "People who were losing during the 1980s didn't know quite what was happening, they couldn't explain how it happened, but they began to see that they could buy less, that their standard of living was either stagnating or declining."

Threlkeld: "So last week when Congress and the White House first came up with a deficit plan that seemed to give the rich still another tax break, that was the last straw."

Woman on street: "If you have more money, then you should pay more money, and that's how I feel."

Man on street: "Target the rich. I'm not one of them."

Carol Cox, 'Committee for a Responsible Federal Budget': "When people from working class families see their taxes go up, they'd like to see people that they think are better off than they have their taxes go up as well."

Threlkeld: "And the Democrats have gotten the message. For the first time in a decade they are not only unafraid to use the T word as in taxes, but they're even using the R word, as in soak the rich."

Rep. Barbara Boxer, 'D-Budget Committee': "Democrats are working for budgets that are fair so the Helmsleys and the Donald Trumps at last will pay their share."

Threlkeld: "So if and when they do sort out that deficit mess it's likely the rich are going to get soaked, at least a little, to make up for the soaking they avoided in the '80s, Dan."

Story B appeared on the June 17, 1993 *NBC Nightly News*:

Stone Phillips: "Hunger in a land of plenty. For thirty-million Americans the cupboard is often bare. In south central Los Angeles, for instance, a new UCLA report says one out of four people doesn't have enough money to buy food. NBC's Sara James."

Sara James: "Janise Banks had to take three buses from her home in south central Los Angeles to this food bank, her refrigerator is almost empty."

Banks: "You just can't apologize to a child that I'm sorry you're hungry."

James: "Banks is an unemployed widow who has two children and a third on the way, and she says one hundred forty dollars in food stamps runs out before the end of the month."

Banks: "We're already at poverty level."

James: "Banks isn't alone. Demand at food banks and soup kitchens jumped nearly 40 percent in Los Angeles last year."

Voice of interpreter for a food bank recipient: "When I have nothing to feed my children I either go to one of my neighbors and they feed us, or I try to find any food shelter."

James: "For Antonia Lopez, getting food on the table is a day to day worry now. She left her alcoholic husband two months ago, and is caring for their ten children alone. Caroline Olney works for the Hunger Coalition which commissioned the new report."

Caroline Olney: "Basically the War on Poverty hasn't been fought in the last twelve years."

James: "Olney says 27 percent of the people in this neighborhood go without food an average of five days a month, and cuts in government programs aren't the only problem. There aren't many supermarkets in the inner city and grocery shopping is more expensive. The same food costs three hundred dollars more a year in this low income neighborhood than it does in middle class suburbs just a few miles away. Hunger isn't just a problem in L.A. Tufts University says, nationwide, twelve million children are going hungry. The UCLA report recommends that the federal government spend an extra twelve billion dollars on food programs, but admits that's a long shot given Washington's cost cutting mood. In her day to day battle, Janise Banks scored a small victory -- trading a few groceries for a ride home. Sara James, NBC News, Los Angeles."

Identify, a final note

At this point you should know how and where to look to determine a journalist's personal political views and how to document that a news story reflects liberal bias. Now, it's time to publicize your findings so others in your community will understand the depth of the media bias problem and members of the media will know their days of unchecked bias are over. That's the subject of the next chapter: How to Expose media bias.

CHAPTER TWO

EXPOSE

In the first chapter you learned how to identify biased news by analyzing a particular story or series of stories. Once you've mastered how to prove that a reporter, newspaper or television station has been biased, how do you let others know about what you've found?

In this chapter we'll tell you how to set up a news monitoring system and conduct studies to prove overall bias on an issue or in long term coverage. You'll learn how to expose media bias to: 1) conservatives in your state or city who share your concern about the impact of biased reporting; 2) political figures and opinion leaders in your community; 3) the public at large; 4) friendly people in the media who will help you publicize your findings, such as talk show hosts and columnists; 5) members of the media who are committing the bias or are their bosses, so that they know their stories are being checked.

Accomplishing these goals will be a three-part process.

■ Step One: Become a dedicated media monitor. On your own you can't watch, listen and read everything, but you can do more than you might think.

■ Step Two: Become an activist. To let people in on what you find, write letters to the editor, call radio talk shows, and make speeches before church groups and business clubs. While doing these things you'll attract the attention of those in your community who share your concern for media bias.

By providing this book to them so they can also learn the basics of media bias you'll be able to enlist them to help you monitor the local media. And they can supplement your publicity efforts. Soon you won't be the only one writing letters and calling talk shows.

■ Step Three: Become a leader. Once you've got people helping you, it will be time to consider increasing your impact by forming a committee or foundation and publishing a newsletter.

Of course, if you already have friends and colleagues upset by media bias and, more importantly, a significant amount of money to invest in this project, then you can go directly to step three. But don't skip over the basics of steps one and two. Systematically monitoring the media and publicizing what you find through talk shows, letters to the editor and speeches to civic groups are the foundation of any successful effort to expose media bias.

Section One:
How to Become a Thorough Monitor

The first major step in exposing bias is to monitor and analyze the media. You should focus on the key sources of news for the citizens of your community -- local newspaper(s), radio stations and local network television affiliates. Everything from a Christian radio station to a weekly alternative newspaper are also part of the media, but they may not be widely accepted news sources. You'll have a big enough job handling major TV, radio and newspaper outlets. Don't burden yourself with minor or alternative media outlets unless the major straight-news outlets either have a pattern of using their less balanced material in their own reports, or add to your own critique against the local media.

What to monitor

Newspapers: Most cities have at least one major newspaper. If you are in a major metropolitan area, you need to start by monitoring the newspaper or newspapers that cover the entire metropolitan area. Houston, for instance, has two competing dailies: *The Houston Chronicle* and *Houston Post*. Boston has the *Boston Globe* and *Boston Herald*. Other big cities have just one metropolitan newspaper, such as the *Los Angeles Times* or Cleveland *Plain Dealer*.

But if you live in a suburb, you may also have a local daily that is the dominate news source for a county or region. The Long Beach *Press Telegram*, *Los Angeles Daily News* and *Orange County Register* all cover suburban areas. The Boston area, for example, has the *Middlesex News* which covers the western suburbs, *Patriot Ledger* which covers the southern suburbs, and *Lawrence Eagle-Tribune* to the north.

Whether you decide to also monitor one of these depends on your scope. People who live north of Boston never see the *Patriot Ledger* and probably won't care much about it, so you would only include it if you think its content interests those you hope to reach. If you're concerned about its coverage of the suburban towns, then include it; if your concern is newspapers read by people metropolitan-wide, then don't.

Some metro areas have their own paper, but many residents also read a newspaper from a nearby city. One example: Orlando has the

Orlando Sentinel, but the *Tampa Tribune* is also well read.

If you live outside a metropolitan area, then you'll want to monitor the local daily newspaper, plus the nearest big city paper available in your town. For example, if you live in or near Rome, Georgia you'll want to monitor the *Rome News-Tribune* and, because its state-wide distribution includes Rome, the *Atlanta Constitution*.

Radio: The importance of radio depends on where you live. Generally speaking, in big cities television news is much more important than radio news. So if you live in a big city, you'll probably want to concentrate your efforts on television and newspapers. In small towns, the opposite is true. You may have a small daily newspaper, but the television stations you see are from a city miles away with little priority for covering your town. So the local radio stations are the only broadcast sources for coverage of local politics.

Most radio stations don't even have news departments. In bigger cities, local news exists only on an FM National Public Radio affiliate and on two to four AM stations with a talk or news format, or a format that combines both. In medium-sized cities, there's also often a AM music station with news on the hour. In small towns, however, there may only be one or two stations and they often emphasize news, at least during the morning and afternoon "drive times," meaning 6 to 9am and 4 to 6pm.

A quick tip for determining the relative audience of different stations: Look at their rate cards, which list their advertising rates. In general, the larger a station's audience, the more it charges. If you know any local businessmen, ask them for the rate cards of local stations. Chances are they've been called upon by station salesmen. Or call each station's sales department and ask where their audience ranks. Keep in mind that they'll probably exaggerate -- claim they are No. 1 when they are actually only first with women of a certain age group. By comparing answers, though, you should be able to figure out the stations that are most popular.

Television: ABC, CBS and NBC affiliates carry daily newscasts; and a growing number of Fox stations and major independents carry a 9 or 10pm newscast. You should concentrate on the main 5 or 6pm newscast aired before, or in the Central Time Zone after, the national network evening news. As the longest newscasts of the day they will include all the stories produced by the local staff. The later 10 or 11pm news show includes less since it's shorter and usually repeats the news of the early evening show. The only exceptions will be to note an armed robbery that night or to report on the Monday night city council meeting.

Stations in larger cities have an early morning newscast airing before the *Today* show, *CBS This Morning* and *Good Morning America*, but they rarely include any new stories produced by the station. Instead, they normally re-run the stories from the night before, note traffic problems and relay overnight developments as reported by the Associated Press.

So, in priority order, you should aim to monitor: 1) the early evening 5 or 6pm newscast weekdays on the ABC, CBS and NBC stations and the 9 or 10pm Fox show; 2) the early or late night newscast on weekends (the late night is often a better choice since it's not pre-empted by sports); 3) the weeknight late night news; 4) other newscasts aired in the morning or at mid-day.

In addition, many stations air a Sunday morning interview/discussion program with a politician as the guest. If you think there is an ideological slant to the host's questions or the guest list favors liberals, then look at this too.

Equipment requirements

To be an effective media monitor, you need to be a thorough media monitor. You need to move beyond cutting an occasional article out of the newspaper or remembering that Channel 8 did a really biased story last week on the need to pass the Governor's tax hike plan. In order to use the skills you learned in Chapter 1 (How to Identify Media Bias), you must have news stories to analyze. For newspapers that's relatively cheap and easy. TV and radio will cost some money.

First, newspapers. Once you've identified the newspaper or newspapers you plan to monitor, start cutting out or making copies of articles that touch on controversial issues. If there's a battle over property tax rates and how much more the school committee gets, cut out all those articles. If a conservative is opposing a liberal for city council, county commissioner, state representative or governor, cut out every article during the campaign.

As the days and weeks go by you may come across an article that reflects bias by commission, omission, placement, selection of sources or labeling. More importantly, when the battle or campaign is over you'll have all the articles ready to analyze for a study. Even if you don't have time to read them all each day, if you put them in a file you can read them whenever you have the time. In a matter of months you'll have dozens of articles, so create a file folder for each newspaper for each topic for each month. In other words, if you are analyzing the *Daily News* and the *Herald Tribune,* you should have a file of all June *Daily News* articles on the debate over raising the state sales tax. Don't forget to write the date on every article.

Try to cut out articles on as many politically-oriented topics as possible, even if the topic doesn't excite you. If you see a big page one spread on a pro-gun control rally in front of the State House, wouldn't it be great if you could go to your "gun control" file and pull out the three-paragraph item the same paper ran on a bigger NRA rally four months earlier? That would be an example of bias by story placement. Gun control may not interest you, but it does many other conservatives. And if you follow the tips on how to write a letter that appear later in this chapter (page 106), an ardent anti-gun control conservative might see your letter and give you a call. That's how you'll build your efforts.

If all goes well, soon you'll be able to assign your volunteers to tasks within their interest area. The gun enthusiast will help you cut out all gun control articles and the woman you know at church who is a pro-life activist will handle stories on abortion protests and legislation.

Television and radio come next. Newspaper monitoring requires little more than the price of home delivery and a few dozen file folders. TV and radio will require a monetary investment in VCRs (Video Cassette Recorders) audio tape recorders and tapes.

If you already own a VCR, start by recording what you can. With one VCR you can at least record one channel's early evening news and another's late night news. Eventually, you'll require three VCRs to record the news at the same time on three channels. If you also want to analyze the Fox or independent news, that shouldn't be a problem with even just one VCR since almost all Fox and independent stations air their news when ABC, CBS and NBC affiliates are showing entertainment shows.

For radio, you could get a reel-to-reel type of recorder, but they are very expensive. Cassette tape recorders with a radio run from $75 to $125. Commonly called "boom boxes," the built-in radio makes them the easiest to use. Radio station news is normally run on the hour, so whether you're in a small town with only one station with news, or a city with several stations, one recorder should go a long way. Record the news from one station at 4pm and another at 5pm. If a station offers continuous news in drive time, record a half hour or a full hour of it.

Cassette recorders don't come with built in timers like VCRs. So be a little creative. For $25.00 to $35.00 you can buy an electrical timer, the kind you'd normally use to turn the lights in your house on and off while you're vacationing. Set the recorder's radio to the correct station, push the record button and turn the timer power to off. When the timer comes on, you'll be recording. A timer with a digital clock will allow you to be most accurate about the on and off time.

VCRs and cassette recorders wear out, so be prepared to replace them. When most people buy a VCR, they use it to play a movie or two a week and to record a couple of TV shows. You'll be putting several months worth of wear on it every week. A heavily used VCR -- two to four hours of recording per day -- probably won't last more than two years.

Creating a videotape library

Here are some helpful tips on video and audio recording:

✔ You don't want to cut off the beginning of the show you are recording. Whether it's the VCR timer or an electrical timer you're using for a audio tape recorder, set it at least 30 seconds fast. That way, when the news starts at 6pm, you'll already be recording. (That said, many local stations actually start the 6pm news at 6:01pm and the 11pm news at 11:01pm. Network shows, however, start exactly on the hour or half hour mark.)

✔ VCR tapes cost from $3.00 to $5.00 each for standard grade VHS tape. There's no need to pay extra for the higher quality stereo or Super VHS tape. Remember, you're taping the news, not a high fidelity concert. The standard tape length is T-120, meaning 120 minutes of recording time in SP (Standard Play) mode. But you should always record in EP (Extended Play) mode. (Some VCR manufacturers use the SLP designation for EP mode). Whether called EP or SLP by the VCR brand that you own, it will give you six hours of recording time, three times more than SP mode. The audio quality is not as good in EP mode, but it will suit your needs.

✔ Like videotapes, you don't need to buy expensive audio tapes. The cheapest brand name or an off-brand tape will do adequately for voices on an AM station, or even for a FM stereo station. Audio tape designations refer to the minutes of recording time on both sides combined. A C-30 tape has 15 minutes on a side, C-60, 30 minutes on a side and C-90, 45 minutes per side. C-120, an hour per side, is the longest size that's widely available. You should be able to find a pack of three C-120 tapes for about $6.00.

✔ Put a priority on labeling video and audio tapes. Number each tape. Three years from now, you won't remember whether tape #788 contains 1994 or 1995 news, so make the year part of your tape number. If you start recording in 1994, number your first tape 94-1. When January 1, 1995 comes around and you're up to tape number 456, number the first 1995 tape 95-457. Or, start over again at 95-1.

Use abbreviations for each show and write it and the date on the tape label. If you are using the numbering system described above, you won't have to write the year for every show, just the month and day. To track tapes, start out by getting a calendar with big blocks for each date, such as a desk calendar at an office supply store, and write down the tape number for each show. When you get a computer database set up, enter the tape number along with the other information. Then you can abandon the desk calendar and see the tape number in the database for every show.

Or, use the database software to create neat notebooks telling the tape numbers for all shows. Database software will allow you to print out only certain fields, such as date, network, show name and tape number. That will allow you to print those four fields on regular 8 and a half by 11 paper, meaning you could have sheets for each show. Say you tape the 6pm news on ABC affiliate KUSA-TV in Denver. One set of notebook sheets would list tape numbers for that show, such as

Date	Net	Station	Show	Tape#
01/01/93	ABC	KUSA	6PM	93-273
01/02/93	ABC	KUSA	6PM	93-277

      etc.

✔ Lower-priced VCRs have two video heads, but it's always best to buy a "four head" unit, a VCR with four video heads. It may cost a bit more, but it will last a lot longer. You should be able to get a good quality, brand name, four head VCR for $300 to $400. If you buy two or three at once, ask for a special price reduction.

✔ With most cable television systems you don't really need the cable box except to tune in a pay movie or sports channel. If that's true in your town, then you don't have to tune the VCR through the cable box. That means you can use the VCR tuner to record different channels at different times on the same VCR. To do this, just put the cable line directly into the "input signal" connection on the back of the VCR. At Radio Shack, any TV/VCR store or movie rental outlet for a couple of dollars you can pick up a short coaxial cable. Run it from the VCR output to your TV. Set up this way, you can record the news on channel 4 while you watch the news on channel 12. If you want to watch what the VCR is recording, set the TV to channel 3 and push the TV/Video button on the VCR.

✔ Most cable signals are strong enough to be split and still provide good picture quality. So if you have two VCRs, buy a two-way splitter and a couple of short cables. Put the cable television line coming into your home into the splitter, with a cable from the A and B output each going to a different VCR. With a six or seven dollar A/B switch, on TV channel 3 you'll be able to see the channel being tuned by either VCR.

But be careful not to get in trouble with your cable company. Many cable companies insist that you pay for any additional connections. So, if you want to set up three or four VCRs ask about getting additional cable connections. Most cable companies offer a second outlet for a very low charge.

Of course, if you receive good quality over-the-air reception, you can have one VCR tuned through the cable service and the other through an antenna. If you don't have cable, you can still use a splitter to send the signal from an indoor or outdoor antenna to more than one VCR. If you have a satellite dish feeding into an electronic splitter with a cable or antenna feed for local reception, the satellite dish instructions should explain how to add a VCR to the system.

How to monitor

In all your activities as a media monitor, apply high professional standards to your effort. Imagine that the newspaper or broadcast station, or a particular reporter, editor, or producer, is on trial for bias. Ask yourself: What evidence would prove in a clear and convincing fashion that the media are unfair? Be patient in your search for evidence; never jump to a conclusion. Occasionally the evidence of bias is dramatically clear, but sometimes it takes weeks or months (even years!) for you to gather enough evidence to prove your case.

Obviously, how much time and money you have will determine how much you're able to do. But always remember the point of recording the news: Creating an accurate record of what was aired, just like clipping newspaper articles. That's been the key to the Media Research Center's success. The MRC uses quotes of what a reporter actually said to demonstrate bias, not a summary of what we recalled hearing the reporter say. If a story is biased, accurate quotes will make a more convincing case than any amount of rhetoric from you.

Anecdotes about biased TV coverage aren't completely convincing. You need the actual tape or transcript. Nothing makes an argument like reading the media's own words back to them. The need to tape and transcribe can't be over emphasized. Historically, complaints by conservatives about media bias were dismissed by journalists. A conservative would accuse Dan Rather of bias in a particular story. The reporter would ask for specific evidence, but the conservative couldn't produce it. The whole debate changes when you can provide the evidence.

How to transcribe. Getting a radio or television story transcribed is a time-consuming task. A two-minute piece could easily take an hour to transcribe completely. You don't always have to transcribe the entire story -- sometimes, only part of a story shows bias, such as bias by labeling. But don't ever do a partial transcript that is misleading, such as taking down the part that summarizes the liberal argument but ending the transcript before the reporter explains the conservative view so it appears to be a one-sided story when it really wasn't.

To transcribe a television story, you have two options. First, using the VCR, push play and take down as much as you can until falling behind. Then push pause. Because VCRs skip a few seconds of tape when going from pause or stop to the play mode, you'll have to rewind for a second or two and then hit play again. Repeat this process until you've finished the story. (If you are a slow typist, you might find it easier to transcribe by hand and then type it on a typewriter or into a computer.)

The second option is to use an audio tape recorder. Place the cassette recorder near the TV speaker and record as you play the story on the VCR. Then transcribe the story from the audio tape. You may find this easier since audio recorders don't tend to skip over any words as you go from pause to play. Obviously, this is the simplest way to transcribe a radio story already recorded on cassette tape. Another audio tape option is to use a recorder made for secretarial use. Dictaphone is a popular trademarked brand name. This type or recorder includes features that are meant to make transcribing easier, such as a foot pedal control and slow speed playback so you can keep up with the audio.

No matter which option you select, go back afterwards and compare your transcript to the actual audio to make sure you didn't make any mistakes. For soundbites in television stories, identify them by how the person is described on-screen. If you know Barbara Jones is a liberal who serves on the board of a welfare rights group, but on-screen she's identified as "Barbara Smith, social policy researcher," put that in the transcript. That way there won't be any confusion when you cite the story as an example of bias by labeling but your transcript identifies her as "Barbara Smith, Board Member, Nebraskans for Fair Funding." (See page 53 in the first chapter for sample transcripts produced by the MRC.)

Tracking broadcast news. Ideally, with unlimited resources and time you would do what the MRC is able to do -- log topic areas and summaries of every story into a computer database. But that may be a bit ambitious for starters. At first, just try to watch or listen to all the shows you tape. When you come across an interesting story write down the date, reporter's name and a brief summary. If you have time, apply the tests outlined in chapter one to see which, if any, types of bias the story reflects. If you find that it is indeed biased by commission, labeling, spin or policy recommendation, transcribe as much of it as you can. If it's biased by omission, story selection or placement, write down exactly how.

Like you do with newspaper stories, put these story analyses in folders by topic and show. If you have a computer, consider purchasing a "database" software package. They cost upwards of $500.00, but the software would allow you to track the date, topic, show and reporter's name for every story you've analyzed. You can do the same with your newspaper stories.

A note about computers. Computers will make your analysis work easier and more complete. They will also be an absolute necessity to publish a newsletter and to implement the suggestions in chapter three for "correcting" media bias. If you don't have one, plan to get one as soon as possible.

Creating a computer database

Both Corel's Paradox and Microsoft's Access are popular database software packages, though not the only ones. A database software package will cost about $200, but "upgrade" packages are often half the price. Corel, Microsoft and Lotus also sell their database software as part of an office "suite" of several software packages.

This kind of software will let you enter the date, station, show title, name of reporter, video tape number and a few topic areas for every story you analyze. You can write your analysis and transcribe exactly what was said in a "memo" field. Then, you can do what is called a "relationship search" of what you've entered. In short, you could call up all the stories by reporter Barbara Smith on a particular topic, such as "Taxes" or "School Funding." Or, find all the stories aired by WMRC-TV on those topics.

The thoroughness of your database will be limited only by how many stories you have time to enter. Even if you only enter a few stories, a computer with database software will be tremendously helpful. Enter four or five stories a week and you'll have 200 or more in just a year! The database software will make it a lot easier to find the date and tape number for that one-sided story channel 12 did on the abortion march sometime last spring. For whatever range of stories and shows you find time to analyze, be thorough. Your summary should convey an accurate understanding of everything important said by the reporter. To save time, use abbreviations. Be sure to note the names and affiliations of every soundbite.

In the MRC's original database design which was created using the dBase III+ software, analysts entered the date, network abbreviation (ABC, CBS etc,), show abbreviation (WNT for *World News Tonight*, EN for *CBS Evening News*, TM for *CBS This Morning*, TDAY for *Today*, 60M for *60 Minutes*), name of the reporter or anchor doing the story, three topic areas, the tape number and a summary of the story.

In 1995 the MRC began using a customized software package created just for the MRC that lets us enter more topic areas, and the names of those appearing in soundbites along with their affiliation, title as well as any label applied to them.

Starting on the next page you'll see the first three pages of a reduced size print-out of a *CBS Evening News* broadcast. These pages were originally printed on 11 by 15 inch tractor-fed paper for a wide-carriage dot matrix printer.

```
SHOW  NET DATE      TAPE     Media Research Center / Media Tracking System     INT        PRINTED: 10/29/96 12:40:51 PAGE: 1
-----------------------------------------------------------------------------------------------------------------------------
EN    CBS 10/10/96  11011                                                      SHK

/00001 TOPIC: DISASTERS        s1: TWA s2: PLANE CRASH

   SUMMARY: dr: search for cause of twa explosion and crash of long island is going in diff direction. bo: 3 mo after
            crash investigators have theories but no proof. now they will ask relatives of victims if they were
            targeted or wanted to die themselves. letters went out to families saying they will soon be contacted.
            fbi agents will pose painful questions to families. target of sabotage for financial gain? was passenger
            on suicide mission?

       HOST: RATHER DAN        PRO: 0  NEU: 0  NEG: 0
   REPORTER: ORR BOB           PRO: 0  NEU: 0  NEG: 0

/00002 TOPIC: DISASTERS        s1: TWA s2: PLANE CRASH s3: CIA

   SUMMARY: dr: invest looked beneath ocean to solve twa 800, but also across the seas. jsi analysts for cia are no
            closer than anyone else to solving the case of twa 800. known terrorist orgs have speculated as to who
            was responsible for crash, but no one has claimed responsibility. may soon offer money for info. has
            worked before.

       HOST: RATHER DAN        PRO: 0  NEU: 0  NEG: 0
   REPORTER: STEWART JIM       PRO: 0  NEU: 0  NEG: 0

/00003 TOPIC: DISASTERS        s1: PLANE CRASH s2: TWA

   SUMMARY: dr: us govt has denied that any kind of so called friendly fire frm any us military source could have
            been involved in explosion of twa 800.

       HOST: RATHER DAN        PRO: 0  NEU: 0  NEG: 0

/00004 TOPIC: CAMPAIGN 96      s1: DOLE s2: KEMP s3: DEBATES s4: POWELL s5: GORE s6: CHARACTER

   SUMMARY: dr: in prez campaign, in ohio colin powell was brought in as a croud pleaser and a teaser to remind
            voters that powell will be involved in any dole admin. look at what public saw today and what was really
            going on in private. pj: in ohio, campaign bus was crowded, had kemp and powell. how did kemp do? dole
            th. day after debates, soem aides were saying time has come to attack clinton on the so called character
            issues. but kemp left hint he would not become the attack dog. kemp th. in powell intro of dole, word
            character is not used, but powell made it a pt to talk about dole service. powell th. to win prez dole
            must win ohio. he is trailing in polls, but says he is gettign through. dole th. in private, aides strong
            sense of disappointment in kemp debate performance. they talk about missed opportunities, fact that kemp
            let gore take credit for welfare reform. as one dole aide asked cynically, did he study much?

       HOST: RATHER DAN        PRO: 0  NEU: 0  NEG: 0
   REPORTER: JONES PHIL        PRO: 0  NEU: 0  NEG: 0

TALKING HEAD: dole bob          republican presidential can        PR: 0  NU: 0  NG: 0
TALKING HEAD: kemp jack                                            PR: 0  NU: 0  NG: 0
TALKING HEAD: powell colin      republican vp candidate            PR: 0  NU: 0  NG: 0
```

/00005 TOPIC: CAMPAIGN 96   s1: CLINTON   s2: INTERNET   s3: OHIO

SUMMARY: dr: clinton campaigned in tennesee today. clinton expanded on fave campaign theme: helping students get on line to widen their knowledge of cyberspace. clinton th. didnt leave ohio entirely to dole. flew there too. both are mindful clinton won ohio by narrow margin in 1992. also aware that no repub has ever won the wh w/out winning ohio.

HOST: RATHER DAN   PRO: 0   NEU: 0   NEG: 0   PR: 0 NU: 0 NG: 0

TALKING HEAD: clinton bill

/00006 TOPIC: CIS   s1: RUSSIA   s2: YELTSIN   s3: ILLNESS

SUMMARY: dr: russian tv showed yeltsin meeting with chief of staff. look at man who will have fingers on heart of prez. tffs dr renot archurin will perform heart bypass on yeltsin. will tell himself that yeltsin is just another patient.

HOST: RATHER DAN   PRO: 0   NEU: 0   NEG: 0
REPORTER: FENTON TOM   PRO: 0   NEU: 0   NEG: 0

/00007 TOPIC: HEALTH   s1: BABIES   s2: CRIB DEATH

SUMMARY: dr: fed health officials underscored advice: place infant on side or back in crib. never face down to avoid crib death.

HOST: RATHER DAN   PRO: 0   NEU: 0   NEG: 0

/00008 TOPIC: ENVIRONMENT   s1: ANIMALS   s2: PANDAS

SUMMARY: dr: new residents of san diego zoo: pair of giant pandas ust arrived frm china.

HOST: RATHER DAN   PRO: 0   NEU: 0   NEG: 0

/00009 TOPIC: CAMPAIGN 96   s1: ADS   s2: WARNER JOHN   s3: WARNER MARK   s4: VIRGINIA

SUMMARY: dr: whole new dimension to prob of distorted polit ads. not what was said in this tv ad for repub sen. john warner of va. demo opponent mark warner, no relation, is labeled a liberal polit insider over this handshake with fmr gov doug wilder and clinton with chuck robb. mark warner's head was pasted onto robb's. warner has now fired his media consultant. greg stevens, who also does work for the dole campaign.

HOST: RATHER DAN   PRO: 0   NEU: 0   NEG: 0

/00010 TOPIC: CAMPAIGN 96   s1: OHIO   s2: CREMEANS FRANK   s3: REPUBLICANS   s4: CONGRESS

SUMMARY: dr: ohio is also imp in congressional race. to gain control of house. demos need to win 19 seats to

EXPOSE

EN   CBS 10/10/96 11011   SHK

regain control. can it happen? bs: 6th congr dist in so ohio is as about as mid america as it gets. place where demo candidate ted strickland will spend campaign morn stirring apple butter. where the repub incumbent congressman frank cremeans will devote middle of campaign day to talking about the flag with 1st and 2nd graders. also example of kind of districts demos need to win to take back the house. strickland won the congr race here the yr clinton won the wh but lost it to cremeans 2 yrs ago when repubs won the house planning to revolutionize washington. now the two are back for rematch that typifies the predicament many repub freshmen are finding. the talk of revolution and its result backfired with many voters. just ask the repub county chmn. remember he is repub not demo chmn. bennett th. where did he make the mistake? in shutting down the govt? bennett th. one reason why cremeans is a gingrich stalwart in dc but stresses the local angle here. is your opponent running against newt gingrich or is he running against you? cremeans th. for sure, opponent promises the same. he has learned a lesson too. strickland th. obvious perhaps, but as election draws near, dozens of repub freshmen are running scared, wondering if its a lesson they learned in time.

       HOST: RATHER DAN   PRO: 0 NEU: 0 NEG: 0
   REPORTER: SCHIEFFER BOB   PRO: 0 NEU: 0 NEG: 0

TALKING HEAD: bennett roger   clinton county republican   chairman   PR: 0 NU: 0 NG: 0
TALKING HEAD: cremeans frank   congressman   republican   PR: 0 NU: 0 NG: 0
TALKING HEAD: strickland ted   democratic candidate   PR: 0 NU: 0 NG: 0

/00011 TOPIC: CENTRAL AMERICA s1: CANADA s2: UNIONS s3: GM s4: STRIKE
    SUMMARY: dr: in canada, autoworkers strike shut down all gm plants there.
       HOST: RATHER DAN   PRO: 0 NEU: 0 NEG: 0

/00012 TOPIC: BUSINESS   s1: AETNA s2: LAYOFFS
    SUMMARY: dr: aetna insurance company announced it is laying off workers, 4400. 13% of workforce.
       HOST: RATHER DAN   PRO: 0 NEU: 0 NEG: 0

/00013 TOPIC: ASIA   s1: AFGHANISTAN s2: TALIBAN s3: FIGHTING
    SUMMARY: dr: 2 wks after capital of afghanistan fell to a army of islamic radicals the country has changed. taliban rulers imposed a strict and harsh version of islamic law. mpi new regieme is already under attack. new opposition alliance. regieme is being condemned for launching a reign of terror. strict islamic wrath being targeted of afghanistan's women. may starve them taliban has closed schools for girls. if tens of thousands of war widows cant work, they wont be able to feed themselves or their children. the taliban see it another way.
       HOST: RATHER DAN   PRO: 0 NEU: 0 NEG: 0
   REPORTER: PHILLIPS MARK   PRO: 0 NEU: 0 NEG: 0

/00014 TOPIC: SPORTS   s1: BASEBALL s2: YANKEES
    SUMMARY: dr: talk of ny and baltimore. report on that kid. hs: not latest child movie star but pic is on every

For the morning shows like *CBS This Morning* and *Today*, the MRC design had a slot for analysts to enter the names of guests interviewed. This design allowed MRC analysts to do a search for all *CBS This Morning* stories in May on the topic of taxes. Or, search for all the dates on which House Speaker Newt Gingrich was interviewed.

A print-out of the first hour or so of a *Today* appears on the next six pages. For the *CBS Evening News* print-out you saw that we tracked the sequential story number, i.e. 01, 02, 03, etc. Knowing a story you want to find was the 14th one on a morning show isn't very helpful when you try to go back and find it. Did the 14th story come just before 7:30am or during the 8am headlines? So, the MRC created a "time" field for the two-hour morning shows. You'll see that the print-out lists the half hour in which the stories aired -- 0700 for 7am and 0730 for 7:30 am followed by the story number, so 07304 designates the fourth story of the 7:30 half hour.

Following the 1996 *Today* print-out is a "list" format of an entire 1993 *Today* show done with the MRC's old database system. A list print-out does not include the story summaries, so it provides as a quick view of a show's topics and guests.

EXPOSE

```
SHOW    NET DATE    TAPE    Media Research Center / Media Tracking System    INT         PRINTED: 10/29/96   13:34:16 PAGE: 1
TDAY NBC 10/16/96 11029                                                       GCD
-----------------------------------------------------------------------------------------------------------------------------

/07001  TOPIC: CAMPAIGN 96        s1: DOLE BOB  s2: CLINTON BILL  s3: DEBATE  s4: NEGATIVE  s5: CHARACTER

        SUMMARY: bg: good morning. pres clinton and bob dole are making final preparations for tonight's debate in san
                 diego. trailing badly in all the polls dole's hopes are desperate so he's expected to focus on the
                 negative and attack the president's ethics and character in their final face to face meeting today.

              HOST: GUMBEL BRYANT          PRO: 0  NEU: 0  NEG: 0

/07002  TOPIC: CAMPAIGN 96        s1: CLINTON BILL  s2: DOLE BOB  s3: DEBATES  s4: CHARACTER  s5: WOMEN

        SUMMARY: bg and kc host: the last debate of the natl political campaign is on tap in san diego. dole is
                 not waiting for that debate to attack clinton's ethics. with more on a campaign that is getting meaner
                 kelly joins us in san diego.

                 kc: the first thing dole advisers will tell you about tonight's town hall debate is that this is a
                 clinton friendly format. so dole is expected to respond with a change in style that is decidly less
                 friendly. aides describe bob dole's evermore aggressive style and plan for tonight's debate as an
                 evolving strategy. in a series of speeches he has gradually turned up the intensity. in san diego tuesday
                 he reached full boil. rd th. advisers have pusher and even some frustrated republicans have demanded dole
                 use this last debate with its huge tv audience to go after bill clinton. republican strategist rich bond.
                 rb th. but the dole campaign does see a downside. their own surveys tell them women voters are more
                 likely to be turned off if dole is seen as too negative. dole's own reluctance put aside he appears ready
                 to take his assault on the ethics of the clinton administration into prime time. and ready to justify his
                 attack. rd th. with a potential gain for dole if enough voters see pres clinton as vulnerable when his
                 ethics and character are questioned. most of dole's preparation for tonight's debate is working on that
                 sharpened attack of white house ethics. aides say he will rely heavily on his study from the first debate
                 for all of the other issues.

              HOST: LAUER MATT           PRO: 0  NEU: 0  NEG: 0
          REPORTER: ODONNELL KELLY       PRO: 0  NEU: 0  NEG: 0

      TALKING HEAD: dole robert          presidential candidate                         repu PR: 0  NU: 0  NG: 0
      TALKING HEAD: bond rich            fmr head of rnc                                      PR: 0  NU: 0  NG: 0

            QUOTES: Matt Lauer: "Good morning everyone. The last debate of the national political campaign is on tap for
                    tonight in San Diego. Bob Dole is not waiting for that debate to attack Bill Clinton's ethics. With more
                    on a campaign that is now getting meaner NBC's Kelly O'Donnell is standing by live in San Diego."

/07003  TOPIC: CAMPAIGN 96        s1: DOLE BOB  s2: CLINTON BILL  s3: DEBATES  s4: CHARACTER  s5: NEGATIVE

        SUMMARY: ml: in new mexico to prepare for the debate pres clinton is not exactly fighting fire with fire. he
                 limited his personal criticism to saying, "bob dole tries to seperate the administration from what goes
                 right and to blame it for what goes wrong? pol analysts predict the president will stay on the positive
                 side even if dole stays on the attack.

              HOST: LAUER MATT           PRO: 0  NEU: 0  NEG: 0
```

/07004 TOPIC: CAMPAIGN 96   s1: WALSH LAWRENCE s2: PARDONS s3: CLINTON BILL s4: DOLE BOB s5: IRAN CONTRA s6: WHITEWATER

SUMMARY: m1: meantine former iran contra prosecutor lawrence walsh has some harsh words for dole this morning. he
         is calling him a hypocrite. it stems from dole's criticism of pres clinton for refusing to rule out
         pardons in the whitewater case. judge walsh says dole himself pushed for pardons for those connected to
         the iran contra scandal. and this morning the judge is in our oklahoma affiliate. judge good morning.
         m1: what exactly was bob dole's role in getting casper weinberger a pardon before he went on trial for
         iran contra crimes back in 1922? lw.
         let me read you something that comes out of the dole camp this morning. it says, quote "judge walsh
         failed to note that prior instances of pardons did not involve sitting presidents who are active
         investigations and stood to personally gain from the promised pardons." lw.
         the dole people also mention that you have a book on this subject coming out in the spring. and they say
         you are taking this opportunity to do a little self promotion and money making. lw.
         so your statements this morning come only for political reasons not promotional reasons? lw.

         HOST: LAUER MATT   PRO: 0 NEU: 0 NEG: 0   PR: 0 NU: 0 NG: 0
         GUEST: walsh lawrence   fmr iran contra prosecutor

/07005 TOPIC: RELIGION   s1: POPE JOHN PAUL s2: SURGERY

SUMMARY: m1: pope spending first full day back at the vatican after recent surgery. greeted well wishers from apt.

         HOST: LAUER MATT   PRO: 0 NEU: 0 NEG: 0

/07006 TOPIC: CRIME   s1: SIMPSON OJ s2: CIVIL TRIAL

SUMMARY: m1: prosecution and defense in oj civil trial expected to finish picking jury by end of week. simpson
         appeared in court today.

         HOST: LAUER MATT   PRO: 0 NEU: 0 NEG: 0

/07007 TOPIC: CRIME   s1: RAPE s2: DEAF

SUMMARY: m1: judge in ca court has turned down unusual request of rapist. defendant jesse masias. the alleged
         victim and all of the witnesses in the case are deaf. mesias demanded that all members of the jury be
         fluent in sign language. judge turned him down.

         HOST: LAUER MATT   PRO: 0 NEU: 0 NEG: 0

/07008 TOPIC: SOCIAL   s1: SMOKING s2: BAN s3: MARYLAND

SUMMARY: m1: a court test in the works for anti smoking law in tiny suburb of wash dc. last night council members

TDAY NBC 10/16/96 11029   GCD

in friendship heights voted to ban smoking on public streets and parks. reaction is mixed. am th. tl th.

HOST: LAUER MATT   PRO: 0 NEU: 0 NEG: 0

TALKING HEAD: muller alfred   friendship heights mayor   PR: 0 NU: 0 NG: 0
TALKING HEAD: lee thomas   resident   dr   PR: 0 NU: 0 NG: 0

/07009 TOPIC: SPORTS   s1: BASEBALL

SUMMARY: m1: quick preview of sports.

HOST: LAUER MATT   PRO: 0 NEU: 0 NEG: 0

/07010 TOPIC: CAMPAIGN 96   s1: DOLE BOB s2: CLINTON BILL s3: BUCHANAN PAT s4: DEBATES s5: CHARACTER s6: NEGATIVE s7: FBI FILES
ALE BILLY

SUMMARY: bg: on close up this morning the last debate. the second and final debate tonight in san diego. and as we've noted dole is expected to go on the attack. pat buchanan joins us in new hamp. pb. i'm fine thank you. good to see you again. pb. what's your advice for dole. what should he do tonight that he didn't in the first encounter? pb. so you make a distinction between the president's ethical integrity and his personal character? pb. (brings up dale and fbi files) but let me ask you again do you think dole should make a distinction tonight between the president's personal character and his ethical integrity? pb. as you know dole has been concerned about looking and seeming mean spirited. do you think tonight he can go on the attack with valid issues, without reminding voters of his reputation as a hatchet man and windup in the negative? pb. coming as they will with just 3 weeks left to campaign and dole trailing badly in the polls aren't these moves going to look like they are born of desperation? pb. do you still think repubs could have made a better choice in the primaries? pb.

HOST: GUMBEL BRYANT   PRO: 0 NEU: 0 NEG: 0
GUEST: buchanan pat   fmr presidential candidate   PR: 0 NU: 0 NG: 0

/07011 TOPIC: CAMPAIGN 96   s1: DOLE BOB s2: CLINTON BILL s3: DEBATES s4: CHARACTER s5: NEGATIVE s6: TRAVEL OFFICE s7: FBI FILE

SUMMARY: bg: paul begala is one of the strategists who helped president clinton prepare for tonight's debate. he is in new mex. what do you and the president expecting from dole tonight? pb. but wait a second, wait a second! is that really a hatchet man? why shouldn't voters view issues like influence peddling or travelgate or the problem of the fbi files as legitimate campaign issues? pb. are you saying the ethics of a presidential administration are not a legitimate issue? pb. how should we expect the president to respond when mr. dole goes on the attack tonight? pb. you say that but the white house has suggested that mr dole raises these issues tonight at his own peril. is the president prepared to fire back? pb. in an interview last weekend dole said quote, "whatever happens i want to be at peace with myself when it's over." do you see him disavowing that wish tonight? pb.

HOST: GUMBEL BRYANT   PRO: 0 NEU: 0 NEG: 0
GUEST: begala paul   political strategist   PR: 0 NU: 0 NG: 0

/07012 TOPIC: CAMPAIGN 96   s1: DOLE BOB s2: CLINTON BILL s3: DEBATES s4: CHARACTER s5: NEGATIVE s6: ETHICS s7: WHITEWATER s8:
LES s9: TRAVELGATE

EXPOSE

SUMMARY: kc: bryant the possibility that tonight's town hall debate could turn on questions of character and ethics made us think back 4 years ago to one of the more memorable questions from the 1992 presidential town hall debate. this was the question. (video of '92 town hall debate about trashing opp't's character question) that question came from kim usry of richmond va. welcome. first of all tell me how your life has changed in the last 4 years? ku. what are you doing now? ku. tell me back then if you were pleased by the response by the candidates. did you feel as if they adequately answered your question? ku. during this campaign year are the candidates addressing the issues in a way that you would have hoped they had in '92? ku. after a few days of vacillating dole has made it clear that he is going to be much more aggressive than he has prior to this debate at tonight's debate. how do you feel about that? about attacking the president's character? ku. some people consider some of the things that have gone on in the clinton administration. we've heard about whitewater and filegate and travelgate as cause for concern. does it impact you at all? does it affect your vote in any shape, way or form? ku. you supported perot back in '92. are you supporting this go around? ku. would you like to tell us who you are supporting or would you rather keep that private? ku.

HOST: COURIC KATIE   PRO: 0   NEU: 0   NEG: 0

GUEST: usry kim   audience member of 1992 pre   PR: 0 NU: 0 NG: 0

/07301 TOPIC: CAMPAIGN 96   s1: DOLE BOB s2: CLINTON BILL s3: CHARACTER s4: DEBATE s5: NEGATIVE s6: ETHICS

SUMMARY: kc and bg host: m1 rpts: president clinton is headed to california today as he prepares to meet dole tonight in san diego. the president has been preparing for tonight's debate in alburque. and on tuesday he dismissed dole's recent attacks on his character as quote, "politics." meanwhile dole continued his attacks tuesday, calling the president, "self righteous and self serving."

HOST: LAUER MATT   PRO: 0   NEU: 0   NEG: 0

/07302 TOPIC: BUSINESS   s1: AIRLINES s2: KIWI s3: BANKRUPTCY

SUMMARY: m1: officials of kiwi airlines say airline will go out of business next week if an investor can't found to keep it running through bankruptcy.

/07303 TOPIC: POLITICAL   s1: POVERTY s2: STATISTIC s3: UNITED STATES s4: CHILDREN s5: BREAD FOR THE W

SUMMARY: m1: a new report says us has more children living in poverty than any other industrial nation. the bread for the world institute says 22% of americans under 10 live in poverty.

HOST: LAUER MATT   PRO: 0   NEU: 0   NEG: 0

/07304 TOPIC: CRIME   s1: SIMPSON OJ s2: CIVIL TRIAL

SUMMARY: kc: jury selection continued in simpson civil trial. da.

HOST: COURIC KATIE   PRO: 0   NEU: 0   NEG: 0

GUEST: abrams dan   court tv   PR: 0 NU: 0 NG: 0

/07305 TOPIC: ENTERTAINMENT   s1: LEE SPIKE s2: MILLION MAN MAR s3: MOVIE

SUMMARY: bg: today is the first anniversary of the million man march on washington. to mark the occasion spike lee has a new film opening nationwide today called "get on the bus." film is about a group of african american men traveling cross country to take part in the march. men who begin their journey as strangers but find they have much in common. it's a film lee directed but unlike his past works he didn't write the screenplay for this one. sl. is it true what i read spike that 3 quarters of the film is shot on a real bus? sl. why did you feel compelled to film it on a real bus rather than cut one in half? sl. in fact you have so many diff elements of the black community represented that you reveal a great deal of conflict? sl. why did you choose to end the film before speeches began? sl. how much a real diff that march made? sl. i know you didn't make this film for white americans but do you think they will go see it? sl. do you think white americans will learn a lot about african americans if they get a chance to get on the bus? sl.

HOST: GUMBEL BRYANT   PRO: 0 NEU: 0 NEG: 0   PR: 0 NU: 0 NG: 0
GUEST: lee spike   get on the bus   director

/07306 TOPIC: INTLIFE   s1: ART s2: ANIMAL s3: APE s4: PAINTING

SUMMARY: kc: a young artist has taken vienna art world by storm. nona. km rpts. organtuan artist. ck th. hp th.

HOST: COURIC KATIE   PRO: 0 NEU: 0 NEG: 0
REPORTER: MILLER KEITH   PRO: 0 NEU: 0 NEG: 0

TALKING HEAD: kment claudia   zoologist   PR: 0 NU: 0 NG: 0
TALKING HEAD: pribil heinz   gallery owner   PR: 0 NU: 0 NG: 0

/08001 TOPIC: CAMPAIGN 96   s1: DEBATES s2: CLINTON BILL s3: DOLE BOB s4: CHARACTER s5: NEGATIVE

SUMMARY: bg and kc host: ml rpts: with second and final debate set for tonight repub bob dole is sharpening his attacks on pres clinton. on tues dole turned up the heat criticizing what he called the "ethical failures of the president and his administration. he also said that no administration has been "more self righteous or shown more arrogance." the president meantime was shrugging off the attacks.

jp: at a news conf in hotel serving as his debate training camp pres clinton turned down several opportunities to swing back hard at dole's blistering character attack. preferring instead to offer a light jab. bc th. but mr clinton's aides were not reluctant to respond. jl th. but some say mr clinton may have difficulty handling questions about ethics. mb th. others say dole will be taking a risk if he makes personal attacks on the pres. ms th. conventional wisdom says the president should stay positive, focus more and more on winning the house of representatives as well as the white house.

HOST: LAUER MATT   PRO: 0 NEU: 0 NEG: 0
REPORTER: PALMER JOHNE   PRO: 0 NEU: 0 NEG: 0

TALKING HEAD: clinton bill   president   PR: 0 NU: 0 NG: 0
TALKING HEAD: lockhart joe   clinton gore campaign   PR: 0 NU: 0 NG: 0

EXPOSE

TDAY NBC 10/16/96 11022   GCD

TALKING HEAD: barone michael   us news and world report   PR: 0 NU: 0 NG: 0
TALKING HEAD: siegel mark   democratic strategist   PR: 0 NU: 0 NG: 0

/08002 TOPIC: POLITICAL   s1: SUPREME COURT s2: ABORTION s3: CLINICS

SUMMARY: m1: a dispute over anti abortion protest today goes to the supreme court. at issue is whether it is legal
to keep protestors away from people going into or out of clinics where abortions performed. .

pu: after enduring 2 years of aggressive protest. some of it blocking clinic doors. supporters of
abortion rights in ny state got a judge to limit protest in a novel way. his order - no demonstrating
within 15 feet of any one entering abortion clinic. a moving bubble zone. free of protest. even on the
sidewalk or the street. womens groups say the zones protect clinic patients from protest that gets out of
hand. jl th. but some of the anti abortion protestors are asking the supreme court to strike down the
bubble zones. they say it is unconstitutional to limit free speech on a public sidewalk no matter how
unpleasant it maybe to those hearing it. js th. how the supreme court rules could affect many other kinds
of protest including labor disputes and civil rights issues.

HOST: LAUER MATT   PRO: 0 NEU: 0 NEG: 0
REPORTER: WILLIAMS PETE   PRO: 0 NEU: 0 NEG: 0

TALKING HEAD: lichtman judith   womens legal defense fund   PR: 0 NU: 0 NG: 0
TALKING HEAD: sekulow jay   attorney for protestors   PR: 0 NU: 0 NG: 0

/08003 TOPIC: CRIME   s1: RAPE s2: DEAF s3: TRIAL

SUMMARY: m1: in other news a ca judge rejected request by defendant who was deaf. do rpts. mf th.

HOST: LAUER MATT   PRO: 0 NEU: 0 NEG: 0
REPORTER: OLIVER DON   PRO: 0 NEU: 0 NEG: 0

TALKING HEAD: feiger mara   defense attorney   PR: 0 NU: 0 NG: 0

/08004 TOPIC: CRIME   s1: POVERTY s2: CHILDREN s3: UNITED STATES

SUMMARY: m1: a new rpt finds more children living in poverty in the us than any other major industrialized
country. bread for world instit.

HOST: LAUER MATT   PRO: 0 NEU: 0 NEG: 0

/08005 TOPIC: ENVIRONMENT   s1: AUSTRALIA s2: WHALE s3: RESCUE

SUMMARY: m1: humpback whale rescue in australia.

HOST: LAUER MATT   PRO: 0 NEU: 0 NEG: 0

/08006 TOPIC: INTLIFE   s1: UNION s2: STRIKE s3: ROME s4: AIRLINES s5: BRITISH AIRWAYS

Record#	DATE	NETWORK	PROGRAM	TIME	HOST	GUEST1	GUEST2	GUEST3	TOPIC	SUBTOPIC	NOTE	TAPE	SUMMARY
1104	11/18/93	nbc	tday	0700	miklaszews				political	nafta	6744	6744	Memo
1105	11/18/93	nbc	tday	0700	levine irv				economy	nafta	ag		Memo
1106	11/18/93	nbc	tday	0700	lauer matt				social	gun control			Memo
1107	11/18/93	nbc	tday	0700	cummins ji				airlines	american air			Memo
1108	11/18/93	nbc	tday	0700	lauer matt				africa	somalia			Memo
1109	11/18/93	nbc	tday	0700	couric kat	gore al			political	nafta	ck		Memo
1110	11/18/93	nbc	tday	0700	gumbel bry	martin lynn			political	nafta			Memo
1111	11/18/93	nbc	tday	0730	lauer matt				airlines	american air			Memo
1112	11/18/93	nbc	tday	0730	lauer matt				political	nafta			Memo
1113	11/18/93	nbc	tday	0730	lauer matt				political	rollins ed			Memo
1114	11/18/93	nbc	tday	0730	lauer matt				britain	bus crash			Memo
1115	11/18/93	nbc	tday	0730	lauer matt				africa	somalia			Memo
1116	11/18/93	nbc	tday	0730	couric kat	russert tim	myers lisa		political	nafta	ck		Memo
1117	11/18/93	nbc	tday	0730	gumbel bry	katzenbach nic	schlesinger ar	hunt al	history	jfk			Memo
1118	11/18/93	nbc	tday	0800	lauer matt				airlines	american air			Memo
1119	11/18/93	nbc	tday	0800	clarke ode				political	nafta			Memo
1120	11/18/93	nbc	tday	0800	lewis geor				political	nafta			Memo
1121	11/18/93	nbc	tday	0800	lauer matt				social	gun control			Memo
1122	11/18/93	nbc	tday	0800	bazell rob				health	premature ba			Memo
1123	11/18/93	nbc	tday	0800	gangel jam				defense	cia			Memo
1124	11/18/93	nbc	tday	0800	miller kei	boothroyd bett			britain	parliament			Memo
1125	11/18/93	nbc	tday	0830	lauer matt				airlines	american air			Memo
1126	11/18/93	nbc	tday	0830	lauer matt				political	nafta			Memo
1127	11/18/93	nbc	tday	0830	lauer matt				political	apec			Memo
1128	11/18/93	nbc	tday	0830	lauer matt				central amer	haiti			Memo
1129	11/18/93	nbc	tday	0830	lauer matt				africa	somalia			Memo
1130	11/18/93	nbc	tday	0830	brown jame	julia raul			entertainmen	movies			Memo
1131	11/18/93	nbc	tday	0830	gumbel bry	mcwhirter norr	crevier bruce		entertainmen	guinness boo			Memo
1132	11/18/93	nbc	tday	0830	shalit gen				entertainmen	movies			Memo

EXPOSE

Here are some tips on selecting database topics and using your database to create tapes of stories on selected topic.

✔ Keep topic areas simple and consistent. You want to be able to remember how you categorized a similar story weeks earlier. Whether you are using a computer database or files in a box in the corner, don't define topic areas too narrowly. File stories by general topic areas like "abortion," "schools," "taxes," and "health." If a story covers several topics, put it under those and a broad topic heading like "politics." When trying to track down a story, you don't want to have remember whether you put it under "city council property tax proposal" or "property tax" or "Fairhaven property tax." The topic "Taxes" should cover all tax stories.

If there are several distinct tax debates going on simultaneously, then use topic headings like "Taxes/Fairhaven," "Taxes/sales," and "Taxes/income surtax." That way, in a paper file they will all be together under T. In a computer database you can enter two or three topic areas for each story, but doing it this way will allow you to most easily find all the tax stories. Database software works by finding all the entries that share the letters you search by. In other words, if you search for the word "taxes" you will get all stories under the topic "taxes," plus all entries in which another word follows "taxes," such as "taxes/sales."

At first, you may be only able to track stories on one or two topics. For example, if you believe the local police are being unfairly accused of brutality, put copies of all newspaper articles on the subject into a file along with a brief summary or full analysis of broadcast stories. With a computer, enter the key information into a database system. As your file on police brutality grows, sift through it to see if you can spot a pattern of biased news coverage.

As time passes, compare transcripts or video of coverage of two opposing events. If you play the tape of a station's story on February's pro-abortion demonstration, followed immediately by the tape of the same station's coverage of a pro-life march in August, you may see a dramatic contrast. It's important to keep all your tapes so you can go back and see how a story was covered months earlier. If you can't afford to keep buying new tapes, make sure you don't record over any story you found important enough to note in your files.

✔ Create tapes of stories on a given subject such as taxes or gun control. It is amazingly effective in proving bias to show a series of stories, on the same station over a period of time, in which only one side is presented. Any video store has "dubbing" cables that will let you connect two VCRs so that you can record from one tape onto another. Remember, VCRs record over the last few seconds of tape. To get the best results, on the recording VCR use the "pause" button, not the "stop" button, between stories. With a little practice you'll learn how to make tapes with fairly smooth transitions between the stories recorded onto them. For best results, use the editing function that comes with many better VCRs.

On page 116 you'll learn about addressing groups. Videotapes showing bias will be extremely helpful in convincing an audience that bias is a problem. Nothing speaks louder than showing actual stories.

EXPOSE

Section Two:
Documenting Bias Through Studies

After you have begun tracking print and broadcast stories, completing studies to prove bias becomes a possibility. Quoting a story or summarizing how the media covered an event is critical. Proving bias in specific stories day after day and week after week shows how reporting favors the liberal viewpoint, but a skeptic can still claim just as many stories are biased to the right as to the left. A study is definitive. When done properly, it provides irrefutable proof of media bias because it covers every story aired or printed on a certain subject. In a study, you use the same rules you've learned to apply to a single story to analyze a set of stories, often over a significant time period, to determine one or more of the following:

● Whether certain topics were mentioned in coverage of an event or policy debate

● How particular groups or politicians were labeled

● The political perspective of those quoted or appearing in soundbites in stories on a particular subject

● Which side of an issue received more time, space or words in stories on a certain topic

● The number of stories and time devoted to two different events or subjects months or years apart

Avoid the temptation to "slant" your study. Your search is for the truth -- "let the chips fall where they may." The more careful you are to ensure that the research itself is objective, the more credibility you will have when you reach a subjective conclusion based on that research.

Here are descriptions, examples and instructions for how to conduct the five types of studies most effectively utilized by the MRC.

Labeling study

This kind of study is used to show a disparity in labeling of politicians or political groups.

Past MRC studies on think tanks, environmentalists and abortion activists proved that reporters tinker with the credibility of political groups by regularly identifying conservative groups as conservative but refusing to label liberal groups as liberal. If news stories label conservatives but not liberals, then conservatives appear to represent extreme views while liberals appear mainstream and thus more credible.

Labeling study example A:

To learn whether reporters for some major newspapers and magazines accurately identify the political viewpoints of the Washington "experts" they quote, back in 1989 the MRC reviewed every 1987 and 1988 news story mentioning two prominent groups on the right and two prominent ones on the left. The study included *The Washington Post, New York Times, Los Angeles Times, Newsweek, Time,* and *U.S. News & World Report*. The result: an astonishing contrast in treatment.

Think Tanks: Brookings and Heritage. Perhaps the national media's favorite source of expert opinion, the Brookings Institution was labeled just 10 times in 737 news stories (1.4%). In 270 of 271 mentions (99.6%), *The New York Times* failed to label Brookings. *Time* magazine applied a label once in 39 stories, while *U.S. News* (45) and *Newsweek* (30) never did.

By dramatic contrast, Heritage was accurately described as "conservative" or a similar term in 217 of 370 stories (58.6%). *The Los Angeles Times* attached a conservative label the most, 71 times in 79 stories (89.9%). *Time* was second with 13 labels in 19 stories (68.4%), followed by *The New York Times* (74 out of 126, or 58.7%), *U.S. News* (7 out of 14, or 50%), and the *Post* (51 out of 129, for 39.5%). *Newsweek* refrained from issuing a label in three mentions of the think tank. *Time* writers Richard Hornik and Michael Duffy best demonstrated the double standard in a December 5, 1988 story: "Neither Bush nor the nation will risk serious damage if he ignores the recommendations of groups ranging from the archconservative Heritage Foundation to the Brookings Institution."

Women's Groups: National Organization for Women (NOW) and Concerned Women for America (CWA). The liberal NOW also escaped categorization, labeled a mere 10 times in 421 stories, (2.4%). *The Los Angeles Times* issued six labels in 166 stories, five "liberal" and one "mainstream." In 124 stories, the *New York Times* never once placed a liberal label on NOW. Out of 100 stories in the *Post*, two included the term "liberal." Among magazines, *Time* used no labels in 10 stories, while *Newsweek* in 9 and U.S. News in 8 applied "liberal" once each.

On the other hand, CWA got labeled 25 times in 61 news accounts (41%). *The Los Angeles Times* issued the lion's share of labels, describing CWA as "conservative" five times, "right-wing" on four occasions, and "New Right" once. In six labels over 16 stories in *The New York Times*, three were "conservative," two were "strongly conservative," and one was "New Right." In 17 *Post* stories, all eight labels were "conservative." Though NOW claims 160,000 members and CWA about 600,000, it's worth noting reporters mentioned the liberal group four times more often.

Labeling study example B:

Though the Children's Defense Fund (CDF) sounds inoffensive, the group is extremely liberal. How liberal? The CDF's own "Nonpartisan Voting Index" routinely grades liberals such as Sen. Ted Kennedy as 100 percent politically correct. CDF founder Marian Wright Edelman regularly scolds the government for not copying Europe's socialist programs.

To determine the tone of news stories featuring CDF, *MediaWatch* analyzed both print and broadcast news stories. *MediaWatch* analysts used Nexis to identify every news story mentioning CDF in the *Los Angeles Times, New York Times, Washington Post* and *USA Today* in 1991 and 1992. The newspapers described CDF as "liberal" only 19 times in 343 news stories (5.5 percent). This still lags far behind the 1991-92 labeling of conservative child advocacy groups like the Family Research Council (FRC), which got tagged with a conservative label in 43 of 92 stories, or 47 percent of the time. Put another way, reporters were almost 12 times more likely to label the conservative FRC than the liberal CDF.

➡ **How to conduct a labeling study.** To complete these labeling studies MRC researchers used the Nexis™ computer system to retrieve newspaper and magazine articles mentioning the groups studied. (For a description of Nexis, see page xx in the previous chapter.) The MRC used the "kwic" feature in Nexis to print out just a dozen or so words before and after the "search term;" such as "Heritage Foundation." Then a researcher read each mention to see whether a label appeared and tallied the number times each type of label was used, such as "conservative" and "right wing."

Many large newspapers, such as the *Chicago Tribune, New York Times, San Francisco Chronicle, Los Angeles Times, Atlanta Constitution and Seattle Times,* are on the Nexis system. Every year Nexis adds newspapers, so you'll have to check to see if it carries the major paper in your area. As mentioned on page 14, the content of all Knight-Ridder newspapers is available through the Dialog database service.

But you can still complete a labeling study for newspapers not on a database service, such as your local paper, by maintaining thorough research files. Nexis lets you go back in time. You'll have to start on a particular date and go forward. This is a long term project. You can't do a study on just few stories that appeared one month. The longer the time period covered, the more convincing a study you can conduct. If your labeling study covers only a few months, critics may discount it, attributing the disparity you found to a particular incident or event. But if the study covers two or three years, it will be impossible for anyone to dismiss it as an aberration. You'll have proven a pattern. At a minimum, study stories over a one year period.

If certain activist groups or politicians on both the liberal and conservative ends of the spectrum are quoted fairly often, (the local equivalent of Senators Kennedy and Helms, of the Children's Defense Fund and Family Research Council) choose one, two or three on each side and cut out every article mentioning them. Then when you've got at least a year's worth of stories filed, read through to count the number of labels applied to the politician or group on each end of the spectrum.

You can also make this an ongoing project: When you cut out an article, underline the person or group's name and, if there is one, the label. At the top of the article, write down the result -- "no label" or "liberal." Then you can flip through the file fairly quickly to tally the result. Remember, a labeling study should be based on percentages. The fact that a liberal was labeled 23 times and a conservative 34 times means nothing. Determine the percentage -- the liberal got tagged 21 percent of the time (in 23 of 107 stories), but the conservative was labeled 69 percent of the time (34 of 49 stories).

If a liberal group or person gets tagged with just one label, say "liberal," while a variety of labels are applied to the conservative, such as "arch-conservative," "far right" and "right wing," compare the total number of labels for each side. Don't just compare "conservative" to "liberal." Then break down the specific conservative labels so you can note how 18 percent of the conservative labels were "far right" (6 of 34), but the newspaper never used the term "far left."

It is possible to conduct a labeling study for radio and television stories, but it's a lot more difficult. In a few years, the transcripts of many local television station newscasts will probably be available through a local computer database service. In the meantime, however, to find every mention of a person or group you'll have to watch or listen to every edition of a particular newscast, and use your computer database to enter a summary of every political story that notes every mention of the persons or groups you are studying. Then, just like with newspaper stories, you can go through your database print-outs to count up the total number of times each person or group was mentioned and in what percent labels were attached.

✔ **Tip:** Create a one or two character field in your database to identify stories mentioning the persons or groups you are studying. Putting an "L" in this field will allow you to easily print out all the relevant stories.

Selection of sources study

Complete this type of study to prove how one side of a debate received a disproportionate amount of attention.

A selection of sources study can be done over the long term, or to prove bias in coverage of a specific event or topic over a matter of days or weeks.

Selection of sources study example A:

After the 1990 Earth Day celebrations, the MRC conducted a study to determine which point of view garnered more media attention during the week leading up to the march: liberal environmentalists who advocate more government regulations or free-market environmentalists who wish to unleash market forces to improve environmental conditions.

MRC analysts watched all morning and evening news shows during the week of April 16-22, in addition to *Nightwatch,* the CBS overnight show. *MediaWatch* compared the amount of time given to liberal environmentalists (Earth Day and major environmental group staffers and ecologists like Barry Commoner) to the time given to free-market environmentalists. We differentiated between talking heads (people appearing in news stories) and in-studio interviews.

Liberal environmentalists were offered more than 30 times as many opportunities to speak as their opponents, tallying 68 talking head appearances, compared to two soundbites by one free-marketeer. Interviews were just as heavily weighted: 26 liberal environmentalists to one free-marketeer.

The majority of morning show interviews came on April 20. For example, the CBS show *Nightwatch* interviewed eight left-wing guests, including West German Green Party leader Petra Kelly, anti-technology activist Jeremy Rifkin, and *Washington Post* reporter Cynthia Gorney, who was writing for *Mother Jones* on how to go green in "this grossly overconsumptive and wasteful society." Rifkin told host Charlie Rose that "A radical reduction in energy use is not a big sacrifice: it's just changing habits...convenience culture is destroying the planet."

NBC's *Today* was the epitome of imbalance. Bryant Gumbel interviewed Ellen Silbergeld of the Environmental Defense Fund, rainforest advocate Thomas Lovejoy of the Smithsonian Institution, and Paul Ehrlich, notorious author of *The Population Bomb*, which falsely predicted mass famines in the 1970s.

What the networks failed to do was offer time to almost anyone who challenged the scientific, economic, and political assumptions behind the entire Earth Day protest. The only exception: meteorologist Patrick Michaels of the University of Virginia, who joined the debate over global warming on *This Week with David Brinkley* (clips of which were later used once each on *World News Tonight* and *Good Morning America*). Earth Day Alternatives, a coalition of free-market environmental groups, held a press conference and made numerous spokesmen available, but was shut out completely.

Selection of sources study example B:

In the wake of the 1992 Los Angeles riots, the MRC undertook a study to learn whether advocates or critics of more federal social spending appeared more often in network television news stories. Did the media give equal weight to both sides?

MRC analysts watched every evening news story in May (from ABC's *World News Tonight*, *CBS Evening News*, CNN's *World News*, and *NBC Nightly News*) on the impact on federal social programs. In 29 news stories, defenders of Great Society programs and advocates for more federal spending outnumbered critics, 79 to 22, or roughly four to one. Thirteen stories aired pro-Great Society sources with zero critics.

CBS had the worst soundbite imbalance, 33-8 (or 80 percent pro-government), followed by ABC (13-3, or 80 percent), NBC (14-4, or 77 percent), and CNN (19-7, or 73 percent). ABC had the most stories that aired liberals with no critics -- five. CBS aired three, and CNN and NBC aired two. Only three ABC stories featured critics, and they were all President Bush, two in Brit Hume stories and one by Tom Foreman.

➡ **How to conduct a selection of sources study.** A selection of sources study is best employed to prove bias in coverage of a major political event or policy debate in which liberals and conservatives have strong, contrasting views. This could be anything from stories leading up to a protest march one weekend to stories that appear on and off over a several month period as the governor and legislature spar over the school aid bill.

The purpose of the study is prove one side got more broadcast soundbites or newspaper quotes than the other, so you must first define the two categories. In the MRC Earth Day study we classified people as liberal environmentalists or free market environmentalists; in the post L.A. riots study, as those favoring or opposing additional federal social spending. Once you've defined the categories, your work isn't done. You must decide into which category everyone fits. Well-known liberal and conservative politicians and activist group representatives will be easy to classify. For others, you'll have to see which side their comment supports. But some won't fit either category -- a professor who makes a neutral observation or a government official who simply notes how the state "distributed $12 billion in school aid last year." Don't count these.

Once you've got the classifications worked out, you're ready to go. As part of your monitoring, you should have already cut out and filed print stories. Go through each one and add up the number of quotes from the liberal and conservative viewpoint. If someone is quoted more than once, count each instance. A newspaper story may quote a liberal legislator at three different points and quote a liberal activist once. That story contains two liberal sources, but four liberal quotes. The number of quotes devoted to the liberal argument is most important, but keep track of both counts. That way, you can report how *Daily Banner* stories included 23 quotes advocating the liberal position from 15 liberals.

For television, check your database for the dates and show names for all relevant stories. If you've been entering thorough summaries into your database which include the names of all soundbites, then you'll just have to read through them. If not, go back through your tapes, watch the stories and for each soundbite write down the name, on-screen identification, and a summary of what the person said. Count both the total number of sources and soundbites aired for each side. In the Earth Day study summarized earlier, the MRC determined that 44 liberal environmentalists tallied 68 talking head appearances, compared to two soundbites by one free-marketeer.

Television news interview shows can also be studied for their selection of interview subjects. In the Earth Day study example the MRC examined the political agenda of those interviewed on *Today*, *Good Morning America* and *CBS This Morning*. If one or more of your local television stations carries a similar morning program or if a noon time or evening show regularly features an interview segment, use the same criteria as you did with soundbites to examine who was interviewed.

Story selection study

Undertake this type of study to show a disparity in the amount of coverage devoted to two events months or years apart.

In the last chapter you read how the MRC employed a story selection study to show how John Sununu's travel arrangements generated many more stories than similar travel habits by then-Congressman Les Aspin.

Story selection study example:

In the Spring of 1992, the MRC compared the number of stories the networks devoted to questions about Democratic candidate Bill Clinton's draft record to the number of stories Dan Quayle's military service had generated in 1988. MRC analysts examined the coverage of four evening news shows (ABC's *World News Tonight, CBS Evening News*, and *NBC Nightly News*, as well as CNN's *Prime News* from 1988 and *World News* from 1992) during times when Clinton and Quayle were under scrutiny over possible draft evasion and other personal issues.

In the ten days following revelations about the two candidates, 1988 Quayle stories outnumbered 1992 Clinton stories by a margin of almost four to one. In the first ten days of Quayle's National Guard controversy (August 18-27, 1988), the four networks did 51 news stories solely on Quayle's National Guard service. (This counts only evening news, not any of the 158 times the networks raised questions about Quayle's controversies during the prime time coverage of the Republican Convention.) By contrast, in the first ten days of Clinton's draft flap (February 6-15), the four networks aired only 13 stories.

When the February 6 Wall Street Journal broke a story questioning Bill Clinton's draft record, how did the networks react? ABC made it story number five. CBS and NBC completely ignored the story. Two days later on the *CBS Evening News*, reporter Bruce Morton declared: "When attacks are made on character, the press ought to report them and then let the voters decide who's right and who's wrong." By contrast, on August 18, 1988, the four networks aired 15 stories on Quayle. ABC did three stories, and CBS and NBC each broadcast five. The Quayle news led all four evening newscasts.

On February 12, 1992 one of Clinton's ROTC officers, Clinton Jones, released a 1969 letter from Clinton thanking the ROTC for "saving me from the draft." The response was again protective. None of the evening newscasts began with it, and each aired only one story.

➥ **How to conduct a story selection study.** Like a labeling study, a story selection study requires a large body of research material collected over at least a year. The MRC could not have compared 1992 Clinton stories to 1988 Quayle coverage unless we had recorded and tracked those Quayle stories from four years earlier. This is another reason to log into your database as many stories as possible: you won't know until months or years later which topics you'll want to examine for a story selection study.

When the media devote a large amount of negative coverage to a controversy about a conservative, try to recall an instance of a liberal charged with committing the same or similar act. When you see studies from liberal groups or which match the liberal issue agenda getting coverage, ask conservative groups if they released studies on the same topics weeks, months or years earlier. If you can find a contrasting event, consider a story selection study.

Begin by identifying the appropriate time periods to study. In the Clinton/Quayle study the MRC decided to check the ten days following the initial revelations about both candidates. If you want to study coverage of liberal and conservative political policy pronouncements or studies, stick to long time periods. A comparison showing a liberal group's study got three stories but a conservative group's study on the same subject six months earlier got one story is not a media study. It's just one instance of bias. For a story selection study, examine how many stories were generated by studies from each side of the spectrum over a one, two, or three year period.

Look through your television news database and/or newspaper files for the appropriate time period and tally up the number of stories.

✔ **Tip:** As part of your regular news monitoring, make a special effort to track coverage of policy studies. For newspaper stories, create a "liberal studies" and a "conservative studies" file. Photocopy any article that reports a study released by a liberal or conservative group and place it in the appropriate file. For broadcast stories, create a database field to mark stories devoted to, or mentioning a study. At the end of the year, print out all study stories and see if policy studies from either side received a disproportionate number of stories.

Commission/Omission study

Engage this kind of study to prove that media coverage of an event or policy either repeatedly stated a false or liberal premise, or omitted a particular viewpoint.

Refer back to the definitions of bias by commission and omission on pages xx to xx in the last chapter for descriptions of what falls into this category.

Commission/omission study example:

After the House and Senate passed President Bush's 1990 "deficit reduction" package which included tax increases, the MRC studied whether network television stories did or did not report certain facts. *MediaWatch* analysts watched every ABC *World News Tonight*, CBS *Evening News*, CNN *Evening News* and NBC *Nightly News* story from the emergence of the first budget bill September 24 to October 28, the day after a budget passed. In total, 231 news stories were reviewed. Questions 1, 3 and 4 show bias by omission; question 2 shows bias by commission.

1) How many reported the actual size of next year's budget, compared to this year's budget? Zero. The federal budget for fiscal year 1990 was $1.26 trillion. The latest figures from the Office of Management and Budget project a 1991 budget of $1.36 trillion. That's an increase of $100 billion in one year or an 8 percent increase, hardly the model of penny-pinching austerity. But not one reporter managed to compare the overall budgets of 1990 and 1991. Instead, the reporters' emphasis on "getting a deal" accepted politicians' promises to reduce the deficit at face value. Reporters led viewers to assume the budget deal will reduce the deficit by $500 billion over five years, or whatever the two sides claimed as talks wound down to the finish.

2) How many reported that many, if not all of the budget's "spending cuts" were not spending cuts at all, but cuts in projected increases? Zero. Reporters did a number of stories on the disastrous effects of spending cuts, particularly Medicare cuts, but not one reporter explained that the "cuts" they were referring to were not cuts, but reductions in spending increases. "Tonight both sides say that unlike budget deals of the past, these cuts are real," emphasized

ABC's Ann Compton on September 30. Simply by reporting phony "spending cuts" as real, the media participated in misleading the American taxpayer. Since 1984, tax revenues have risen by an average of $78 billion a year. If spending had been held to the rate of inflation, we would have had a surplus years ago. Federal revenues are projected to rise $397.8 billion dollars over the next five years -- without the coming tax hikes.

Medicare is a perfect example. Every network told viewers Medicare would be "cut" $60 billion and devoted at least one entire story to "profiles in suffering." Reporters didn't say that Medicare is the fastest growing program in the budget, and without "cuts," is scheduled to grow 12 to 13 percent a year. Over the five years of the new budget deal, Medicare spending is still projected to grow from $105 billion to $168 billion, a 60 percent increase.

3) How many reported the actual effect of a full one-year sequestration on next year's budget? Zero. Reporters also ignored the basic facts and figures on the sequester. A full one-year sequester would have cut spending by $85.4 billion. Even after the sequester, overall federal spending would increase $15 billion. Instead of reporting the actual numbers, reporters bought the government line that the allowed spending increase required a shutdown, calling it a "disaster," a "train wreck" that "cripples the country," in which "everyone loses." NBC showed the least restraint, reporting "it appears we are going over the precipice," "an awful precipice," "the guillotine coming down," an "alternative too horrible to contemplate," and "a long nightmare with no morning."

4) How many reporters concentrated on the savings from cutting government waste? Zero. "Waste, fraud, and abuse" may sound like an empty catch phrase, but Charles Bowsher, head of the General Accounting Office, estimates there is $180 billion a year in waste, fraud, and mismanagement. The networks ignored the hundreds of GAO reports identifying waste, and even the $60 billion in annual savings identified by the Congressional Budget Office. Citizens Against Government Waste has issued a report calling for $305 billion in waste reduction over the next five years. All these arguments were ignored.

➡ **How to conduct a commission/omission study.** You must know the arguments forwarded by liberals and conservatives in any policy debate in order to conduct this type of study. If you notice that coverage of a policy debate hardly ever mentions conservative views or repeatedly includes false statements, or liberal premises stated as if they were beyond question, then you may wish to do a study.

First, write down a specific description of all the points made that you believe are false or one-sided along with all the views you think were omitted. Go through your list to see if any of the items can be combined with others that are similar. Then, like the MRC did with the budget study above, draw up specific questions about what was said or omitted. Try to keep the list to five or fewer questions. Any more will make for an unfocused study.

Second, after you've figured out what you're looking for, determine a reasonable time frame to examine. For the budget study, the MRC looked at all stories from the time the budget was proposed through its passage. If you study a policy debate, make sure to include all stories from the beginning to end of the process. Otherwise, you'll leave yourself open to criticism for not including all the coverage.

Third, write down your questions on a sheet of paper, leaving an inch or two of blank space below each. Put places at the top of the sheet for the date, show name or newspaper, story or page number and name of the reporter. Go through your newspaper files and computer database to identify all relevant stories. Photocopy enough sheets to match the number of stories you identify. Read or watch each story, filling in a sheet for each. When finished, go through all your sheets to tally the study result.

Spin study

Utilize this type of study to show how the media interpretation of an event matched the liberal spin far more often than it did the conservative spin.

Spin study Example A:

The Republican defeat of President Clinton's stimulus package drew a great deal of media attention, but the defeat was hardly unique: the Democrats did the same to George Bush and his "stimulus" tax cut proposal in his first year.

To compare the TV treatments of the blocked Bush and Clinton proposals, MRC analysts reviewed every evening news story (on ABC's *World News Tonight, CBS Evening News,* CNN's *Prime News* or *World News,* and *NBC Nightly News*) and morning news report (on ABC's *Good Morning America, CBS This Morning,* and NBC's *Today*) from the House passage of the bills to their deaths on the Senate floor (from September 28-October 26, 1989 for Bush, and March 19-April 23 for Clinton).

Analysts found that in 1989, the Bush plan was never described as a "jobs bill," but simply as a "capital gains tax cut." So, in 1993 did the networks call the Clinton bill an "emergency spending-increase bill?" No, they were more promotional: 46 percent of stories used the Democratic term "jobs bill" to describe the plan, and only 15 percent explained the GOP opposed the bill as pork-barrel spending. CBS set the pattern for bias. While the other networks described the Clinton package as a "jobs bill" or "job creation bill" in 31 percent of news stories, CBS used the terms in 83 percent. The evening and morning totals were nearly identical.

Spin study Example B:

Just when Judge Clarence Thomas looked to be a shoo-in for Senate confirmation, someone with the Senate Judiciary Committee leaked an affidavit from Anita Hill charging Thomas with sexual harassment. If, as suspected, Democrats did the leaking, it could clearly be characterized as hardball politics or playing dirty.

But when network television covered the hearings live over the Columbus Day weekend, Democrats were not subjected to tough questioning about their possible role in the leak, or how committing this crime was a new low in playing dirty. Instead, reporters accused the Republican committee members of playing hardball politics, while criticizing the Democrats for not being tough enough on Thomas, a *MediaWatch* study documented.

The study covered all ABC, CBS and NBC news broadcasts (both live coverage and normal shows) between the start of the hearings at 10 AM EDT on Friday, October 11 through the Wednesday, October 16, 1991 morning programs. The study also covered all CNN and PBS live coverage, plus CNN's *World News*.

In total, the five networks' anchors, reporters and affiliated analysts singled out the Republicans for cynical or hardball tactics on 28 separate occasions. On another twelve occasions, the network personalities complained that committee Democrats went too easy on Thomas. (On two occasions, CBS vaguely blamed both parties, calling the hearings "smear and counter-smear," for example.) No anchor or reporter deplored the likelihood that the Democrats leaked in an effort to stop Thomas at all costs.

During an October 14 *Today* roundtable discussion, NBC News Washington Bureau Chief Tim Russert exemplified the attack on Republicans: "You had Senators accusing people of perjury; Senator Simpson, 'I have faxes, I have letters' -- the closest thing to McCarthy that we've seen. It was not a kinder, gentler Republican panel." On *Today* the next morning, Andrea Mitchell complained about Thomas: "The Democrats did not ask him tough questions about the facts of her charge and they did, the Republicans did a great job of hammering her. It's basically what happened in the '88 campaign. The Republicans know how to fight dirty."

➡ **How to conduct a spin study.** A spin study can best be done when the Democratic and Republican Parties both have the discipline to push the same spin on a story day after day. When the Democrats always refer to the Governor's "jobs creation stimulus package" and the Republicans consistently describe it as a "tax hike job killer," see which spin the media most often repeat.

A spin study can simply look at stories done over a few weeks on a certain event. Or, you can compare the spin on a current event to the spin on an event that occurred months or years ago. Either way, determine the phrases used to express each side's spin. Then go through all the stories on the topic you're studying to see how many express one of the phrases.

Three notes about studies

First, not all studies work out. Sometimes you might see a biased story and assume it's typical of all stories on the same topic. In fact, you may be very surprised to find that media coverage of the event is not biased, or that it's pretty close to being balanced.

Second, don't ever fudge the facts to prove a contention. Assume a reporter or liberal activist will try to destroy your credibility by taking your study apart. So keep a well-ordered record of what you did. Set aside in a file all the question sheets, database print-outs, photocopies of newspaper articles, television news story transcripts and tally sheets you used to conduct the study. A study should be replicable, meaning that someone else could do it and come up with the same result. You should always be able to show others how you came to your result.

Third, you can complete more than one kind of study simultaneously. Remember the selection of sources study the MRC did after the L.A. riots? Well, the MRC also studied how many stories omitted mentioning that social spending had grown in the '80s. In the MRC commission/omission study on 1990 budget deal coverage, we also studied the selection of sources: "When the networks went to outside analysts on the politics and economics of the budget, liberal analysts outnumbered conservatives 33 to 11."

Section Three:
Publicizing Your Findings

With a system in place to monitor the news media, you will soon come across a biased story or a pattern of bias on a particular topic. Your next move: Bring the evidence to the attention of the community through letters to the editor, editorial response time on television and radio stations, calls to talk shows and speeches before church and civic groups, such as the Knights of Columbus, Kiwanis Club, Rotary Club, Lions Club and veterans groups.

Fulfilling these publicity activities should bring you in touch with fellow conservatives who share your concerns. Ask them to help you out. If someone else with a VCR can tape the Channel 12 news, that's one less show you have to handle. And the more people writing letters to the editor and calling talk shows, the more attention media bias will receive.

To be most effective, keep this in mind: Conservatives already believe the media are biased. They are a ready audience for solid proof. But you don't want to turn off the skeptical media executive or reporter with conservative rhetoric. Emphasize quotes. Back up your case with numerical analysis and studies -- the story in question omitted the conservative argument or included three officials explaining the tax hike's necessity to only one person advocating spending cuts. Don't lead with rhetoric. That will only let the skeptic dismiss your case. Make the skeptic respond to fact and solid analysis.

In this section you'll learn how to:

- Write letters to the editor
- Submit op-ed pieces
- Take advantage of the ombudsman
- Submit a TV or radio editorial response
- Call radio talk shows, provide information to hosts & become a guest
- Send evidence of bias to friendly media contacts
- Give speeches to local civic groups
- Develop an e-mail list and create a Web site

Letters to the editor

The letters column is a very popular feature, especially with readers interested in politics and the affairs of the community. When you find bias in a newspaper, write a letter to the editor.

It is one of the best ways to become known for a particular point of view, for the courage to express it, and for the knowledge and skill to express it well.

Some newspaper people don't have much respect for their television colleagues, so you can also write a letter about broadcast coverage. When writing about television or radio news, don't critique just one story. An editor might consider that too narrow a focus. Stick to a broad topic like the one-sided coverage of the state senator race on channel 12. On the other hand, if you're concerned about newspaper coverage it's better to write about one particular story in that newspaper than about the paper's general coverage.

Always remember that your work will appear in the letters column by the good graces of the editor. If he thinks you are unreasonable, he will simply throw your letter away. But if you seem like a reasonable person and have a valid point, even if the editor disagrees, he will print your letter so that (a) he will appear fair to the readers and to his friends in the business community and (b) it will make the letters column more interesting and help sell newspapers.

Here are some rules for a written letter, but their general principles also apply to letters sent by fax or e-mail. (Newspapers want their letters to be as current as possible, so a letter sent immediately by fax or e-mail will often have a better chance of being run. If they accept letters by these methods, the fax number and/or e-mail address will be listed on the editorial page.)

● Type or print your letter neatly, double-spaced on white 8 1/2-by-11-inch paper. Check spelling carefully.

● Sign all letters. Many editors will not print letters unless they can verify the authorship, so include your address and both daytime and nighttime telephone numbers, if possible. If it is relevant to the issue you are discussing, you may sign your name with a professional title. If your letter contains personal information, the editor will usually withhold your name upon request when he publishes it. But almost all editors require that you sign your letter if you want it considered for publication.

● Keep it simple. Do not attack every point made in a biased story, no matter how tempting that might be. Pick out one point, two at the most. If you make your case effectively that he is wrong on one or two points, no one will remember the other points. But if you try to make too many points, you may confuse the reader.

• Keep it short. The shorter the letter, the more likely it will be printed. You are a guest on the editor's page, and guests who stay too long don't get invited to many parties. An editor only has so much space, and you are competing with all the other features in the newspaper and all the other letter-writers. And an editor only has so much time to read the letters; the long and complex ones get thrown away first.

Many newspapers have a hard-and-fast rule against letters of over a certain length, such as 300 words. Be sure to know the limit, if any, for that particular paper.

• Make doubly sure you are correct. If possible, check your facts with someone who is an expert on the issue. Don't hesitate to call the head of the local or state anti-tax group, if the subject is taxes. Consider calling an authoritative source such as the State Revenue Department or the Chamber of Commerce. Never be shy when your own reputation for accuracy is at stake.

• Remember the difference between fact and opinion. For example, if an editorial says that "military spending under President Reagan, as a percentage of Gross National Product, was the highest in peacetime history," that is a question of fact and a good letter would provide proof that the statement is false. But if the editorial simply argues that "Reagan spent too much on the military," take the opportunity to refute the argument itself. An editorial, remember, is supposed to take a position on an issue; it is not evidence of bias. But that doesn't mean you can't respond to editorials as part of an ongoing, respectful debate.

• Stay on the main point or points. Do not engage in ad hominem (personal) attacks such as "What would you expect from Editor Smith? She's an atheist, and her father was a draft-dodger." Remember that it is the editor's *argument* that you're criticizing, the reporter's *facts* that you're correcting.

An occasional friendly poke in the ribs is okay, of course, particularly if you're a regular critic of a particular journalist. A good model is Ronald Reagan in the 1980 debate with Jimmy Carter, chuckling "There you go again." He did *not* call Carter, then the President of the United States, names; he amiably implied that he had countered Carter's arguments before.

• The best defense is a good offense. Don't write letters only in response to articles or editorials you disagree with. Take the initiative;

help set the agenda for public debate by finding issues the newspaper has failed to address. Make a point, then suggest that the paper cover the issue. This technique is especially effective when you suggest follow-ups to old stories: "I read all these stories about how the world faced a new ice age. Now the same people are warning us about global warming. Well, which is it?" Even if the letter doesn't get printed, it might spur the reporter or editor to cover the issue.

● Use the carrot as well as the stick. Reporters and editors need to be rewarded when they do a good job, not just punished when they perform poorly. Write a favorable letter when you see an article or editorial that you like. Do this especially if you're a frequent critic. But base your comments on the journalistic merit of the piece.

● Be timely. Respond quickly to errors or to comments with which you disagree. After several days, only a few readers will remember and even fewer will care about an error. You must strike while the iron is hot.

● Keep a calendar to remind you of upcoming events -- congressional hearings or debates, protest demonstrations, important anniversaries, etc. -- and do an early draft expounding your points several days before the event. Editors love to print letters about the hot topic of the day, but they can only do that when someone sends a letter quickly.

Here are some sample letters: Say the local newspaper claims the city council "came at health spending with the budget ax," but notes later in the article that spending increased in the past year by $1 million instead of the $2 million the city's health department wanted.

> **WRONG:** "Put a dunce cap on your reporter, Jeff Smith, and buy him a calculator while you're at it. One million dollars in new city spending isn't a 'cut.' My third grader can figure this out." Not only is this too personal an attack, but it isn't specific enough about the date or actual wording or numbers in the article.

> **RIGHT:** "In Jeff Smith's article on city health spending ('Health cuts strain local hospitals,' 6/13), he claims the city council 'came at health spending with the budget ax,' but ten paragraphs later, he notes that spending 'increased in the last year by $1 million.' Even if the health department wanted a $2 million increase, an increase half that size is not a 'cut.' I hope your reporters can do a better job in the future calling an increase an increase and a cut a cut. We like our news straight."

This version is more factual in tone, identifying exact quotes and their location in the story, notes the source of the reporter's confusion, and ends on a hopeful, almost non-ideological "good journalism" note.

Take another example: a local reporter does a story on unconfirmed rumors that the female mayor is gay. The reporter notes that women aren't letting gossip get them down "since Anita Hill showed women how to fight back."

WRONG: "Jessica Jones just can't keep her feminist views out of the newspaper. Not only does she stick up for her feminist buddy Mayor Anderson, but she has to drag Saint Anita Hill into it. Like birds of a feather, the feminists stick together, and your newspaper is turning into nothing but a manifesto for their agenda." This version makes the following mistakes: it doesn't condemn rumors, it isn't specific enough about the article, and it doesn't grasp the real irony.

RIGHT: "Jessica Jones is completely right about rumor-mongering about the Mayor's personal life ('Anderson suffers slings, arrows of sleaze,' 2/10). No one should have to tolerate the stain of unproven gossip. So how can Jones celebrate Anita Hill for teaching women to fight back? Is Hill's testimony about Clarence Thomas any more proven than the allegations against the mayor? If a woman stepped forward and claimed she'd had an affair with the mayor, would that make it so? Jones should use the same standard of evidence for Anita Hill as she does for the whispers about Mayor Anderson."

In this version, you've come out against gossip and suggested a single standard of evidence for good journalism.

Even your letters of praise should be carefully considered.

RIGHT: "You are the first reporter who has covered property seizures, which is important to people on the south side of town. Thank you for covering our neighborhood's concerns."

WRONG: "I'm glad to see there is at least one reporter who agrees with us that the city's fascist bureaucracy is stealing our land on the south side."

Praising a reporter as a supporter of your point of view is usually not helpful to a journalist's career.

Submit an op-ed piece to your newspaper

Op-ed articles, so named because they usually appear opposite the editorial page, are basically just longer letters to the editor. Most run from 500 to 1,000 words. Some papers run only syndicated columnists on the op-ed page, such as Mona Charen, George Will, Ellen Goodman,

Tom Wicker, William F. Buckley and Pat Buchanan. Others also run local columnists and an occasional contribution from a reader. If you see op-eds from local residents in your newspaper, then this is another option for you to pursue.

Larger newspapers have an op-ed page editor; at smaller ones it's just one of the duties of the editorial page editor or the editor of the whole paper. If you can't tell, call to find who's responsible at your newspaper. Then write that person to see if the paper has any special requirements. (Include you phone number so he can call you, but don't call him. If he's very busy, he'll find your call annoying.) Do this ahead of time so you'll know exactly how to make a submission when the time comes.

Many newspapers don't run op-eds about just one incident; they think that's better handled through a letter to the editor. You may have better luck with an op-ed that doesn't dwell on just one report you didn't like. Write about a broader topic, like an issue you think the newspaper has misrepresented or underplayed, but still include specific examples. Try to tie a broader topic to a specific, timely event. An example: If you see bias in coverage of the tax limitation committee's effort to roll back a tax hike, write an op-ed on it, but hold onto it. Then, when the newspaper shows bias in coverage of the city hall march on Saturday, update the article to start with reference to coverage of the march.

Timing is critical for any article about a current event or analyzing coverage of a story. If you're upset by coverage of the march on Saturday in front of city hall, it will be old news a week later. So, you want the appropriate editor to see your op-ed within a matter of days. Ideally, in this case, you'd hand deliver it to the newspaper's front desk by Monday morning. Then he could run it on Tuesday, when the event is still fresh in people's minds.

When you do submit an article, include a brief cover letter with your op-ed that explains in a couple of sentences its thesis and conclusion.

Take advantage of the ombudsman

Many large newspapers employ an ombudsman. Taking a critical look at how the paper covers the news is the ombudsman's job. His column normally appears on the editorial or op-ed page at least a couple of times a month. An ombudsman is employed by the newspaper, but is totally independent. The newspaper guarantees him a certain amount of space to write whatever he wishes. Often the ombudsman is a retired editor or reporter, or a professor on leave. If your paper has one, take advantage of it. Ombudsmen have a lot of credibility. When an ombudsman criticizes his paper for imbalance or lack of fairness toward a news subject, it puts the issue in the forefront. Talk show hosts, for instance, are likely to make it a subject that day.

Following the same general rules that apply to letters to the editor, write the ombudsman with a specific complaint about a story you saw, or a pattern of imbalance you've found. One difference from a letter to the editor -- within reason, your letter can be a bit longer in order to provide a few more details or examples. Always provide your address and a daytime phone number. A good ombudsman may call you to ask for further details.

Just as with op-eds and letters to the editor, timeliness is critical. If you explain your complaint about a Tuesday newspaper story to the ombudsman within a day, he'll have time to investigate it and write about it for his regular Saturday column. If he doesn't hear about your complaint until Friday, he's already written his Saturday column and it will be old news by the following Saturday. So, if he has a fax number, use it. If he's on-line for computer electronic mail, learn how to send him a letter through your computer.

TV and radio editorial responses

Television and radio stations don't have the equivalent of a letters to the editor page, but many do provide time for an "editorial response" or an open forum to offer an opinion on an issue of concern to the community. This response time goes under a lot of different names, such as "Sound-off" and "Opinion Line." Given the large number of people asking stations for time, you face tough competition. But considering the large audience you'll reach, it's worth a shot.

As with letters to the editor, brevity is the key. Most stations will want you to keep it to two minutes or less. That's less than two double-spaced pages. Unlike letters to the editor, specific criticism of a story isn't the best way to go. The television or radio station staffer combing through editorial response requests is looking for well-known topics familiar to listeners, something with a point of view. So talk in more general terms about how the station's coverage of the abortion march or the General Assembly's tax debate favored one side. Base your comments on your analysis, but mention a specific story only briefly and only to support your thesis.

Finally, don't forget to say thank the station. A station is under no obligation to run your response. So if they do, be appreciative. Send a thank you letter to the station employee responsible for selecting your response and to the station's general manager.

Using radio talk shows

It is said that radio talk shows have taken the place of town meetings as the best example of direct democracy in America. Remember the public explosion over the congressional pay raise in 1990? That was the result of the exposure the issue got on radio talk shows. Scandals such as congressional pay hikes and the Keating Five got much better coverage on radio talk shows than in the rest of the media. Talk shows were way ahead of the rest of the media in pursuing questions about Bill Clinton's background and tax plans. During the fall of 1992, media bias became a hot talk show topic.

Radio is probably the one segment of the media where there is the greatest degree of competition and where, therefore, average people have the greatest influence. As a result, radio is one of the few areas in which conservatives are strong nationally; conservatives currently hold the titles of top radio newscaster/commentator (Paul Harvey) and top radio talk show host (Rush Limbaugh).

The same goes at the local level. So many people with conservative values have come to distrust newspapers and television news that they've turned to talk radio for information. There are many liberal talk show hosts, but at least as many are conservative. Boston has WBZ's David Brudnoy, Milwaukee has WISN's Mark Belling; Denver has KOA's Michael Rosen; San Francisco has KGO's Jim Eason; Kansas City has KCMO's Wes Minter; Dallas has KLIF's David Gold and WBAP's Mark Davis; and Pittsburgh has KDKA's Mike Pintek. And that's just a few names.

There are four ways you can help conservative ideas get a fair hearing through radio talk shows.

❶ **Call in.** Only about two percent of the listeners to a radio talk show call in; some 98 percent never do. So the callers are not representative of all the listeners. Rather, the people you hear calling in with comments and questions are the ones with the most patience and the most determination to be heard.

Make a note of the telephone number for the shows you listen to. Memorize the number, write it down next to your phone or, if you have a programmable telephone, enter that number in the telephone memory. Listen to the show often enough so that you have a good idea of its format and quirks. (For example, people who call the Rush Limbaugh show are supposed to say "dittos Rush" if they agree with him).

When you have a comment or question, dial the number. If you get a busy signal, immediately hang up and call again, and again, and again, until you get through. (If you have an automatic redial button on your phone, use it. If you have a car phone, use it.)

✔ **Tip:** All radio shows are on a five to eleven second delay so that the engineer can bleep out profanities. Use that to your advantage. Five to eleven seconds before you hear the current caller hang up was when he actually hung up. So, when you hear a call nearing completion, start dialing. If you're calling when that caller hangs up you'll get that now-open line.

Remember: The callers you hear on the radio are the ones who had a little patience. Most people, once they get in the habit of calling, are surprised at how often they get on the air.

It is not hard to get through. If it were difficult, would you hear the same people call repeatedly, to the point that you and the show's host recognize their voices? Even the TV cable call-in shows on C-SPAN, which has viewers around the world, has a "30-day rule" to keep the same people from calling over and over. So the concern that "I'll never get through" is no excuse for failing to call the local talk show or even a nationally syndicated show such as Oliver North's or Mary Matalin's.

Don't limit yourself to shows hosted by conservatives. Liberal and moderate hosts often value callers with whom they disagree; it makes for a more lively show.

When you do get through, remember to turn your radio volume way down. The "delay" mentioned earlier means that if you listen to the radio while you try to talk, you'll hear your own voice from several seconds earlier and you will get very confused.

Some people get nervous when they call, as if they were the President addressing the nation. The best way to handle "stage fright" of this sort is to just talk directly to the host and/or his guest. If you feel confident that your question or comment is a valid one, you have no reason to feel self-conscious.

❷ Provide fodder to conservative talk hosts. Radio talk show hosts are always looking for something interesting to talk about. Identify the conservative hosts in your radio market and send them material. Attach a brief note telling them how you enjoy their show and thought they might get a kick out of the enclosed item. What could you send?

● A biased article from the paper along with an explanation of why you think it's biased.

● A transcript of a television news story with an accompanying note explaining why it's biased (you can also underline the biased parts). The host may have even seen the story, but only you can provide a word for word rendition of what the reporter said. If the host finds the story particularly imbalanced, or contains a ridiculous assertion or conclusion, he'll love to read part of it on air.

● A study you have done on coverage of a particular issue by a local media outlet or outlets.

If you can obtain the radio station's fax number, that's even better. A story from last night's news will be considered current the next day, but a few days later, the host may think it's out of date.

● E-mail. Don't forget about e-mail. If the host plugs his e-mail address on the air, use it but don't abuse it. Don't send lengthy messages detailing your personal opinions about life and politics. Do send short messages alerting the host to an interesting item you saw.

❸ Be a guest on a talk show. Later in this chapter you'll learn how to form a formal committee or organization. In the "Correct" section you'll learn about public relations. If you follow the suggestions in both of those sections, you'll be able to establish yourself as a media bias expert. Then, and only then, will talk show hosts and producers start inviting you on to talk about media bias. Once you've been on, and assuming you are a good guest, you'll find that the talk show producers will invite you back fairly often. That's because he'll put you in his Rolodex™ under media bias. Whenever the issue comes up, he'll see your name.

You can be the best friend a talk show producer ever had. You see, producing a talk show is a hazardous occupation. Guests cancel at the last minute or get stuck in traffic. A producer (who, at a smaller station, is also the host) has guests lined up to discuss urban renewal or the movie rating system when suddenly war breaks out in the Middle East or the Supreme Court hands down a landmark decision; then the topic for today's show suddenly changes.

Talk show producers love the kind of guest who is always prepared, who is available on a moment's notice, and who won't complain if his segment is cut short or canceled without warning.

You can be that kind of guest.

But don't forget to be a valuable research resource for the host and producer. If the producer calls you at 11am and says they would like some examples of bias from the anchorman they just booked for the 1pm hour, jump into action. Gather everything you can and fax it or drop it off as soon as possible. That will earn you the appreciation of the host and/or producer, making it all the more likely that they will ask you over someone else to be a guest at a later time. In the meantime, your examples of bias are being publicized on the show.

❹ Encourage stations to hire a conservative host. If a local station has a liberal but not a conservative talk show host, lobby for a conservative talk show. If you have a business that advertises heavily on the radio, or if you know a committed conservative who does, you can use that economic power to create a forum for conservative views. Tell the folks at the radio station that you won't allow your ads to go on programs that treat conservatives unfairly, but that you would be glad to buy extra ads on a conservative-oriented show.

There are many places where a conservative talk show would do well, if only someone would take the time and trouble to get one on the air. You probably know someone -- perhaps yourself -- who has the gift of gab, the knowledge of the issues, and the dynamic personality necessary to be a successful talk show host.

If a major station in your town does not have a local talk show -- it has music with news on the hour or runs national talk shows midday and at night with local news in drive time -- then suggest a point/counterpoint segment. Suggest the names of two or three liberals and conservatives willing to participate. A station will be most likely to take up your idea if you can provide an enthusiastic sponsor.

So talk to local businessman about being a sponsor. A point/counterpoint can come in any length, but the shorter it is the more likely a station will be able to squeeze it into its programming schedule. With 90 seconds for each side, a station might only need one sponsor for a one minute spot each day, making for a total length of four minutes. Sell potential sponsors on the idea by telling them how much prestige they will gain in the community if WMRC listeners hear the "Brown's Hardware *From Both Sides*" debate every morning or afternoon.

✔

EXPOSE

Send information to friendly media

Just as suggested above with talk show hosts, send information to friendly figures in the media. Besides conservative talk hosts, most newspapers have at least one conservative columnist or editorial writer. While the national media are quite liberal, many smaller newspapers have conservative publishers and/or columnists. They may be stuck with the Washington Post, New York Times or Knight-Ridder news services for national news stories, but they control the editorial and op-ed page. Often they write a weekly column themselves.

These people are often a receptive audience. They realize the media are biased. Professional rivalries mean talk show hosts and those in the print media frequently look down on their television brethren. The local newspaper columnist or publisher might love to do a column on biased reporting on the local or nearby big city television station if he only had the necessary facts. You can provide the information.

On the national level the Media Research Center has found this one of the most effective ways to get our research to the public. Like talk show hosts, columnists and editorial writers need ideas everyday or week for what to write about. Send them your story analysis or example of contrasting coverage.

When you first write, they won't know whether or not your information is reliable, so always include photocopies of any articles you cite. Note that you have a videotape of the particular story or stories that you can provide if they wish to verify your transcript. Don't expect everything you send to be used. But if you keep sending good material you should soon find quotes you provided popping up in editorials and columns.

If after several months the particular columnist, editor or writer hasn't used any of your material, enclose a note in the next letter asking whether he's interested in continuing to receive information from you. If not, it's not necessarily a bad reflection upon the quality of your material. Media bias just doesn't interest everyone.

Giving speeches to local civic and church groups

Civic, community and church groups are always struggling to find entertaining and interesting speakers. Why else would the local Kiwanis Club form a "speakers committee"? Between you, your family and friends you probably know someone who belongs to the Chamber of Commerce, Kiwanis Club, Knights of Columbus, Rotary Club, Elks Lodge or Masons. At church, do you attend the Tuesday Men's Breakfast or Wednesday night Women's Club? Are you a veteran? Do you know any? The VFW and American Legion tend to a have a conservative membership.

Make members of these clubs know you are available to talk about media bias. Chances are, with the frequent cross-membership, someone who hears you address the Chamber of Commerce lunch will recommend you to the Kiwanis Club.

Prepare a short speech outlining why you think the local media are biased. Illustrate it with specific examples. You can photocopy newspaper articles and pass them around. If you have a particularly egregious television news contrast -- say, the disparate coverage of two marches -- consider showing the stories. One caution: Playing a videotape on a 19-inch TV in a huge room won't work. Half the people won't even be able hear or see it, so only do this in a small room or when you have the proper equipment available, meaning a large-screen TV and adequate sound system.

Don't feel you have to prepare too much material. A short talk with some interesting points or examples will prompt plenty of audience questions. If you're given a half hour to talk, keep it to ten minutes or so. Q and A will easily take up the rest of the time.

Try to cater your examples to the audience. A church women's club will be a lot more interested in coverage of abortion, sex education or condom distribution in schools than bias against guns used by hunters. The Chamber of Commerce membership is most concerned with policies toward businesses, such as taxes and health care benefits.

You're an expert on local media bias, but don't let that preclude you from discussing the networks and newsmagazines. Cite some examples from the latest *MediaWatch* or *Notable Quotables*. You may find the local media are biased in favor of more taxes and abortion just like the national media. If so, when discussing how network news favors making businesses provide health care coverage, note parallels to local media coverage. Explain that you and the audience may not be able to do much about the networks, but you and they can impact the local newspaper or radio station.

Offer suggestions for what your audience can do. Encourage them to call talk shows, write letters to the editor and alert you to instances of bias they see, hear or read.

If you've started your own newsletter, pass it out. You have a captive audience, so make sure to tell them how to subscribe. If you've written letters to the editor or been quoted in a newspaper article, distribute photocopies. If you are in the process of forming a committee or already have one, encourage them to join your efforts. This is an opportunity to recruit people to join your cause. You not only need volunteers to help you analyze the news, but people who don't have the time to help out personally -- they can make a financial contribution.

Make contacts: You need experts to call upon to tell you how a story was biased. Who knows the local tax code better than a lawyer or accountant who helps businessmen comply? Who knows more about studies on teenage sex and condom distribution than a parent battling with the school committee? These are the kind of people you'll be addressing, so make an effort to meet them. Get their phone numbers and addresses. Later, when you have a question or need something explained, call them. When your letter appears in the paper send it to them. These people can form the initial core of the informal group or official committee you eventually form. Get as many names and addresses as you can. When you do form a group, you'll have a list of potential donors to solicit to help get things up and running.

Develop an e-mail list

E-mail a very powerful tool to expose bias. It's immediate and it's much cheaper than regular U.S. mail. All you pay is a monthly fee for on-line time. In early 1996 the Media Research Center began sending "MRC CyberAlert" e-mail messages to about 50 friends in the media, such as talk show hosts and columnists. By election day in November our recipient list had soared to over 800 names. The MRC CyberAlert messages started out weekly but soon became daily as campaign bias grew.

Sent at night, the MRC CyberAlert messages cited the latest examples of bias and other developments of interest to those wishing to follow media bias. A message, for example, may have quoted biased questions or comments from Bryant Gumbel on that morning's *Today*, given a network by network breakdown of which did and did not report the latest revelation in a Clinton scandal and relayed the results of a new poll showing the public found coverage to be biased.

What you need to start an e-mail service:

● By this point, you've bought a computer. You'll need a modem, a device that lets your computer communicate via phone line with another computer somewhere else. Always buy the fastest one you can afford. Modem speed is measured in the number bytes per second (bps) it can transfer. In 1994 a 14,400 bps modem (commonly referred to as 14.4) was considerd cutting edge. By 1996 a twice as fast modem, 28.8, had become standard. Expect to spend about $150.

● Subscribe to an Internet service provider (ISP) or on-line service. ISP's are local and national companies that provide access to the Internet's World Wide Web and allow you to use e-mail.

Getting an on-line service, such as America Online (AOL), Compu-Serve, Prodigy or Microsoft Network (MSN), is probably the easiest way to go. Computer magazines run their ads and they often put free copies if their disks in the magazines. Many computers now come with one or more of these services already installed. All you have to do is call it up, enter your credit card number and then dial in through your modem. Usually the first month is free. Then you pay $10 per month for five hours, or $20 for either 20 hours or unlimited time.

When you sign up you'll be prompted to choose an e-mail address. If you go with an on-line service you'll have to follow their protocol. CompuServe, for instance, only has numbers. So, the MRC address on CompuServe is: 73041,2757. On AOL you can have letters, such as your name, but given the large number of subscribers, they'll probably add on some numbers. So, if you're John Brown, you may get JBrown8792.

● Develop a list of e-mail addresses. As you talk or exchange letters with reporters, talk show hosts and columnists ask if they'd like to be on your list. When you address groups, announce your e-mail address and encourage those in the audience to send you their e-mail address. All e-mail software has an address book where you enter the recipient's name and e-mail address.

People don't like getting e-mail in which they are not interested, so don't add people to your list unless they ask first. If you think someone would be interested, send them one of your messages with a note at the top stating it's a sample and you won't send more unless they ask.

✔ **Tip:** Send your message using the Blind Copying (BC or BCC) option. This has two advantages: First, people won't see the addresses of all your other recipients. That's important if you obtain the e-mail addresses of prominent members of your community. They won't appreciate getting a lot of unwanted e-mail from others on your list. Second, it will make your message a lot cleaner. If you have 40 recipients carbon copied (CC), with many e-mail services each recipient will have to scroll through several inches of addresses before being able to read your message.

To join the MRC Alert list, e-mail the MRC: mrc@mediaresearch.org.

Create a Web site

A "Web site" is a graphical page that you can create which anyone with Internet access and a "Web browser" can view. If you've never seen a Web site, ask someone familiar with them to show you one. Web sites are an excellent way to make your material available to others, especially conservatives looking for alternative sources of information.

How much you can do depends upon your time and financing. If you are proficient with computers, AOL, CompuServe, MSN and Prodigy all allow subscribers to create simple personal Web sites. If you've formed a group, then you should contact a local Internet Service Provider. An ISP should be able to handle the procedures to obtain a "domain name" for you, that's what follows the @ in an e-mail address and serves as the name of your web site. You can then use software from a company like Corel or Microsoft to create a simple Web site.

If you have some money and want a top notch, professional looking site, an ISP provider should also be able to help you find a Web site creator to "build" you site. Expect to pay upwards of $5,000 for this service and at least several hundred dollars per month for a company to maintain the site, that is, add material to it on a regular basis that you provide.

If you don't add or update material regularly, people won't return. So put a priority on giving people something new whenever they visit.

The MRC Web site includes a section for each of our divisions, with text of all our newsletters, special reports and MRC CyberAlert e-mail messages. Plus, information on becoming a member and on how to order our books and publications.

The MRC Web address: http://www.mediaresearch.org

Does all this sound like a lot of work? It is, but the results will be worth the effort. Obviously, no single individual can handle all the projects we have suggested. That's why you should follow the old liberal technique: If you can't do it by yourself, form a committee.

Section Four:
Form a Committee or Foundation

Now that you've learned how to analyze news to prove bias and how to expose your findings to the community, it's time to take the next step: Form a committee or more formal foundation. There's only so much you can do alone. Getting more people involved will multiply your resources, impact and credibility.

A committee can be as far as you go. Or, your goal can be to establish a foundation dedicated to documenting bias in your metropolitan area or state. In short, a local version of the Media Research Center. How far you go will be determined by how much time you and your colleagues can dedicate to the project and the extent of your funding.

Over the next few pages you'll learn how to create a committee of volunteers and a foundation staffed by salaried employees. For a foundation you'll also learn how to:

● Meet legal requirements, including a Board of Directors, IRS application rules, and applying for a trademark

● Set up a fundraising system

● Establish an administrative structure

● Organize a research and publications operation

● Fulfill promotion and marketing needs

Forming a committee/club

If you've followed the recommendations outlined in the first half of this chapter, putting together an informal committee should be relatively easy. Talk to friends, neighbors, co-workers and folks you know from church or civic clubs. Don't forget people you met in the course of a political campaign. Virtually every state has a least a couple of conservative groups, such as an anti-tax committee. Contact them to get the names of contributors and volunteers in your area. When speaking to groups tell them you are looking for volunteers to help you out.

Later in this chapter you'll learn how to produce a newsletter; In the next chapter you'll read how to issue press releases, hold press conferences and organize conferences with media figures. All these tasks will require an organization with a name.

For the purposes of discussion, let's say you live in suburban Omaha, but hope to eventually cover the media statewide. Instead of using an Omaha-specific name, choose one that reflects your wider goals, such as Nebraskans for a Balanced Media (NBM).

Following standard by-laws that your lawyer can provide, NBM must first select officers, including a President, Secretary and Treasurer. You need to decide who will be authorized to sign checks. Choose a treasurer who's good with numbers since he'll be responsible for balancing the checking account and filing tax statements.

Under the group name, NBM can open a bank account, print letterhead and rent a P.O. box. Now you can pay for computer, television, video and storage equipment, as well as postage, out of a common account instead of your own.

NBM could remain as a group of people who meet regularly to decide who will watch and read what and who will call and write whom. But NBM has the opportunity to do much more. Most importantly, you can begin to raise money to pay for your activities. Many people who share your concerns for media bias but don't have the time to volunteer will be willing to contribute. That's how you'll afford to buy that new VCR or box of letterhead.

With a committee you're looking to find more eyes and ears to identify bias, more letter writers and talk show callers, and more hands to help you conduct studies. But you will need to keep things organized. Hold regular meetings so all involved can discuss what they're watching and reading.

Organize your group like you would a political campaign. Set goals and aims that you think you can realistically achieve. If you think you can thoroughly monitor one newspaper and two TV stations, make that a goal. Additional goals could be sending information to certain local columnists and talk show hosts at least once a week, writing at least two letters to the editor each month, and making at least one address per month to a civic group. Don't set out to do everything described so far in this chapter immediately. You can always do more as time goes on.

To achieve your goals, assign responsibilities to particular people. Have people read or watch what most interests them. If, for instance, a businessman always watches the news on channel 4, have him record it and take some brief notes as he watches. If he has the time, use this book to teach him how to analyze stories. If he doesn't have the time or initiative, then get the tapes from him so that you can complete the analysis. Either way, you've saved yourself the cost of a VCR and tapes to record channel 4.

If a member of the church women's group is concerned about education issues -- teacher competency testing, merit pay, school choice, etc. -- have her analyze those stories. Whether she, another member of the group or you cut those stories out of the paper, have her analyze them. During your weekly meeting you can exchange clips or videotapes.

Follow the same rules for publicizing what you find. Have people do what most interests them, what they know the most about or what they have the best opportunity to do. Those home in the daytime can call daytime talk shows. Those with computers at work can help draft letters to the editor and op-ed articles.

Don't worry about too many calls to talk shows or letters to the editor. The more the better. Talk shows put on whomever calls, so the more callers talking about media bias the more listeners will hear and learn about it. A newspaper is more likely to run a letter if a biased story generated ten letters than just one or two.

The better your volunteer colleagues get at identifying and analyzing biased stories, the more you'll be able to rely upon them for accurate analysis. The more they know, the better they'll explain why a story was biased in their letters and phone calls. When they're comfortable that they know enough, encourage them to speak to civic and church groups.

Who has better credibility with the church women's group than a church woman? Same goes for a Rotarian speaking to the Rotary Club. Your volunteers can also start spreading the word to more exclusive groups. The lawyer you first met at the Kiwanis Club, or who happens to be your next door neighbor, can speak to the local bar association meeting. In bigger cities or regions, specialists may gather for a monthly lunch, such as real estate lawyers. The same goes for medical doctors, accountants and other professionals.

Keep these meetings in mind when you start a newsletter. Members of these professions will be able to distribute your newsletters to their colleagues. During your meetings, discuss what points should be made in a letter, article or talk show call. It's often helpful to talk through your points with others. They may pick up on how your wording could be misconstrued by non-conservatives in the public and the media. They can offer suggestions for better ways to make the same point. If you are President, you have the final say. Obviously, you don't want to alienate your volunteers, but protecting NBM's reputation should always be your main concern. In fact, you should be trying to enhance it by making sure those who best understand an issue are the ones to write about it.

If five people want to write a letter to the editor about a particular story, but you fear one of the people will write a really bad letter that makes points you don't agree with as a group, then it's up to you to prevent it. You'll have to summon your inter-personal diplomatic skills. You could steer that person toward another topic or project, or gently explain that you think the other letters have a better chance of being chosen by the newspaper. Keep in mind what you're trying to avoid: Having the newspaper choose a letter that least reflects your views and, in the worst case, would connect NBM to embarrassing comments.

Don't let anybody run out and "do his own thing" under the group name. As individuals who shared a common concern about media bias, you signed your own name to letters, articles and packets of information sent to friendly columnists and talk show hosts. Now, these items should come from "Barbara Smith, a member of Nebraskans for a Balanced Media." That means everything Barbara Smith writes or says reflects upon the whole organization. If she writes something that could be construed as racist or derogatory, NBM's credibility could quickly be destroyed. You can't afford any "loose cannons." Remember, many reporters assume conservatives are racists or "hate-mongers" and are just looking for an excuse to dismiss your cause.

✔ Designate two or three people you trust, including yourself, to serve as official spokesmen. Have all volunteers refer reporter's questions to them. Have the spokesmen screen letters before they are sent. Have volunteers describe to a spokesman what they plan to say when they call a talk show. This will allow you to control what people say under the group name, while not putting all of the burden on one person.

If you are to the point where volunteers can't handle all the work needed to be done, if you have to start paying people to do work for you; then it's time to consider becoming a foundation. If you aren't prepared yet to create a foundation, but wish to produce a newsletter, read section five of this chapter to learn how to create a mailing list, obtain postage permits, and design and create a newsletter.

Create a foundation

If you already have a group of dedicated volunteers willing to put up a significant amount of money, then you can skip right to this step. Or, if you have managed to create and run an informal organization, then you can change your structure to take advantage of what a foundation offers.

Establishing a non-profit educational foundation will allow you to run like a business, with two big advantages: a foundation can accept tax-deductible contributions and, with some exceptions, does not have to pay federal or state taxes. (See page 132 for a description of these exceptions.) Of course, a foundation must pay the employer share of FICA and deduct from pay checks federal and any state income taxes for its employees.

On the other hand, a foundation must remain non-partisan. This is a key point that you can never overlook: A foundation cannot lobby a legislature, donate money to a political campaign or align itself with a political party. In short, no political activity.

Legal requirements

To establish a foundation legally, you must first create a legal entity, such as a charitable trust or a non-profit corporation; establish a Board of Trustees or Board of Directors; file an IRS application, and trademark your name.

Board of Directors. To meet IRS requirements, you will need to elect a Board of Directors and name a President, Secretary and Treasurer. The signatures of the President and Secretary will be needed for any official financial documents, such as IRS forms and office space leases.

To fill the three officer positions, choose people you trust. These positions can be most easily filled by people who are also foundation employees, including yourself. If you start with three people, make yourself President and the other two Secretary and Treasurer.

The Board of Directors ultimately controls the foundation. Once elected, their majority vote is determinative, so be very careful about who you choose. Theoretically, they could even get rid of you! Select people for the Board of Directors who can work together and whose views are compatible with your own. At a minimum, you should have three Board members. You can have more, but any more than seven or eight will get too cumbersome.

How many you decide to have and the length of their terms will be determined by the by-laws. Initially, your lawyer can provide some standard by-laws and options. It's up to the actual Board to adjust and approve them. At first, you could just have three Board members, but at the first meeting those three could decide to nominate and approve additional members.

Of course, you can serve on the Board, or even be Chairman of the Board. At the MRC, L. Brent Bozell serves both as President and Chairman of the Board. Other Board members can give you credibility and help raise money. Consider asking:

● Retired or current Congressmen or other well-known former or current elected officials, such as a city councilman or state representative.

● Former news people concerned about bias in their industry.

● Community leaders, including Rotary Club or Chamber of Commerce officials.

● Advertising executives, who can advise you on ways to put pressure on the media to be fair.

● Business people, including some with media clout due to the size of their advertising budgets.

When deciding upon Board members, ask yourself if you can answer yes to at least one of these four questions:

● "Will this person help our foundation raise money?"

● "Is this person a well known, respected community leader who will bring credibility to the foundation?"

● "Will this person give the foundation positive publicity?"

● "Will this person bring talents and abilities helpful to creating or operating the foundation?"

If you already had been a regular public speaker and had set up an active volunteer organization before forming a foundation, then hopefully, you've already enlisted these kinds of people. The wealthy businessman in town who has been recording channel 4 for you is a perfect Board candidate. He can contribute money personally, he's a respected business leader who will encourage other businessmen to contribute, and he probably has the trust of many people in the community who will be willing to contribute once they learn he's affiliated with the foundation.

Among others who meet one of the criteria: A current or former elected official or major media figure can generate publicity. When they make a comment, the media will pay attention. A lawyer can handle the foundation's legal needs. A businessman with marketing experience can direct the foundation's marketing and promotion.

IRS application. Referring to the IRS tax code, non-profit foundations are commonly identified as "501 (c) (3)'s." The IRS application process for 501 (c) (3) status involves some pretty complicated tax codes, so a tax lawyer will be absolutely necessary. Ask a lawyer you know to refer you to a tax specialist. The state Bar Association can also provide a list of tax specialists in your area. Unless you have a lawyer in your volunteer organization willing to provide pro-bono work, be prepared to pay a lawyer upwards of $2,000. The IRS will probably take at least 180 days to process your application. The IRS must also be paid a fee between $150 and $465 when your application is filed. If you are interested in learning the details of what information the IRS requires, get a copy of IRS Form 1023 and instruction booklet from your local library or IRS office.

While waiting for the IRS to complete the process, you can operate as a foundation. Your lawyer can advise on the specific wording, but basically you must let every potential donor know that their contribution is tax-deductible pending IRS approval of your 501 (c) (3) application. The catch: If your application is turned down, you'll have to notify all donors that they cannot deduct their contribution from their taxes. That could make for some very unhappy donors, so don't claim donations are tax exempt until you, and more importantly, your lawyer, are confident you meet all the IRS requirements. Your lawyer should also make sure you comply with any applicable laws in your state.

Trademark. Choosing a name and creating a logo are top priorities. Assuming you want to operate in more than one state or expect to send your newsletter to someone in another state, then you'll want to trademark your organization's name with the U.S. Patent and Trademarks Office near Washington, D.C. (Even if you do not plan to have anything to do with another state, this is still a smart move: It protects you from having anyone else in the U.S. use your name. You don't want someone to create another media group using your name.)

The trademark protection includes not only your organization name, but also your logo. Delta Airlines, for instance, has a trademark on "Delta Airlines" and the triangle shaped blue and red above the word Delta. The Media Research Center logo (see the back cover of this book), includes the square TV set frame with globe inside, as well as the type style used to spell out "Media Research Center." Taken together, the whole unit is what the MRC has trademarked.

The trademark application fees run about $250. The approval process could take a year or more. In the meantime, you can use the name and logo, but should always place a small ™ next to it. The TM indicates that you have applied for a trademark. Once approved, your lawyer will instruct you to replace the TM with an R in the middle of a circle. The ® means you have a "registered" trademark.

A local design artist can create a logo, or you can make one yourself using a "desktop publishing" computer system. Even if you do know how to use desktop publishing, going to a professional still makes sense. The logo you choose will represent the foundation. It will be on every letter you send, in your newsletter, on your brochures and envelopes. You want one that enhances your image. You don't want anything tacky. Don't give those in the media an excuse to dismiss you. A cheap-looking logo will do that.

To find a designer, talk to local businessmen. They've probably used one for a company logo or to design a newspaper ad or promotional brochure. If that doesn't work, check the yellow pages under "Designers," "Artists," and "Typesetting." Some work for an hourly rate, others will offer to design three or four rough sketches for a set fee. Either way, be prepared to spend at least $500 in total -- $200 to $300 for an initial set of design ideas, another $200 to $300 to finalize the one you choose. Before you commit to hiring a designer, ask for the names of clients you could call for a reference. Designers should also be able to provide you with samples of their work.

Foundation needs and personnel

To create a successful foundation dedicated to documenting media bias you'll need to fulfill four needs:

- Fundraising
- Administrative structure
- Research and publications
- Promotion and marketing

Without money, you can't do much. So let's start there with a brief overview.

Fundraising

You'll need a Finance Director, someone to coordinate all fundraising efforts. This is a full-time job for a good fundraiser. The Finance Director needs to be the kind of person who can sell your foundation in one-on-one meetings with businessmen; can organize fundraising events committees; and can write and present proposals to philanthropic foundations and business philanthropy committees. At first, he may also have to handle marketing duties – produce brochures and annual reports; and sell your newsletter through display ads and direct mail.

Whomever you choose, it must be someone dedicated to the cause of identifying, exposing and correcting media bias. The success or failure of the foundation will rest heavily on this person. Don't choose yourself, although you will always be intimately involved. If you already have an active group of volunteers, you could select from among them. A retired businessman active in local civic, church and political activities would be ideal. He has business knowledge and community leader contacts.

Who to ask for money. The Finance Director's first job: Getting seed money from your most active and enthusiastic volunteers. Who would support a venture like this? It's time to put together a list.

- Yourself/your family. Do you, or family members, have the financial means to put up a grant to start the venture? Do you, or family members have the means to offer a loan, to be repaid when the venture has enough funds to do so?

- Your Rolodex™. Many people assume they don't know people of financial means, but oftentimes that is not the case. Go through your rolodex of friends, business associates, etc. and names will pop up. Are they conservative? Do they have money? Are they, too, upset at the problem of media bias? If the answer is yes to all three, that person should become a donor.

● Other organizations. Every community has a network of conservative groups, be it the local NRA, the local Focus on the Family or the local Chamber of Commerce, and all have one thing in common: they probably have been blistered at some point by the local press. Meet with their leaders, explain the concept, and ask them to help you get started. How? They can provide you with direct financial grants. They can make available loans. They can approach local conservative philanthropists for you. Or they can just provide you with the names of local donors. Take what you can get and be grateful for it -- they didn't have to do anything, remember.

● Local business leaders. Every community has conservative business leaders who take a particular interest in supporting local causes. Who are they? Ask around, look for them on the mastheads of other local groups, scan the papers for their names. With legwork you'll find them.

Once your list is compiled, what do you do? You have no track record, just a concept -- so use it. Visit with these people personally if at all possible. Explain your plan by defining *why* the venture is important, *how* you will undertake it, *what* you hope to accomplish, and *how much* it will cost.

Set some specific goals for yourself for the first year and present them to the prospective donor. Tell him that if he supports your effort you will, in turn, make those goals a reality. Commit to meeting with him in exactly one year to demonstrate what you have accomplished.

Why is this last step critical? First and foremost, most donors never really learn how their gifts are utilized, even when wonderful things are done as a result of them. You have, at the outset, promised to answer this dilemma. Second, if you do what you promised, you can probably expect another (and possibly greater) gift in Year Two. On the other hand, if you didn't do what you promised, you probably aren't deserving of additional support, either.

Prospectus. The Finance Director needs to put together a prospectus and package of information about the new foundation. The prospectus should explain the media bias problem in your community and how your new foundation will work to identify, expose and correct it. Include a proposed budget, specifying the expected costs of major expenses, such as electronic equipment, computers, office space, printing, postage and salaries. (See the next two pages for an example of a past MRC budget. To make it fit on two pages, we cut out several lines, but it should give you a good idea of the types of items a budget should cover.)

Put the written prospectus in a folder with:

➤ Biographies of the foundation's key personnel. Keep these to one double spaced page.

➤ Copies of any published articles or letters to the editor by you or your volunteers.

➤ If you've been quoted by a columnist or editorial writer, include photocopies. Same goes for any articles that cited your incorporated group's studies or analysis of news coverage.

➤ Press releases you've distributed.

➤ The foundation's budget.

➤ Letter from the IRS stating that you are a tax-exempt foundation.

➤ After your first year, the annual audit performed by an outside accounting firm, if you can afford it.

➤ When created, the latest issues of your newsletter.

➤ A list of endorsement quotes from well-known conservative politicians, columnists or talk show hosts. (These will be obtained by whomever is handling marketing and promotion. See page 135.)

Always update the packet with the latest examples of articles, press releases and newsletters.

Remember, the purpose of the prospectus and accompanying information packet is to persuade potential donors that you are a sound investment. You must convince prospectus readers that their money will be well spent. To do that, the prospectus must show that you are media bias experts, have the respect of the media and political figures, have a sound budget plan, and will have an impact on the media bias problem.

Once you're established you can begin to utilize direct mail for fundraising. See page 197 in the newsletter marketing section to learn the basics of how to best implement a direct mail program for a foundation.

```
                    MEDIA RESEARCH CENTER
                      Budget Projections
                     Jan 1-Dec 31, 1990


Section A: Operations, Programs & Funding

INCOME
Contributions.......................................  $1,207,240
Tape Rental.........................................       2,000
Interest Income.....................................      13,500
TOTAL INCOME                                         $1,222,740


EXPENSES
OPERATING AND ADMINISTRATIVE
Salaries and Wages..................................     $35,000
Consulting Fees.....................................           0
Labor Related Costs.................................       2,720
Virginia Unemployment Tax...........................       3,650
Workman's Comp. Insurance...........................       1,430
Legal and Filing Fees...............................      30,000
Auditor/Accountant Fees.............................       7,500
Rent................................................     100,000
Utilities...........................................       6,400
Insurance...........................................       1,000
Telephone Equip. Maintenance........................         500
Local Phone Service.................................       5,400
Long Distance Service...............................       1,200
Printing ...........................................         750
Postage  ...........................................         350
Letterhead & Office Sup.............................       2,550
Bldg Maint. and Janitorial .........................       2,500
Parking  ...........................................       5,800
Office Moving Expense...............................       3,200
TOTAL OPERATING COSTS                                  $209,950


RESEARCH AND PUBLICATION
    (MEDIAWATCH & NOTABLE QUOTABLES)
Salaries and Wages..................................    $276,750
Labor Related Costs.................................      29,310
Printing and Production.............................      32,390
Postage  ...........................................      76,200
Reference Publications..............................       2,800
Cable Service.......................................         750
Typesetting.........................................       1,500
Computer & File Maintenance.........................       8,550
MEDIAWATCH & NQ PUBLICATION COSTS                      $428,250


RESEARCH AND PUBLICATION
    (ENTERTAINMENT DIVISION)
Salaries and Wages..................................    $104,500
Labor Related Costs.................................      13,420
Printing and Production.............................      17,300
Postage  ...........................................      15,000
Reference Publications..............................         750
Cable Service.......................................         670
Typesetting.........................................       1,500
Computer & File Maintenance.........................       2,500
TV ETC PUBLICATION COSTS                               $155,640
```

```
EQUIPMENT RELATED
Equipment Rental.....................................     $5,990
Equipment Maintenance................................      2,780
Equipment Supplies...................................      5,950
Furniture Rental  ...................................          0
Depreciation.........................................     10,580
TOTAL EQUIPMENT RELATED COSTS                           $25,300


FUNDRAISING
Salaries and Wages...................................   $130,500
Labor Related Costs..................................     14,420
Consulting...........................................     30,000
Printing & Computer..................................      9,000
Postage  ............................................      7,500
Long Distance Service................................     10,500
TOTAL FUNDRAISING COSTS                                 $201,920

PRESS, PUBLIC RELATIONS & MEETINGS
Consulting Fees......................................    $36,000
Press Release Service....,...........................      3,780
Press Clipping Service...............................      3,600
Press Conferences & Meetings.........................      2,000
Travel and Lodging...................................      5,000
Media Awards Dinner..................................     25,000
Special Events.......................................      7,500
TOTAL PRESS, PR AND MEETINGS                             $82,880


MISCELLANEOUS
Interest Expense.....................................         $0
Bank & Credit Card Fees..............................        750
Overnight Delivery...................................        750
Courier Fees.........................................      3,000
Contributions........................................      5,000
Other Misc...........................................      1,000
Contingency..........................................     10,000
TOTAL MISCELLANEOUS COSTS                                $20,500

TOTAL SECTION A EXPENSES                              $1,215,640

CAPITAL EXPENDITURES
Office Equipment.....................................     $5,700
Office Furniture.....................................      1,500
Telephone Equipment..................................        300
VCR Tapes............................................     10,180
TOTAL CAPITAL EXPENDITURES                              $17,680

TOTAL SECTION A EXPENSES.............................  $1,215,640
PLUS: TOTAL CAPITAL EXPENDITURES     .................     17,680
LESS: NON-CASH ITEMS (DEPRECIATION) ..................     10,580
SECTION A: TOTAL REQUIRED FUNDING....................  $1,222,740
```

EXPOSE

Administrative Structure

Office space. To be taken seriously, a foundation needs its own address and phone number. At first, you may not be able to afford much. That's fine. The key is to get enough space to provide a reception area, a conference room big enough to accommodate all involved in launching the foundation, and working space for your key employees. Until you raise enough money, some people can continue working at home.

Ask your volunteers if they know of any space owned by fellow conservatives. For years, a conservative businessman in Boston provided free space two floors above a pizza restaurant to two conservative groups. It wasn't the nicest space (visitors had to use the restaurant's service elevator), but it was free. Maybe there's a store owner in town using only a corner of his second floor space for storage. You could use the rest. Start small, and when you can afford it, move to a bigger and better place.

The same goes for furniture. See if anyone can provide it at a discount or at cost. Maybe a volunteer knows someone who works for a company that's moving. They may be interested in getting rid of some of their used furniture.

Taxes. To handle taxes, accounts payable and receivable, and payroll you'll need an accountant. You could hire one full-time, but at first a part timer or outside company can handle your needs. Every city has accounting services companies that cater to filling the needs of small companies. If you desire more hands-on service, you could hire someone part-time; or accounting could be part of a full-timer's job duties -- a receptionist/accountant or fundraising assistant/accountant.

Foundation tax and reporting requirements aren't simple things. Foundations, for instance, must file detailed reports revealing the source of all donations and where the money went -- amount for salaries, equipment, postage etc. In addition, though foundations don't have to pay corporate income taxes, they do have to pay federal and applicable state taxes on "unrelated business income;" that is, income derived from things not related to the foundation's educational purpose. You don't pay taxes on a newsletter subscription, but if you sell a used VCR to someone for $100.00 that's subject to tax.

If your state has a sales tax, you'll have to pay that for all publications sold to state residents, but not on subscriptions purchased by those from another state. This can be pretty complicated, so find someone with some accounting experience who already knows, or can quickly learn, foundation tax law.

Research & publications

To have material to analyze, you'll have to establish a research operation. Taping and reading stuff at home is fine when you are just starting out, but as a research foundation you need comprehensive analysis brought under one roof so that you can assure quality control.

You can't say "In all of last year, channel 4 never aired any comments from any State Representative opposed to the tax increase" unless you've taped and watched every show. Remember, once you criticize the media, they'll scrutinize you too. So you don't want to make any misstatements.

You must establish standards as to what your foundation considers biased. When you were a bunch of volunteers and one of you got upset about a particular story, you wrote a letter under your name. When you moved to the incorporated organization stage, everything started going under the group name. Remember, anything said or written by one person in your organization or foundation reflects on the institution as a whole. You or whomever you choose to run your research operation must have the final say as to what is and is not biased. One mistake could kill you. It's not fair, but liberals in the media will never let you forget a mistake. Wrongly accuse a newspaper or station of never mentioning a particular point of view, and reporters will always write, "NBM, which once falsely accused WMRC-TV of..."

Not all conservatives agree on everything. Some are more libertarian and won't be upset by stories implying misunderstanding is behind opposition to hiring gay teachers. Others might be violently opposed to gay teachers, but view free trade as a fine theory, yet a disastrous policy that will cost jobs. Ultimately, it's up to the Board of Directors to set policy. On a day-to-day basis, it's up to the President or whoever he has running the research operation.

In general, try to emphasize issues on which you all agree, de-emphasize issues where you split. It won't be easy, but you created the foundation to document and correct bias against conservative ideas. Fighting amongst yourselves won't help. If some key people are vehemently anti-tax, but pro-choice on abortion, they'll just have to live with the fact that "pro-life" is the widely accepted conservative position.

Running the research operation is something that you could choose to handle. Or, assign this to whomever has been doing the most news story analysis for you. Raising money is necessary to launch the foundation, but an ongoing research and publishing operation will be necessary to sustain the foundation. If you don't produce anything within a few months of your creation, people won't continue to fund you.

Ideally, you will have adequate initial funding and space to allow you to hire enough people to analyze all the local broadcast news and newspapers and put them all in one place. Initially, you may only have a finance director, yourself and one other person able to devote their full-time to this project. Just remember: the key is thoroughness. It's better to choose a few programs and watch all of them than to try to watch many programs, but only analyze three or four shows a week.

However many people you start with, having all your analysts under one roof makes for easy exchanges of ideas and quick answers to questions. Research will be made a lot easier if all your videotapes and back issues are in one place. If you want to compare how the network affiliates covered a story, you don't want to have to drive to Bob's house to pick up the news from the ABC affiliate and then to Barbara's house to watch the NBC station.

At a minimum, put five or six VCRs in your office. Record all the newscasts and store the videotapes there. The same goes for radio recording and tapes. Get the local newspapers delivered to the office. This way even if you have people working at home, all the news will be stored in one central location.

If you followed the recommendations on page 73 about how to analyze television news, then you're already using a database system. If you haven't yet purchased computer database software, now's the time. As soon as you have it installed, start having your volunteer analysts come to the office to watch the news. As they watch, they can enter their analysis directly into one central computer.

Computer database system. The MRC now has a very sophisticated customized software system. But when the MRC began, it simply used a popular database software package available at any computer software outlet. If you have $10,000 or more available you could get a software writer to produce a unique system for you. Following the MRC's path is cheaper and will let you learn how database systems work so you'll know what features and abilities to demand if you ever decide to create a customized one.

The MRC purchased the DOS version of dBaseIII+ for an individual PC, or personal computer. About a year later, the MRC expanded and purchased the "network" version. A "network" lets several computers in a building connected by cables all work off of one "fileserver," a standard computer dedicated to storing information entered through all the computers on the network.

Deciding which topic to use for a particular story is a lot easier when analysts can talk among themselves. But if people must work at home, you could connect them to your system through a "modem," a device that uses a phone line to connect one computer to another. Modems run about $150 each and you need one on both ends, for the computer in your office and another for the one in a home.

Assign specific shows and newspapers to specific analysts. If there are only two of you, you each can do the evening news on two channels. Remember, there's news on weekends too and news never goes into repeats. Whether you're on vacation or out sick, the news never stops. Factor that into your estimate of how many hours it will take to analyze a certain program. The two of you can also split the newspapers.

One way to communicate amongst yourselves, especially if your full-time jobs are at different hours, is to use e-mail. If you can all access the same computer at the office, then you should be able to use the e-mail on your network system. If not, then share e-mail addresses and communicate through your on-line or internet service. You can tell each other what shows you've analyzed and what bias you've found.

Promotion and marketing

At first, you may not have the money to allocate someone full time to this task. It may have to be handled by your fundraiser or newsletter editor. But don't let this position go unfilled for too long. The success of your fundraising and newsletter will depend on it. Promotion will let people in your community know you exist. Among those who will hear about you will be a few willing to donate money or subscribe to your newsletter.

Marketing will help convince people to make significant financial contributions by, among other things, gathering quotes from opinion leaders endorsing the foundation's work, by creating brochures and by linking the foundation's programs with the efforts of already established conservative groups. Marketing will also get newsletter subscribers through direct mail letters and magazine ads.

Endorsement quotes. The first priority: Gather endorsement quotes. Ask sympathetic media figures, such as columnists and radio talk show hosts, and well-known conservative politicians to endorse your effort.

A sample endorsement: "Every day Nebraskans are bombarded by left-wing, anti-free market messages from television news and newspapers. The media are an ally of liberal politicians dedicated to rasing taxes and increasing government control over our lives. But finally a solution is at hand. Nebraskans for the Balanced Media provides the irrefutable evidence of media bias. NBM's meticulous research exposes the media's agenda. They are invaluable in the battle to level the media playing field." Such a statement will go a long way to earn credibility for your foundation, both in the eyes of prospective donors and members of the media community.

Brochures. Like a regular company or store, foundations must "sell" themselves to potential customers. In your case, your customers are conservatives and politically aware people in your community who realize the destructive impact of liberal media bias. To let these people know of your programs and goals, create a brochure. A brochure will provide a convenient vehicle to describe all your programs and publications. Some of the people who see it will be so impressed by your goals and programs that they will want to help you out financially.

How much money you have will determine the kind of brochure you can produce. On the cheaper end, you could produce what is commonly called a "flyer," an eight and a half by 11 inch sheet of glossy paper folded twice to create an 8 and a half by 3 and two-thirds inches sized final product. This size will fit perfectly in a legal size envelope. Check any tourist spot brochures you may have around the house, such as from an amusement park or historical site. Chances are, it's this size.

You should be able to print a two color flyer for less than 20 cents a piece. On page 175 you'll learn about buying a desktop publishing system to produce your newsletter. You can use it to produce a flyer, or go to a professional designer. Either way, make it look nice. Leave plenty of white space. Make clear headings for each section. In short, make it easy to scan. Someone should be able to read it in just a couple of minutes.

The flyer should explain why the foundation was created; describe its research operation (how you record all local TV news shows, etc.); list some endorsement quotes; and, assuming you've begun a newsletter, describe it. Given limited space, you will probably only be able to fit a couple of sentences on each of these topics.

✔ Allocate one panel to a return device, a panel people can cut out and send to you after filling in their name and address. Have boxes people can check to request further information or to receive a sample copy of your newsletter. Tell people to put the panel in an envelope along with a check if they wish to subscribe.

In subsequent years, or if you have enough money initially, produce a better quality brochure. Ideally, something that looks like a corporate annual report -- ten to twenty pages with color pictures. Ask some of your major donors if they mind being identified publicly. If not, list them in the brochure. Wealthy people are often much more willing to contribute if they know others they respect have done so already.

Whichever type of brochure you print, send it to anyone who calls to ask what you do, or who says he heard a foundation representative on a talk show. Whenever anyone from your foundation speaks to a group, distribute it to all attendees. Talk to the leaders of already established conservative groups, such as an anti-tax committee or parents group battling a plan to distribute condoms in school, about attending one of their meetings. Pass out copies to members of the group and describe your plans. Emphasize how your foundation can help them by documenting and countering media bias they encounter. Ask that they alert you to instances of bias they observe.

Do not, under any circumstances, produce a tacky brochure. Your brochure is your written representation to the world and if it looks cheap, so will you. It's worth the investment to make it (and you) look good.

Web site. Consider a web site a kind of billboard on the information super highway. Creating one will help spread your message and serve as an access point for the public and the media to view your research. Everything you do, newsletters, e-mail messages, special reports and speeches you've given should be on your site. It can also serve to promote your activities. If someone with your group will be on a talk show, highlight that upcoming appearance. Don't forget to tell people how to donate money, subscribe to your newsletter or join your group.

As with a brochure, your web site will be the first thing many see from your group. Make sure it reflects well on you.

Also be sure to promote the web site in all your publications and whenever you are on a radio show.

If you start a newsletter, its marketing and promotion will be a major project for whomever handles your foundation marketing.

Section Five:
Creating & Publishing a Newsletter

As soon as you have the foundation up and running -- you have money, have met the legal requirements, have been set up administratively with accounting and office space, have a research operation identifying biased stories -- start publishing a newsletter to distribute your findings. With a newsletter, your foundation can become the "ombudsman" of the local media, calling attention to instances of bias.

Until now you've been sending examples of bias to sympathetic people in the media. With a newsletter you can let everyone in the media see your findings. Liberals in the media will know their days of unchecked bias are over. Conservative political activists will get the ammunition, the quotes, examples, studies and analysis they need to prove their viewpoint is not receiving a balanced hearing. In short, the media, your supporters, conservatives in the community and the general public will all learn what you find through the newsletter. A newsletter will establish your group or foundation as a serious player with the local political and media community.

The content of your newsletters should consist of articles describing biased stories or coverage of an issue, studies you've completed that prove bias, examples you come across of someone moving between media and political jobs, and recitations of off-the-job comments from reporters that show their liberal viewpoints. As mentioned earlier, your foundation or committee should emphasize quotes and facts over rhetoric. Follow the same rule with your newsletter. A quote from a story will do a more convincing job of showing how a story was biased than your summary of it.

In this section you'll learn the steps to produce a newsletter:

- Understand fonts
- Choose a name and trademark it
- Determine a design
- Develop mailing list, find a list maintenance & mailhouse service
- Learn newsletter production, obtain a desktop publishing system
- Copyrighting your newsletter & running copyrighted material
- Finally, five ways to market your newsletter

Fonts

Before we get into how to create and produce a newsletter, we must look at fonts. As you design your newsletter logo, and choose a text and headlines typestyle, you'll be dealing with them. A "font" is a particular typestyle. Look at your newspaper. The typestyle of the text type is different than the type style of the headlines. Each of these is a different font. The text of this book is set in Palatino.

Fonts are usually put into two categories: "serif" and "sans serif." Palatino is a serif font, a font with curves and some character to it. Sans serif fonts are plain, like block letters. This sentence, as is the Fonts heading above, is set in Helvetica, the most popular sans serif font. This sentence is set in Avant Garde, another often used sans serif style. Serif fonts are much more plentiful like this one, Nebraska.

The size of a font is measured in "points." There are 72 points in an inch, so the height of letters set at 72 points equals an inch. The text of this book is set in 10.5 point type. Here are the names of some serif fonts and what they look like in various point sizes:

Aardvark at 10 points

Bookman at 12 points

Britannic at 14 points

Brooklyn at 16 points

New Century Schoolbook at 10 points

Clearface at 20 points

Cooper Black at 18 points

COPPERPLATE AT 21 POINTS

Garamond at 19 points

Nebraska at 23 points

Ottawa at 28 points

Paradise at 14 points

Times Roman at 10 points

Timpani at 14 points

Switzerland at 18 points

Windsor at 15 points

Look now at the MRC logo on the back cover. You'll see the the words "Media Research Center" are typeset in the Garamond font.

Name & trademark

You can't have a nameless newsletter. Choose a name that tells what your newsletter covers, but isn't too complicated, lengthy or abstract. The MRC's *MediaWatch* newsletter name makes it obvious that it covers the media. *TV, etc.* makes it clear the newsletter deals with television plus other things.

Since there are tens of thousands of newsletters already in existence, not every name will be available to you. Choose two or three names that you can live with and have your lawyer run a trademark check for any "prior registrations." In short, to make sure no one else is already using the name for a newsletter dealing with politics and/or the media. (Remember, as noted on page 125, trademarks are very specific. Someone could create a magazine on peanut processing techniques and call it *MediaWatch*, but no one other than the MRC can publish a newsletter called *MediaWatch* which deals with politics and the media.)

✔ One way to avoid a name problem: come up with one you know is unique, such as *Nebraskans for a Balanced Media Report*. It may be dull, but it is unique. If you go this route, your lawyer will probably advise you that you can skip the prior registration check and go right to making a formal application for trademark approval. (As part of this process, an Office of Patents and Trademarks examiner will check for prior registrations anyway.)

Assuming the initial check (which could take up to 90 days) finds nothing for at least one of the names you selected, or if you decided on a unique name (one that includes your group's name), it's time to design a logo. Look at the top or cover of any newspaper, magazine or newsletter and you'll see its logo. By "logo" we mean the design of the lettering used to spell out the publication's name. You could come up with a unique design, or simply write the name in a font style that already exists.

When you talk to a designer about a foundation logo, do the newsletter logo at the same time. Or, look at magazines, newspapers and advertisements to find a typestyle you like. Then use it to spell out your newsletter name. A designer should have the particular style, or one close to it. A desktop publishing system comes with dozens of font styles, so if you have purchased such a system, scan through the font styles that came with the software.

Finally, you could find a font style you like, and then have a designer make it unique by adding something to it. In a couple of pages you'll see the logos for the MRC's newsletters. All three were created with standard fonts. The *MediaWatch* logo for instance, was made with Switzerland Condensed. We added the lines to give it a unique look. The *MediaNomics* logo was created with Nebraska in italic.

Once you've finalized your logo design, it's time to follow the same trademark procedures as you did with the foundation logo. Your lawyer can file the application with the Office of Patents and Trademarks. Again, the application fee should run about $250.

A final note: As part of the trademark application process, people have up to one year to challenge a new trademark application. Someone might believe that your trademarked name, even if not identical, is close enough to confuse the public and therefore constitutes an "infringement" of their trademark. The only way to know is to see if anyone files a challenge.

Newsletter size & frequency

First, decide the size of your newsletter. Four pages? Eight pages? Twelve pages? Keep a few things in mind before making a choice.

Printing presses are set up to cut paper to 11 by 17 inch sheets which are folded in half to give you a four page, 8 and a half by 11 inch newsletter. So the printer's collating machine can easily create newsletters by four page jumps -- 4, 8, 12, 16 etc. Making a six page newsletter requires a lot of extra work, which translates into a higher price for you. In fact, a six page newsletter will cost more to print than an eight page one.

Postage cost is based on weight, so figure out what it will cost to mail the newsletter. With third class mail, your envelope and newsletter can weigh up to two ounces for no additional cost. With first class, you'll almost double the postage price if it goes over one ounce. Assuming standard paper and envelope weight, an eight page newsletter will weigh exactly one ounce. So go with a four or eight page newsletter if you plan to mail first class. If you plan to use third class mail, then you could create a longer newsletter. (See page 171 for pluses and minuses of mailing first versus third class.)

How many pages, realistically, do you think you can fill with good, quality material? A four page newsletter made up of top quality research, quotes and analysis is a lot better than an eight or 12 page newsletter filled with weaker material. By the same reasoning, it's better to have a smaller monthly newsletter than a longer, less frequent publication. Ask yourself: Would you be more likely to read a 16 page newsletter every other month, or a eight page one which arrives monthly?

One solution: Start small; you can always grow. Make the first issue four pages. If after a few issues you find yourself unable to squeeze in a lot of good material, then expand to eight pages. If you're not so sure about how much time you'll have to work on the newsletter, then start as a bi-monthly. When you've got more time to dedicate to the newsletter, go monthly.

Remember, it's always better to increase frequency and size over time than to do the opposite. If you start as an eight page monthly, but your second issue is a four pager that isn't published until two months later, the whole world will know you're having problems.

Newsletter design

Once you decide on size and frequency, it's time to work on its design. First, determine the length and type of articles you plan to run. Long, in-depth articles that cover several pages may offer thorough analysis, but few will read them. Most people just won't dedicate that kind of time to reading an article. That's why virtually every newspaper in America has changed its layout in the past few years to make itself more conducive to the quick reader.

Among the basic rules you should follow: Keep articles as short as possible, divide the newsletter into several "departments" that always appear on the same page or pages, and avoid having articles continue to a non-facing page.

A reduced reproduction of *MediaWatch* starts on the next page. As you'll see, we run "Newsbites," short articles on a particular instance of bias, across the bottom of the first seven pages. For a uniform look, the Newsbites box is the same size on each page. We created departments called "Revolving Door," "Janet Cooke Award," "Study," "Back Page" and "On the Bright Side." They each appear in the same location each month, so readers don't have to hunt for them. Other than Newsbites, all articles are contained on one page or on two facing pages. To draw people into the longer articles, each includes a smaller sized subhead in addition to the headline, and a "bridge," the three line, large lettered pull-out from the article. Finally, to help separate the "Newsbites" from the rest of each page, the Newsbite box is shaded.

To give you some additional design ideas, after the *MediaWatch* pages we've reprinted two other MRC newsletters -- *MediaNomics*, a four page newsletter published by the MRC's Free Market Project and *Flash*, an eight page report to members of the MRC. You'll see that all three use screens (the technical term for a shaded area), to set off articles or sections. Screens help break up the page so it's easier to find and follow articles. However, the screens here appear darker than they do in the actual newsletter.

Networks Declare Dole Criticisms "Mean," "Harsh" and "Nasty"

Clinton's Character Off Limits

The networks spent early October on referee patrol for Bill Clinton, ruling out of bounds anything critical or negative about him.

World News Tonight anchor Forest Sawyer announced October 3: "Bob Dole decided to step onto center stage with a harshly worded attack not only on the administration's work in the Middle East, but its entire foreign policy....The administration has so far answered softly." The "soft" response? ABC didn't show it, but Clinton Press Secretary Mike McCurry retorted that Dole advisers are "nattering naysayers of gloom."

MSNBC's *The News with Brian Williams* that night showed new ads from the Dole and Clinton campaigns: "We're going to begin with the latest ad from the Dole campaign which takes the campaign into a bit of nasty territory." Dole's ad simply showed clips of Clinton talking about taxes to illustrate he's really a liberal. Williams failed to tag the Clinton ad as "nasty," but it included this negative attack line: "Dole and Gingrich tried to slash school anti-drug programs. They'd take us back."

Bozo became the big news on October 8. A man in a crowd yelled at Dole that he should "get Bozo out of the White House." Dole shot back: "Bozo's on his way out." CNN's Bernard Shaw opened *Inside Politics*: "Was he borrow-

> Katie Couric: "It turned decidedly nastier in the Dole camp yesterday."

ing the words of an over-enthusiastic supporter, or did Bob Dole lower the level of civility a notch in his contest with Bill Clinton?"

On the next morning's *Today*, Katie Couric asked NBC's Tim Russert: "As you've heard Tim it turned decidedly nastier in the Dole camp yesterday. He was talking about a moral crisis. He refused to answer a question if President Clinton was morally and ethically capable of being President. You heard that Bozo exchange. Effective strategy or is this going to come back to haunt him?"

Swift network condemnation followed Dole's October 14 decision to raise the ethics issue. On *NBC Nightly News* David Bloom declared: "In his harshest, most personal attack yet on the President, Bob Dole today charged that the Clinton Administration is unethical, that Bill Clinton himself is slipping and sliding away from questions about possible illegal campaign contributions."

The next day Dole again discussed what he termed "public ethics," leading CBS reporter Phil Jones to worry that Dole "runs the risk of looking desperate and mean-spirited."

Dole's speech prompted Matt Lauer to begin his *Today* newscast on October 16, the morning of the second debate: "Bob Dole is not waiting for that debate to attack Bill Clinton's ethics. With more on a campaign that is now getting meaner, NBC's Kelly O'Donnell is standing by live." ❑

INSIDE

4 Cooke Award: PBS Portrays Clinton as Victim

6 Study: Blackout Imposed on Clinton Scandals

8 Bias So Bad that Even Sam Donaldson Sees It

Volume 10

Issue 10

October 1996

MEDIA RESEARCH CENTER®

Bringing political balance to the media

www.mediaresearch.org

NEWSBITES

Extreme Agreement. Tagging Republican House freshmen as extremists is Democratic mantra. And, it's an assessment endorsed by CBS News. On the October 10 *Evening News*, Bob Schieffer examined the Ohio re-match between GOP rookie Frank Cremeans and the man he beat in 1994, Democrat Ted Strickland.

Schieffer found a GOP official who thought Newt Gingrich had gone "too far" and asked him a question that incorporated the Democratic spin on last year's budget showdown: "Where did he make his mistake? In shutting down the government?"

Strickland insisted that "people want moderation and when extremes are presented, whether they be from the left or the right, I think people have a tendency to turn away from that." Schieffer then concluded by endorsing the "extreme" assessment: "Obvious perhaps, but as Fall comes to the heartland and the election draws near, dozens of Republican freshmen are running scared, wondering if it's a lesson they learned in time."

Crediting Clinton. For the media, bad news is usually good news. Right? Well, not when the good news helps Bill Clinton. On *continued on the next page*

Clinton: Moral Leader

The chief White House speech-writer got his job because candidate Bill Clinton so liked his reporting. In the September 23 *Weekly Standard*, Christopher Caldwell relayed why chief speech-writer **Donald Baer**, who had been Assistant Managing Editor of *U.S. News,* was tapped in 1994: "Clinton liked the articles Baer contributed to *U.S. News* during the 1992 campaign" since "Baer wrote with extreme empathy about Clinton's background."

Caldwell quoted a journalistic colleague: "'Being of the South and still being rooted there, yet being driven and ambitious enough to prove oneself in the larger world -- the two of them have a lot in common.' While Baer has always been a loyal Democrat, he's not necessarily a liberal. Like Clinton, he has an idiosyncratic, instinctive, generally progressive politics that winds up at beyond-left-and-rightism."

Beyond ideology maybe, but not beyond idolizing Clinton. Caldwell learned: "This enthusiasm can appear like ideological non-commitment or caginess. One New Democrat who met Baer at a dinner last year described him as 'bland beyond description, a fount of cliches. 'Clinton was the moral leader of the Universe,' and all that.'"

Up and Out at *U.S. News*

James Fallows took the helm at *U.S. News* in late September. The new Editor promoted one veteran of Democratic politics while another decided to resign. Now in the number two slot as Managing Editor: **Harrison Rainie**, an Assistant Managing Editor since 1988 when he jumped from the office of New York Senator Daniel Patrick Moynihan where he had spent most of 1987 as the Democrat's Chief-of-Staff....

Deciding to depart: **Kathryn Bushkin**, Director of Editorial Administration since 1984 when she put in a stint as Press Secretary with Gary Hart's presidential effort. Bushkin has joined a PR firm.

NBC's on the Mark

A professional flack for a liberal Senator is the newest member of the on-air reporting team at the NBC News Washington bureau. **Alexandra Marks**, Press Secretary to Senator John Kerry (D-Mass.) from late 1993 to mid-1995, signed on in early September. Before joining Kerry and again since 1995 Marks worked as a *Christian Science Monitor* reporter. But she's not new to TV. Prior to flacking for Kerry, Marks reported for the *Monitor*'s since-failed cable channel and for the *10 O'Clock News* on WGBH-TV, Boston's PBS station.

Democratic Cable

Among the on-air talent brought aboard MSNBC, the new NBC News cable channel in partnership with Microsoft, were a Clinton speechwriter and an aide in a Democratic presidential run. Political correspondent **Eric Liu** composed speeches for Secretary of State Warren Christopher in 1993 before becoming, at age 25, the youngest speechwriter for President Clinton. *The New York Times* reported that Liu moved to the White House speechwriting office in November 1993 where he toiled until June 1994....

Chip Reid, hired to cover the White House and Capitol Hill, was general counsel in 1987 for Democrat Joe Biden's unsuccessful run. For the previous four years Reid had been chief investigator for the Senate Judiciary Committee's Democratic Senators. After Biden, Reid accepted a producer slot with ABC News and was a reporter for Washington, D.C.'s ABC affiliate, WJLA, when tapped by MSNBC. ❑

June 30, *The New York Times* reported that "the share of national income earned by the top five percent of households grew at a faster rate than during the eight years of the Reagan administration, which was often characterized as favoring the rich." ABC's *World News Tonight* ran no story. But on September 26, when the Census Bureau reported that median income had risen as poverty fell, who got the credit? Bill Clinton.

Reporter Barry Serafin reported that median income grew 2.7 percent, but remained lower than 1989. Serafin started his story: "The number of Americans living in poverty fell. There were 36.4 million people below the poverty level, 1.6 million fewer than the year before. The poverty rate for African-Americans dropped to its lowest level since 1959, 29.3 percent. What does it add up to?"

Following a soundbite from Clinton, Serafin continued:

"Citing the income gains, the President declared that the country is on the right track. He heralded progress on narrowing the gap between the richest and poorest Americans." Serafin used a single expert source for his story, a professor from MIT. Whom did the professor credit? Clinton and Fed Chairman Alan Greenspan. Serafin closed the story: "All in all the new numbers added to a very good day for Bill Clinton." Thanks to ABC.

Gore: Too Important to Criticize. If you are powerful enough to get between a microphone and Clinton then you're personal hypocrisy doesn't matter. At least that's what a CBS story portrayed.

During the Democratic convention in Chicago Vice President Al Gore was widely praised by reporters for his emotional attack of tobacco by highlighting his sister's

Media Scoff at Far Right...

But Buy Wacky Left

While the media are quick to dismiss crazy right-wing conspiracy theories about black U.N. helicopters they granted credence to the charge that the CIA introduced crack into black Los Angeles neighborhoods as a way to fund the Nicaraguan Contras. The theory was forwarded in an August *San Jose Mercury News* series by reporter Gary Webb. The four major networks aired a total of 12 stories with CBS laying claim to five. CNN ran three followed by ABC and NBC which aired two stories each.

ABC's *Good Morning America* and CBS *This Morning* brought on far-left U.S. Rep. Maxine Waters. She pushed the charge as proof that outside forces created urban drug addicts.

CBS's Bill Whitaker accepted the charge and placed the plight of crack babies at the feet of the CIA. His October 1 *Evening News* piece opened with a shot of woman holding a crying baby: "The decade and a half crack epidemic has exacted a ruinous toll. For ten years Eloise Dangerfield has been rescuing the littlest victims, crack babies, from the death grip in which the drug has ensnared much of South Central Los Angeles....So when L.A.'s black citizens heard of the *San Jose Mercury News* reports claiming CIA backed Contras opened the first

pipeline for Colombian cocaine to their communities their first reaction: shock. Their second: anger."

Whitaker aired a soundbite from Webb's source, a drug dealer, but offered this ambiguous defense of the CIA: "There is no evidence directly linking the CIA to the drug sales and the CIA says its own internal investigation has found no connection. Yet here at Ground Zero of the crack explosion the story simply won't go away." He ended with more emotion over reason: "Eloise Dangerfield says it is all too horrible to contemplate."

Knowing might ease the pain, she says, but it won't end the suffering."

In the September 30 *Weekly Standard* Tucker Carlson questioned Webb's reporting: "Webb came up with no evidence to support his claim ....Instead of actual evidence, Webb relies on a series of unrelated events to show a conspiracy was afoot." Carlson noted that Sen. John Kerry's two year investigation failed to prove CIA involvement. "Indeed ample evidence surfaced that CIA officials had worked to remove drug traffickers from the Nicaraguan resistance." ❑

ATTENTION READERS! The Govt. blew up the Oklahoma City federal building!

ATTENTION READERS! The CIA flooded America's inner cities with drugs!

QUIZ: WHICH ONE'S THE WACKO, REDNECK, MILITIA CONSPIRACY NUT AND WHICH ONE'S THE REASONED, METROPOLITAN JOURNALIST?

NEWSBITES

death from lung cancer in 1984. On CBS Bob Schieffer called it "a barnburner." However, reporters failed to recognize that in 1988, four years after his sister died, Gore made an enthusiastic appeal to voters in tobacco states by stressing his own efforts in growing tobacco.

The October 3 *CBS Evening News* included a profile of Gore by Rita Braver. For the first time, CBS viewers heard about Gore's hypocrisy, but Braver excused him."He's in on every key White House meeting and decision. Just last month in his role as environmental guru, Gore convinced the President to create a controversial national monument in Utah. Of late, Republicans have attacked him for making a convention speech about his sister's death from lung cancer caused by smoking...While for several years after her death he let tobacco be grown on land he owned." But instead of seeing this as a character flaw, Braver relayed Gore's spin about how he "dismisses that attack as politics,

an attempt to sully a man so close to the President he feels free to interrupt him." Viewers then saw video of Gore stepping in front of Clinton at a microphone.

Media to Dole: Just Stay Home. Is it wrong for a presidential candidate to address an ideological political organization? Only if it's a conservative one.

When Bob Dole spoke September 14 to the Christian Coalition, on the NBC *Nightly News* David Bloom was concerned: "Dole decided only this morning to speak to the Christian Coalition despite worries inside his campaign that a bow to the religious right might send the wrong message to moderate, swing voters....Clinton's campaign spokesman said in a statement: 'Watching Bob Dole arm in arm with Pat Robertson speaks volumes to the extreme agenda being pursued by the Dole-Kemp-

Continued on next page

How to Identify, Expose & Correct Liberal Media Bias   149

PBS Special Argues Media Out of Touch, But Show Proves PBS Out of Touch with Reality

Clinton Doesn't Get Enough Credit

Civility was not the rule at PBS when *Frontline* asserted the Reagan administration had funneled drugs into American cities to fund the Contras, that Reagan's CIA attempted to kill Contra leader Eden Pastora, or that the 1980 Reagan campaign conspired to delay the release of the Iranian hostages. Congressional investigations later unraveled these conspiracy theories with no apologies from PBS.

But now that Bill Clinton is President, PBS has funded -- without any rebuttal -- Hedrick Smith's four-hour documentary on how Washington works, *The People and the Power Game*. For devoting his first hour on September 3 to his claim that Bill Clinton has been abused by an uncivil news media, Smith earned the Janet Cooke Award.

Smith began: "By focusing on scandal and conflict over substance, and by our increasingly negative

> To distinguish the most outrageously distorted news story of the month, *MediaWatch* presents the Janet Cooke Award. The award honors the *Washington Post* reporter who won the Pulitzer Prize for a story later proven completely false.

tone, the media has distorted the nation's agenda and lost touch with the public we claim to serve."

But Smith made only two brief asides about coverage of conservatives: how reporters drilled Steve Forbes with personal or tactical questions on *Meet the Press*, while average people asked questions of substance; and Newt Gingrich complaining about the "childhood games" reporters played at his press conferences. Smith introduced Gingrich: "A politician on the make knows that the sure way to command press attention is with sensationalism and extremist polemics. Newt Gingrich, as a junior Congressman, built his power on media fireworks."

The rest of the hour brought example after example of scandalous Clinton coverage, from the supposed $200 haircut with Cristophe on Air Force One, to *New York Times* reporter Maureen Dowd: "President Clinton returned today for a sentimental journey to the university where he didn't inhale, didn't get drafted, and didn't get a degree."

Gennifer Flowers. Smith decried the networks "going with a questionable story that almost felled a future

President." Smith never investigated the substance of the Flowers story, choosing instead to force anchors to defend themselves for even touching it. But Smith's version was at variance with the actual record.

He reported ABC's Jim Wooten asked Clinton about the *Star*'s Flowers story on Thursday, January 23, but decided not to air a story. ABC's local affiliates did -- as did *Nightline*, which booked three guests decrying the story as tabloid trash. Smith claimed: "By the next day, ABC's *World News Tonight*, lagging behind its own affiliates, decided to broadcast the story." Smith asked Peter Jennings: "In this instance, you tried it [to check the story out] on the first day, and on the basis of that standard, you didn't run it...With not much different facts the second day, you did run it." Replied Jennings: "Yeah. I think that's a fair and slightly painful characterization for me. But the truth of the matter is that by the second day, we were pretty much swept along by events."

Smith then interviewed Dan Rather: "I said 'Gosh, I don't have the stomach for doing that. And the first day, even the second day, we said 'Nah, not for me.' I mean, frankly, I

Gingrich team.' A top Clinton campaign official was all smiles, saying, 'if you see Dole, tell him thanks for me.'"

But although Clinton was not criticized for refusing to speak at the Coalition meeting, NBC cast in racial terms Dole's July 10 decision to decline the NAACP's speaking invitation. Back then reporter Jim Miklaszewski claimed the group considered it "an insult to African-American voters....By not showing up here, Bob Dole may reinforce those racial divides along party lines and fuel the anxiety among some Republicans that in this presidential campaign, Bob Dole may not be up to the challenge."

Christian Contradiction. Following David Bloom's piece chastising Dole's Christian Coalition speech, Brian Williams claimed the Coalition was "no longer the lone voice for conservative Christians." What new group of

conservative Christians had NBC discovered?

Bob Abernethy described a group "uncomfortable" with the Coalition's "partisanship and with what seems to many critics its divisiveness and its neglect of the poor." Abernethy described the new group's agenda as a "new kind of political action that defends the poor and brings people together." But at their convention, they "heard from children right's advocate Marian Wright Edelman," and Christian Marxist Jim Wallis.

The group, Call To Renewal, hardly fits Williams' "conservative" label. Yet Abernethy didn't apply a single liberal label, even though "children's advocate" Edelman's speech garnered applause for this line: "Let's guarantee a job. Let's guarantee health care and children care. Let's turn this welfare repeal into real welfare reform."

Abernethy simply described Wallis as "Reverend," but

don't care, and I don't think most viewers care. And then somebody came in and said 'Look at this. Last night, one of our major competitors, they went with it, they went with it strong,' and that bridges over from the sleazy press into the mainstream."

But any look at the tapes of ABC's *World News Tonight* demonstrates that they aired no story on January 24, the day after *Nightline*, but waited until the 27th -- after the Clintons had appeared in an exclusive post-Super Bowl interview on *60 Minutes*. And for Rather's version of events -- that a

---

Clinton's "thoughtful deliberation is seen as indecision and compromise as backsliding."

---

competitor "went with it strong" -- seems strange since he waited until *60 Minutes* did the story. Only NBC's Lisa Myers made passing reference to the Flowers story before that.

Brit Hume. Smith claimed: "The once-cozy relationship between the President and the White House press corps has dissolved into permanent combat...Increasingly, critics argue, the balance is out of whack, and the traditional skepticism of the White House press corps has slid into cynicism, where a President's thoughtful deliberation is seen as indecision and compromise as backsliding."

What kind of cynical question did Smith have in mind? When Clinton appointed Ruth Bader Ginsburg to the Supreme Court after long considering Stephen Breyer, ABC's Brit Hume asked Clinton: "We may have created an impression, perhaps unfair, of a certain zig-zag in the decision making process here. I wonder if you could walk us through it and perhaps disabuse of any notions we might have along these lines. Thank you."

Eric Engberg. The CBS reporter may have been criticized by colleague Bernard Goldberg for attacking Steve Forbes' flat tax, but Smith was only concerned about Clinton: "Critics contend that Engberg's Reality Checks have gone beyond investigative journalism and become saturated with opinion, almost always negative...Just seven days after Clinton's inauguration, for example, Engberg was on the air with a Reality Check declaring the infant administration a failure."

But Engberg's actual report never came close to "declaring the infant administration a failure." Engberg noted Clinton had not followed through on promises to have plans on the economy and energy available "on the first day" of his presidency. Engberg also brought up news reports that the White House was considering a gas tax, recalling Clinton ruled out raising taxes on the middle class in 1992. Engberg concluded: "Overall, the first

week showed the President willing to jump into controversies that can slice away some of his early support. The promise to focus on the economy like a laser seemed to come unstuck in the Washington centrifuge."

CBS's State of the Union. Smith declared: "CBS and others in the Washington media were criticized for relying on inside-the-Beltway punditry in their coverage of Clinton's State of the Union address." The program quoted Joe Klein saying: "It was a very, very long speech. This guy loves to give long speeches." He left out Klein's next sentence: "But it was also a very effective one."

Smith rebutted Klein: "But polls showed the public loved it." Where would Smith have learned that polls showed the public loved it? CBS aired its instant poll results showing that 85 percent "approve of the President's proposals," that 74 percent "now have a clear idea what President Clinton stands for" and 56 percent said Clinton "better understands the major problems facing the country today" than the GOP. Rather signed off by repeating all the pro-Clinton poll results.

Taxpayers fund public broadcasting to be offered an alternative to the commercial networks. Smith's program shows taxpayers aren't getting an alternative, but are paying for PBS to scold the media on how they're not liberal enough. ❏

NewsBites

in the past Wallis has voiced hope that "more Christians will view the world through Marxist eyes." By failing to disclose Call To Renewal's ideological agenda, Abernethy committed sin by omission.

Media Flew the Koop. Former Surgeon General C. Everett Koop endorsed the Clinton health care scheme early on, making him a ubiquitous presence on the networks. Koop made news again when he criticized Bob Dole for suggesting nicotine is not addictive. He appeared on *Good Morning America* and was featured in stories on other networks castigating Dole. In the infamous July interview in which Dole and Katie Couric sparred over liberal bias, Couric cited Koop: "C. Everett Koop is pretty nonpartisan wouldn't you say? He criticized you quite severely for your comments. You're saying the liberal media had a problem but even Dr. Koop had a problem."

But when Koop criticized President Clinton for vetoing in April the partial-birth abortion ban passed by Congress, he fell into TV's memory hole. The former Surgeon General did not appear on any network to talk about his condemnation of the President. The lesson? When a nationally known figure announces he is for a liberal proposal, he is much in demand by the media. When the same figure comes out in support of a conservative cause, the media silence is overwhelming.

Dole Behind: Blame Conservatives. Conservatives argue that Bob Dole's lack of identity with issues that excite conservatives explained why he failed to early on secure his Republican base. But more than a month before the election, ABC's Dean Reynolds instead assigned Dole's low standing in the polls to his being "too conservative."

Continued on next page

How to Identify, Expose & Correct Liberal Media Bias   151

Revelation After Revelation Reported by Newspapers, But Never Make TV News

Networks Blackout Clinton's Bad News

On September 26, the House ethics committee announced it would expand an investigation of Speaker Newt Gingrich's college course "Renewing American Civilization." ABC, CBS, CNN and NBC reported the story, ultimately adding up to eleven broadcast network morning and evening segments in five days.

The next morning, NBC's *Today* led off with an interview with NBC Washington Bureau Chief Tim

---

The networks have virtually ignored eight revelations embarrassing to President Clinton.

Russert, who proclaimed: "It's awful, it's serious, it's potentially devastating." On October 8, *Today's* Matt Lauer asked Gingrich six questions about ethics, including two about whether Gingrich would resign. But a *MediaWatch* review of recent scoops on the Clinton administration's character shows a much different approach to stories which could damage Democrats.

September 23: The Federal Deposit Insurance Corporation's in-

spector general concluded that Hillary Clinton had drafted a real estate document with the intent to "deceive" federal regulators. That real estate transaction, a sham deal selling a property named Castle Grande to a straw buyer, later cost taxpayers $4 million in the bailout of Madison Guaranty Savings and Loan.

The Washington Post put the news on its September 24 front page. Network coverage? Nothing -- until October 4, when NBC's Jim Miklaszewski mentioned it in a *Nightly News* story on a speech by independent counsel Ken Starr: "Whitewater prosecutor Kenneth Starr was invited to appear by outspoken Clinton critic Pat Robertson and the audience was very conservative. The White House claims that's proof Starr is out to get Clinton for political reasons, but Starr says he'll stay the course."

(ABC and CNN did report the story last February 29, when the FDIC released a more favorable assessment, recommending the FDIC not seek legal recourse against Mrs. Clinton or the Rose Law Firm.)

September 24: A House committee held hearings on charges that the

administration has let criminals become citizens. *The Washington Times* story the next day began: "Immigration workers yesterday told a House Government Reform and Oversight subcommittee of rampant abuses in the Citizenship USA program that apparently let thousands of immigrants with criminal records become citizens." The networks? Zilch until the October 18 *CBS Evening News*.

Also on September 24, a federal jury convicted Sun Diamond Growers, one of the nation's largest producers of fruits and nuts, of illegally showering former Clinton Agriculture Secretary Mike Espy with nearly $6,000 in gifts, a conviction for Independent Counsel Donald Smaltz. The story made *The Washington Post* front page the next day. Network coverage? Nothing, but *The NewsHour with Jim Lehrer* on PBS did a brief anchor-read item.

September 25: Sen. Orrin Hatch revealed a six-month gap in the log which listed who at the White House was accessing FBI background files on Republican White House employees. *The Washington Times* bannered the news across page one the next day. Coverage? A CNN *World*

For the September 23 *World News Tonight* Reynolds traveled to Lansing, Michigan where he found that "many of the voters we spoke with blame Gingrich for last year's government shutdown, for a mean-spirited attitude generally, and for attempts to trim Medicare specifically." Then while interviewing a "lifelong Republican" Reynolds asked, "Your party, did it move too far to the right?"

Reynolds next talked with Republican women in a restaurant who opposed Dole on abortion. Of the eight talking heads aired from Lansing, seven were anti-Dole and only one offered "lukewarm" support for Dole.

▪ **Speedy Judgments.** When the Republican Congress obliterated the 55 mph national speed limit last year reporters warned of the coming carnage on the nation's highways. "As Congress moves toward allowing states to

raise the limit," CBS' Bob Orr sounded the alarm in a June 20, 1995 piece, "safety regulators warn highway fatalities will climb... Doctors say if only lawmakers could see what goes on each day in trauma rooms, they would keep the lid on speed." On November 28, 1995, the day President Clinton signed the bill to raise the speed limit, Bob McNamara intoned on the *CBS Evening News*: "Raising the speed limit may be popular with the public, but there could be a deadly downside...Soon, politicians here may find out that sometimes giving the public what it wants could be a fatal mistake."

Now the statistics are in: Many states have actually seen their traffic fatalities decline. In the August 26 *USA Today*, Carol J. Castaneda reported that newspaper's review of states that increased their speed: "Three states reported decreases ranging from 4 percent to 28 percent within a five- to eight-month period after limits were raised. Fatali-

---

Today story and a mention on ABC's *Good Morning America.*

Also on the 25th, the *Times* reported that Rep. John Mica (R.-Fla.) sent a letter to Clinton's "drug czar" demanding release of a four-month-old Institute for Defense Analysis report that concluded Bush's interdiction policy was far more effective than Clinton's emphasis on drug treatment. Network coverage? Nothing until a story by David Martin on the October 15 *CBS Evening News.*

September 26: Three days after President Clinton refused to rule out pardons for Whitewater figures on *The NewsHour with Jim Lehrer,* 170 members of Congress, including three Democrats, sent a letter to the White House demanding Clinton promise not to pardon anyone. The September 29 *Washington Times* reported that House Democrats were prepared to shut down the government if Republicans demanded a vote on a resolution calling for President Clinton to renounce pardons. Network coverage? With the exception of one general question on the 29th about pardons from *CBS Evening News* Sunday anchor John Roberts to commentator Laura Ingraham, absolutely nothing until Dole raised the subject later.

October 1: The White House claimed executive privilege to withhold from House investigators a memo to President Clinton from FBI Director Louis Freeh said to be highly critical of federal drug policy. Network response? Zero.

October 4: Sen. Orrin Hatch released the deposition of White House aide Mari Anderson before the Senate Judiciary Committee. Anderson verified that pages of the log used to record the taking of FBI files were missing. Anderson also asserted, in contradiction to White House aide Craig Livingstone's assurances, that he knew they were procuring the FBI files of Republicans. Even *The Washington Post* put this story on its front page the next day. Network coverage? Only CNN, in two Linden Soles anchorbriefs on *The World Today,* mentioned the news. (ABC's *World News Tonight* didn't report it, but the revelations were raised in an interview on the October 6 *This Week.*)

Also on October 4, former FBI Special Agent Dennis Sculimbrene, who was the senior agent assigned to the White House from 1986 to April 1996, told *The Wall Street Journal:* "There were senior people as well, senior aides and advisers to the President who used drugs recently -- people in policy positions, or say, the director of an office...Some senior people even said they had used drugs as recently as the Inaugural." Sculimbrene estimated that "about 25 percent of the incoming administration, about one out of four cases, had a problem with illegal drugs. Not just casual experimentation, but a pattern of usage." Network coverage? Zero.

An aide contradicts Livingstone's FBI files story. Silence from ABC, CBS and NBC.

October 10: A House panel investigating the Clinton administration's secret foreign policy initiative to encourage the Iranian government to arm the Bosnian Muslims asked the Justice Department to probe administration officials for possible criminal charges for false statements. Since the Iran-Bosnia secret foreign policy emerged in the *Los Angeles Times* April 5, CBS and NBC have aired absolutely nothing on the evening news about the story. CNN and ABC aired only anchor briefs, only in the first days of the story. Network coverage for the latest development? Zero.

On CNN's *Crossfire* Sept. 20, *Chicago Tribune* reporter Ellen Warren declared: "Reporters want nothing more, this year and four years ago, to have a horse race. That's what we're in love with, is the fight, the close call....So it's in our interest to make it look close, to make Bob Dole look good."

The omissions documented here suggest otherwise. ❑

✔

EXPOSE

---

ties remained relatively the same in four states." Six states saw increases, but in "California and several other states [that saw increases], it was unclear whether fatalities occurred on highways where the speed limit was raised."

Grand Canyon Gap. On September 18, 1991, when President Bush visited the Grand Canyon, ABC and NBC used it as an opportunity to review his record on the environment. On *World News Tonight,* anchor Peter Jennings announced that Bush "promised that he would be the environmental President and today he went to the Grand Canyon. It was a trip critics charged was nothing more than grand standing." Reporter Ann Compton opened her story: "This morning there was only a slight haze drifting through the Grand Canyon, so the South Rim was a picture perfect spot for President Bush to claim an environmental victory, but on many days smog from a nearby power plant makes it impossible to see across to the Canyon walls just two miles away." Who did Compton use for a soundbite? Then Senator Al Gore.

What a difference a President makes. When President Clinton and Vice President Gore visited the Grand Canyon exactly five years later to designate 1.7 million acres in Southern Utah as a national monument, no network used this photo op as a chance to tear apart Clinton's environmental record, quite the contrary. On the *CBS Evening News,* reporter Rita Braver started her story: "With Al 'Earthman' Gore by his side, the President signed a bill designating 1.7 million acres of land 70 miles away in Utah as the Grand Staircase-Escalante National Monument." ABC's Sam Donaldson was no different: "Dressed in appropriate western attire, boots and blue blazers, the top guns of the Democratic team came to the South Rim of the Grand Canyon to make points as conservationists." ❑

How to Identify, Expose & Correct Liberal Media Bias   153

TO OUR READERS

"Team Clinton" T-shirt

The MRC has created T-shirts with "Team Clinton" above a drawing of three network anchors. Below, the shirt reads: "The Starting Line-Up of the Pro-Clinton Press Corps."

Order a shirt and you'll get a free copy our *Team Clinton* booklet, packed with pro-Clinton and anti-conservative quotes from 28 media stars.

For a T-shirt and free booklet, send $15.00 to: Media Research Center, T-shirt Offer, 113 South West. St., Alexandria, Va. 22314

PUBLISHER
L. Brent Bozell III

EDITOR
Brent H. Baker

ASSOCIATE EDITOR
Tim Graham

CONTRIBUTING EDITOR
Tim Lamer

MEDIA ANALYSTS
Geoffrey Dickens
Gene Eliasen
James Forbes
Steve Kaminski
Clay Waters

MARKETING DIRECTOR
Kathleen Ruff

CIRCULATION MANAGER
Peter Reichel

PRESS REPRESENTATIVE
Keith Appell (703) 683-5004

MediaWatch (ISSN 1053-8321) is published 12 times a year ($36.00) by the Media Research Center, 113 South West St., Alexandria, Virginia 22314. Phone (703) 683-9733. E-mail: 73041.2757@compuserve.com. Copyright© 1996 by the Media Research Center. Reproduction without written permission prohibited. Excerpts may be quoted if full credit is given to *MediaWatch*. Send address changes to the address above or call the number below.

Customer service: 800-304-6388 (8:30am to 11:30pm ET daily). Call for subscription problems, to change your address or to subscribe to *MediaWatch* or *Notable Quotables*.

BACK PAGE

Wall of Denial Breaks Down
Media Actually Admit Bias

Sam Donaldson, *USA Today*'s Richard Benedetto and the Chairman of CBS all agree: the media are biased.

With Brit Hume out ill for a few days, Donaldson returned to the campaign trail for the first time since Reagan's years. And he found things have changed, *USA Today*'s Peter Johnson reported September 23: "Have the boys on the bus lost the fire in their bellies, the one that fueled their cries of 'Mr. President! Mr. President!' during President Reagan's years in office? ABC's Sam Donaldson isn't saying, exactly, but suspects something's going on. Except for CBS' Rita Braver, 'I have heard no reporter trying to ask the President any question,' Donaldson said....

"What's this, Sam? Reporters going easy on Clinton? 'You're not going to get me in a fight with these guys. They're my friends,' said Donaldson, who covered the White House from 1977 to 1989. 'But there seems to be a change in attitude or a different attitude toward covering the President.'"

A *USA Today* reporter concurs. In his "Politics" column the same day, Richard Benedetto wrote: "As President Clinton's re-election campaign rolled through six states in four days last week, it did so virtually unimpeded by a White House press corps known for setting up roadblocks now and then....He was left free to make a string of feel-good speeches that won great play in the media and gave the desired impression that the Clinton campaign is on a roll....

"In 1992, a tough White House press corps rightly kept President Bush's feet to the fire on domestic issues he would rather have downplayed. But the 1996 crew appears less aggressive with Clinton."

The realization of media bias extends to the top of CBS. Michael Jordan, the Chairman of Westinghouse, parent of CBS, revealed in a magazine profile that he agrees with CBS reporter Bernard Goldberg's charge that network reporting tilts left.

In a *Wall Street Journal* op-ed back in February Goldberg cited a specific CBS story to support his contention that "the old argument that the networks and other 'media elites' have a liberal bias is so blatantly true that it's hardly worth discussing anymore." CBS reaction at the time: "It's such a wacky charge," commented a baffled Bob Schieffer. CBS News President Andrew Heyward called the charge "absurd," took Goldberg off the air for two months and then canceled his bylined *CBS Evening News* feature, "Bernard Goldberg's America."

In the Summer *Forbes MediaCritic*, Terry Eastland found that in a May *USAir Magazine* profile, Jordan sided with Goldberg: "I think his criticism is fair. I think all the networks can do a better job at providing a more objective and balanced perspective." Now, if only Jordan would put his concerns into action. ❑

ON THE BRIGHT SIDE

Impartial on Partial-Birth

Cutting through the rhetoric forwarded by both sides of the partial-birth abortion debate, in *The Washington Post*'s September 17 Health section reporter David Brown found wanting some media-held assumptions about the issue.

Brown exposed inaccuracies in many abortion supporters' arguments. At the veto ceremony of the partial-birth abortion bill, Clinton said, these women "'represent a small, but extremely vulnerable group... They all desperately wanted their children. They didn't want abortion. They made agonizing decisions only when it became clear that their babies would not survive, their own lives, their health, and in some cases their capacity to have children in the future were in danger.'" But Brown uncovered that "Doctors say that while a significant number of their patients have late abortions for medical reasons, many others – perhaps the majority – do not."

Brown also examined the procedure from a perspective not usually focused on by the media: the baby's point of view. Since the partial-birth procedure is usually done in the second and third trimesters of gestation, is it possible the last minutes of the child's life are spent in excruciating pain? Brown determined the answer is not fully known: "Scientists must deduce pain's presence (or absence) by looking for the psychological signs of the sensation. Those include hormones and other biochemicals that appear in the bloodstream when pain is produced, as well as more subjective signs, such as facial grimaces or the movement of limbs. Nobody can say, for certain, however, whether these things denote pain in a developing human being." ❑

October 1996
Vol. 4, Issue 10

MEDIA RESEARCH CENTER®

MediaNomics ™

What the media tell Americans about free enterprise

Ten-Part Series Bashes International Trade, Foreign Workers

Reporters Say American Dream Stolen

"America: Who Stole the Dream?" was the provocative title of a recent ten-part *Philadelphia Inquirer* series, published nationally in Knight-Ridder newspapers, by Pulitzer-Prize winning journalists Donald L. Barlett and James B. Steele. Their answer to the series' title question: free-market proponents and foreigners. But in their lengthy series they didn't mention some important facts that critics have since pointed out.

Free trade was one of Barlett and Steele's main villains. Instead of creating jobs in export industries, low American tariffs have "wiped out jobs and driven down wages." Barlett and Steele lamented that in 1996, "the United States will record its 21st consecutive merchandise trade deficit – a record unmatched by any other developed country." America's other big economic problem, according to Barlett and Steele, is immigration to the U.S. "No other industrial country has allowed in so many workers in so short a time, depressing wages and living standards."

While these policies are good for big business in the short term, the two reporters suggest that American workers may be on the verge of starting a revolution. They quoted a Kansas factory worker as saying:

Inside This Issue:

✔ Network trade coverage down from 1992 – Page 2.
✔ Review: *Traders'* Canadian investment bankers – Page 3.
✔ Guest Editorial: Tweaking tax facts – Page 4.

"Are we just going to keep lowering our standard of living? When that happens, nobody is going to have money to put food on the table. Then you are going to see a revolution, because people are not going to be able to feed their families." A Pennsylvania factory worker told the duo that "there's going to be bloodshed before we get out of

> Workers who believe that there will be a revolution in the United States "reflect a largely silent but growing sentiment," according to Barlett and Steele.

this." These workers, Barlett and Steele informed readers, "reflect a largely silent but growing sentiment" in the U.S. Profiles of people with such sentiments dominated the series. The two reporters proposed restricting immigration and hiking tariffs.

The reaction to the series was quick and severe. Economics columnist Robert Samuelson called it "junk journalism" in a September 18 *Washington Post* column. "What [the series] doesn't say is that the trade balance and employment are hardly connected," he wrote. Samuelson pointed out that the trade surpluses of Germany, the Netherlands, and Sweden – which Barlett and Steele envy – haven't kept those countries from having far higher unemployment rates than the United States. According to Samuelson, Barlett and Steele reported such matters "so select-

ively...that ordinary readers are misled."

The reporters' selective use of anecdotes and statistics bothered George Washington University's Steve Suranovic. In a September 25 letter to the *Inquirer*, Suranovic wrote that it is easy for reporters "to choose individuals whose stories confirm their conclusions." He argued that Barlett and Steele could have "found workers with new jobs in export industries earning higher-than-average wages" and "profiled a couple of millionaires with middle-class backgrounds who created export industries employing thousands of workers. Bill Gates springs to mind."

The Cato Institute's Stuart Anderson argued that Barlett and Steele misled readers about the economic effects of immigration. In an October 14 *Investor's Business Daily* editorial, Anderson pointed out that having more people in the U.S. does not lead to more unemployment. The reason: "While immigrants do increase the supply of labor, they also increase the demand for labor." His proof: As immigration and trade deficits have increased over the past 20 years, and total employment has increased 59 percent, "the unemployment rate has dropped from 7.7 percent to 5.2 percent." According to Anderson, "Even the total number of unemployed people in the country has dropped."

The views of Samuelson, Suranovic, and Anderson are held by enough economists that they should be discussed in any major, ten-part economic series that purports to be serious journalism.

✔ EXPOSE

Issue Analysis: Global Economy As a News Story, 1991-1992 vs. 1995-1996

Deficit in Trade Reporting

International trade has almost ceased to be an issue to report on for the network news media. This is in stark contrast to 1991 and 1992, when the media reported heavily on trade as an election-year issue. As a result, the trade deficit – though large – is not nearly the negative story (except in Knight-Ridder papers, see page one) for President Clinton that it was for President Bush.

Media Research Center (MRC) analysts reviewed all of the stories about foreign trade on ABC's *World News Tonight, CBS Evening News* and *NBC Nightly News* between July 1, 1991 and June 30, 1992. There were 134 trade stories during this period. MRC analysts also reviewed all of the stories about foreign trade on the same shows between July 1, 1995 and June 30, 1996. There were only 39 trade stories during this period.

There was also a large difference in the tone of the stories. During the 1991-1992 study period, many stories focused on how trade, especially with Japan, was harming America. Trade was like war. According to NBC's Garrick Utley, on the January 12, 1992 *Nightly News*, there is a "new superpower rivalry. We, of course, won the old one with the Soviet Union. The outcome of the new one with Japan is much less certain." Stories focused on union demands for tariffs and the views of protectionist economists.

Reporters adopted a different attitude during the 1995-1996 study period. Spurred by Pat Buchanan's criticism of free trade, the networks began pointing out the benefits of a global economy. Before the South Carolina primary, NBC's Mike Boettcher contrasted the "new South," flush with foreign investment and high-tech jobs" with "the old South, shuttered textile mills, unemploy-

ment, and pleas for protection from foreign competitors." ABC's Aaron Brown reported that "while Buchanan says you can protect industries with high tariffs without driving out foreign companies here, economists say that is nonsense."

There was also a dramatic change in the amount of coverage given to the trade deficit. In a 1988 study for the Media Institute, Virginia Commonwealth University's Ted J. Smith III found that as the American economy improved during the 1980s, reporting on the economy decreased in volume and became more negative in tone. In

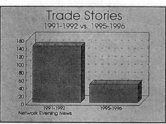

Trade Stories
1991-1992 vs. 1995-1996

There were 134 stories about trade during July 1991-June 1992, but only 39 during the same 1995-1996 period.

particular, he found that the media became more interested in one statistic – the trade deficit – when it widened and less interested in other indicators as they improved.

The trend in trade reporting that Professor Smith found during the 1980s was present during the 1991-1992 study period, when the U.S. economy was coming out of recession. There were 21 reports about the trade deficit, about the same number he found when the economy was coming out of recession from 1982-1983. But during the 1995-1996 study period, when the economy was fully out of recession and the trade deficit was expanding, there were only eight

such reports. During the Reagan era, when the economy was fully out of recession, trade deficit reporting increased dramatically.

During 1991-1992, even decreases in the trade deficit were treated skeptically. "Some mixed signs on the U.S. economy today," reported ABC's Forest Sawyer, on the March 19, 1992 *World News Tonight.* "The U.S. trade deficit grew smaller in January, down $5.8 billion. Still, many economists say they are concerned that American exports were also down."

Trade deficits, though, have not been big news more recently. In two instances, only CBS mentioned reports of widening trade gaps. On July 18, 1995, Dan Rather announced: "The United States has taken another beating in world trade, posting a record-high deficit in May." Nearly two months later, on September 12, 1995, Rather used almost identical language: "The U.S. took a beating in the world markets for the second quarter of the year, posting the biggest quarterly trade deficit ever." ABC and NBC ignored the news.

Trade deficits may not be such bad news. Many economists point out that prosperous countries often run trade deficits because they have a lot of money to spend, and that imports constitute a great benefit to an economy. So perhaps ABC and NBC were correct to play down the trade numbers. Still, this was a new standard not applied to GOP presidents.

And trade in general could be a bigger news issue in this election year than it has been. Will Bill Clinton, if reelected, again defy union backers and work to expand the North American Free Trade Agreement? Reporters, who seem to have lost interest in trade, aren't asking.

October 1996

Review: Lifetime's Traders

New Business Show Better Than Most

"This is the battleground of the modern world, where war is waged daily. Fortunes are made or lost in seconds. These are the men and women of Gardner/Ross. They're brilliant, ruthless, only as good as their next deal...They work hard and play harder and agree on just one thing – winning is everything."

From this promo for *Traders*, a Canadian program now being shown on cable's Lifetime network, one would think that it would be another typical TV caricature of business: A world dominated by rogue greedheads who have no redeeming qualities and whose work does nothing beneficial for society.

While this tendency is present in the show, it doesn't always dominate. *Traders* instead treats investment banking the way television usually treats some other vocations, which is a step above the way business is normally portrayed. *Traders* focuses on the Toronto-based investment firm Gardner/Ross. The plots center on the firm's senior executives:

Sally Ross – An idealistic economics professor, Ross steps into her father's role as senior partner when he is arrested for illegally skimming $5 million off of a $47 million deal. She is immediately at odds with the firm's other senior executives, who want to make money at all costs. She wants to make money, but also wants to preserve her family firm's good name. When she doesn't allow the firm's head trader to trade on inside information, he yells: "You know, you've got a really unhealthy sense of morality."

Adam Cunningham – Ross's alter ego, Cunningham is willing to blackmail government officials to land a deal. He has no conscience, but a great knack for cliches: Investment banking is a "zero-sum game. No-

body wins unless somebody loses" and "We all know the game. You buy on rumor, you sell on fact. Look, if enough people believe that fertilizer is worth more than gold, the next thing you know crap is selling at $600 an ounce." When the Russian mob threatens the family of the editor of the firm's newsletter, Cunningham worries that the editor will care more about her family than the firm.

Jack Larkin – A very hungry young trader, he makes his way to Gardner/Ross by landing a seat-of-the-pants mining deal. He's willing to risk everything for a big deal, but he's no Cunningham. He cares

The cast of *Traders*, a show about the rugged life of Canadian investment bankers which airs Sunday nights on Lifetime.

deeply about mending his poor relationship with his father, and his father's illness occupies as much of his time as does the firm's business. It also gives him some perspective. When a young trader almost ruins her career by not placing an order out of concern for a client who is a compulsive gambler, Larkin tells her: "I'll deny I ever said this, but it's just a job; it's just money." By steering the firm into investing in an emerging medical drug, Larkin shows viewers that investment banking can help society.

Marty Stephens – The firm's head trader, Stephens is a younger Cunningham. When the firm's building

catches fire, he threatens to fire any trader who leaves the floor. Is extensive flooding in South Africa bad news? Not for Stephens, because the firm will make money from the flood's effect on the markets. His family life is a mess: He doesn't know the name of his son's girlfriend, even though she eats dinner with the family every week. When Stephens is suspended for 30 days because of unethical trades, his life seems to change. He finds a support group and learns that he is obsessed with money to compensate for his own insecurities. He resolves to change his ways, but once he's back on the floor the old Marty returns.

Suzanna Marks – Marks runs the firm's investment newsletter. She becomes the target of the Russian mob, which wants her to recommend a stock she doesn't want to recommend. She stands on principle, refusing to compromise her integrity. The Russians then threaten her family, including her young daughter. Though terribly tempted, she still doesn't cave. The situation is resolved when Larkin, whom viewers learn has some mysterious tie to the Russian mob, finds out about the threats and intervenes. The stress, though, ruins her family life. Her husband, believing she places too great a priority on work, files for divorce and custody of their daughter.

Traders has often been compared to *ER*, but it is more like *L.A. Law*. On *ER*, there is no question that the doctors are engaged in noble work. On *L.A. Law*, sometimes the lawyers helped people and society; sometimes they harmed people and society. Some of *L.A. Law*'s lawyers were extremely unethical, some morally upright. *Traders*' traders are a similar mix. For business, as portrayed on television, this is a step up in the world.

October 1996

Guest Editorial, by Stephen Gold

Media Tweak Tax Facts

Many journalists swarmed like hornets after the first presidential debate, their stingers aimed at a Bob Dole soundbite statistic. Maybe the numbers seemed implausible to them. Maybe they deemed Dole's private source for the statistic less reliable than comparable government sources. Or, just maybe, they were simply expressing their knee-jerk bias against conservative economic principles.

Whatever the reason, the day after the first debate, several media outlets challenged Dole's Tax Foundation-inspired statement – that the average American household today pays more in taxes than it does for food, clothing, and housing combined.

In a front-page story, for example, the *Los Angeles Times* hinted at a Dole blunder. The article related that while Dole relied on a conservative think tank for his data, "the Bureau of Labor Statistics' consumer expenditure survey found that the average household spent more than twice as much on food, clothing and shelter as on taxes in 1994." Eric Engberg of CBS News was more forthright in his analysis. Asserting that "some [of Dole's] facts got mangled," Engberg stated the GOP nominee's claim was an "exaggeration" that could be disproved by the Bureau of Labor Statistics (BLS) study.

Ironically, while these and other news organizations used the opportunity to show how Dole, in the words of the *Times*, was "tweaking" the truth to his advantage, it appears the media were doing the same thing. By accepting the BLS data as unimpeachable, the reporters made an error of such magnitude that, if committed by either of the presidential candidates, it would have made front-page news nationwide.

The problem is the BLS survey greatly understates taxes paid. While the national survey is considered an accurate portrayal of consumer expenditures, in the tax category the report only covers individual income taxes (federal, state, and local), real and personal property taxes, and an amorphous category called "other taxes."

Among the most recognizable

> **The Bureau of Labor Statistics survey – relied on by so many reporters to knock Bob Dole's argument for lower taxes – understates total taxes paid by more than four times.**

omissions from the survey: Social Security taxes paid. While the BLS survey doesn't have a category for such payments, the Tax Foundation estimates that the average household will pay about $1,100 for the employee's share of payroll taxes alone this year. Similarly, the BLS survey doesn't specifically report sales and excise taxes paid. In the only entry in the survey in which these taxes might fit ("other taxes"), households earning between $50,000 and $69,000 are said to pay $77 annually. By comparison, based on Bureau of Economic Analysis (BEA) data, the Tax Foundation estimates that households in that income group average over $2,000 in federal, state, and local sales and excise taxes paid.

Also, the BLS survey results altogether ignore the effect of indirect levies, such as business taxes, on American society. Unlike the survey, the Tax Foundation incorporates all taxes at all levels of government in its annual analysis, including those levies hidden from

taxpayers. For example, business taxes (including corporate income taxes) must be borne by the general population somehow, whether through lower wages for workers, lower shareholder dividends (which harms anyone with a pension fund), or higher consumer prices. So, while the typical American won't ever see a tax bill for these taxes, they're certainly paid by everyone.

In total, the BLS survey – relied on by so many reporters to knock Bob Dole's argument for lower taxes – understates total taxes paid by more than four times, according to the Tax Foundation's analysis based on BEA data.

The flaw here isn't the BLS survey. It lies in the way the survey's results were used by reporters. The search for truth by the media is undeniably critical, especially during an election year. Unfortunately, the public is hurt when reporters, to prove a point, choose to accept certain economic premises without verifying their legitimacy.

Stephen Gold is associate director and communications director of the Tax Foundation.

Publisher L. Brent Bozell III
Editor Timothy Lamer
Circulation Peter Reichel
Publicist Keith Appell (703) 683-5004

MediaNomics (ISSN# 1072-785X), a supplement to *MediaWatch*, is published twelve times a year by the Free Market Project of the Media Research Center, 113 S. West Street, 2nd Floor, Alexandria, VA 22314. Phone (703) 683-9733. Copyright © 1996 by the Media Research Center. Reproduction without permission is prohibited. However, excerpts may be quoted provided full credit is given to *MediaNomics*.

Bringing Political Balance to the Media

October 1996

Media Research Center's Monthly Members' Report

volume 1
issue 8
AUGUST 1996

http://www.mediaresearch.org

EXPOSE

Dear MRC Member,

By the time you read this letter the Republican Convention will have come and gone, but Bill Clinton will still be leading Bob Dole in public opinion polls.

Before he picked Jack Kemp, Dole had been running a terrible campaign, one designed, it seemed, to see how many conservatives he could alienate. Hopefully, he's stopped pandering to the left and the so-called moderates and will continue campaigning with a truly conservative agenda. But when he does that he will face a real enemy: the left-wing media, which have waged an all-out war against our policies and leaders by distorting everything we stand for.

Just look at what the leftist press did to the Contract with America. When the Republicans, the party in favor of *reducing* government, introduced the Contract, the media immediately and consistently slammed them. Over and over, hundreds of times in fact, the media labeled the Republican agenda and its leaders as "far-right," "extreme," "intolerant," "mean-spirited," "cruel" -- the list goes on and on.

But the media aren't stopping at distortions and lies like these. They are performing shameless damage control with each new Clinton scandal, or "snafu." Every time a Clinton detractor surfaces, they attack him, fast and furiously.

Witness the case of former FBI agent Gary Aldrich, whose newly released book

Unlimited Access detailed all sorts of nefarious acts taking place in the Clinton White House. It was after Aldrich's appearance on

MRC Chairman L. Brent Bozell III

This Week with David Brinkley, where the author's credibility was mercilessly attacked, that -- what a surprise -- the left-wing media dropped the subject of Aldrich and his Clinton expose. In fact, after the *Brinkley* appearance, CNN and NBC both nixed their plans to interview Aldrich. And no other network has invited him on.

The moral of this story: If the media are not confronted, exposed, and neutralized in this campaign, Clinton will win the election. It's as simple as that.

The Media Research Center is making great strides to combat the left-wing press in this election, demanding fairness and balance for conservatives. Thank you for helping us.

Sincerely,

L. Brent Bozell III, Chairman

INSIDE

The Media Research Center battles the media at the **Republican National Convention** ...on page 2.

Rush Limbaugh lauds the MRC and the book *Pattern of Deception* ...page 3.

The PTC lobbies for some **family-friendly** shows to receive **Emmy nominations**. See page 4 for details.

Brent Bozell takes over **Mary Matalin's** radio show for two days... Page 8.

MEDIA
RESEARCH
CENTER

MEDIA RESEARCH CENTER

Chairman L. Brent Bozell III

FLASH Editor Kerrie L. Mahan

News Division
MediaWatch & *Notable Quotables*
**Editor and MRC Executive
Director** Brent Baker
Associate Editor Tim Graham
News Media Analysts
Geoff Dickens, Gene Eliasen,
James Forbes, Steve Kaminski,
Clay Waters
Interns
Jessica Anderson and Matt Turosz

Entertainment Division
Director Sandra L. Crawford
Senior Writer Thomas Johnson
Entertainment Analysts
Christine Brookhart, Carey Evans,
Alice Lynn O'Steen
Intern Jennifer Lobaugh

Parents Television Council
Director of Operations
    Mark Barnes
Board of Development
    Peter C. McCarty
    Wendy H. Borcherdt
333 South Grand Avenue, 29th
Floor, Los Angeles, CA 90071
(310) 277-6951
FAX (310) 277-6959

Free Market Project
MediaNomics
Director Timothy Lamer

Development
Finance Director Richard Kimble
Assistant Finance Director
    Lawrence Gourlay
Development Assistant
    Michelle Sharp

Marketing Director Kathy Ruff
Administrator Evelyn Reichel
Assistant to the Chairman
    Sara Harris
Circulation Manager
    Peter Reichel

FLASH (ISSN # 1087-5077) is
published monthly by the Media
Research Center, 113 S. West
Street, 2nd Floor, Alexandria, VA
22314 Phone (703) 683-9733.

MRC in the Trenches

A
t press time, on the eve of the Republican Convention, the Media Research Center is positioned to launch several major projects designed to counter the media's liberal agenda. These projects are an essential part of our Tell the Truth! campaign to stop media distortions during the election season.

From our convention headquarters in San Diego, the MRC will print and distribute a daily newsletter -- *Media Reality Check '96* -- containing analysis of the networks' convention reporting. Early each morning, the MRC crew will hand-deliver these newsletters to each of the major convention hotels, centers, and press outlets, ensuring *Media Reality Check '96* receives maximum coverage. Our findings on the liberal media will also be blast-faxed to members of the press outside the convention city, including a nationwide roster of conservative talk show hosts.

In addition, MRC Chairman Brent Bozell will be issuing a daily media bias update on three nationally syndicated radio talk shows: the Oliver North Show, the Blanquita Cullum Show, and the Michael Reagan Show.

The MRC will also have a convention booth featuring *Team Clinton: The Starting Line-Up of the Pro-Clinton Press Corps*, a unique new guide for Republican Convention delegates containing quotes from 28 of the most liberally biased reporters. *Team Clinton* includes infamous quotes

from journalists such as *Newsweek*'s Eleanor Clift, CBS's Eric Engberg, and NBC's Bryant Gumbel, informing convention delegates of which reporters will give their views a fair hearing, and which members of the press will distort everything they have to say.

At the MRC booth, convention delegates will also be able to purchase "Team Clinton" T-shirts featuring caricatures of ABC's Peter Jennings, CBS's Dan Rather, and NBC's Gumbel; bumper stickers, pens, and magnets with the tag line "I don't believe the liberal media" will also be available.

Sure to be huge hits at the Republican Convention, all of these items are available to MRC members at a special discount. See page eight for ordering details.

Next month in *Flash*: a full disclosure of the media's performance at both conventions.

How to Identify, Expose & Correct Liberal Media Bias

Dittos for *Pattern of Deception*

In the August 1996 issue of *The Limbaugh Letter*, talk show host extraordinaire Rush Limbaugh gave his stamp of approval to *Pattern of Deception: The Media's Role in the Clinton Presidency*, authored by Tim Graham of the Media Research Center's News Division.

In the article, the nation's premier conservative spokesman described the work of the Media Research Center as "superb," and noted that *Pattern of Deception* is full of "invaluable information," and "especially useful now, to put this campaign season's media behavior in context."

Limbaugh added that *Pattern of Deception*'s "impact is simply overwhelming" while it lays bare "the sorry record of press manipulation of every memorable milestone of this Administration."

"This book should be intensively studied in every journalism course and newsroom in the country," Rush raved. "Sadly, that is unlikely to happen."

If you don't already have your copy of *Pattern of Deception*, see page eight for the details on how to order the book Limbaugh says is "invaluable information." Plus, order

Rush Limbaugh says the Media Research Center is "superb" and *Pattern of Deception* is full of "invaluable information."

through *Flash* and get your **members' only discount!**

Radio Active: MRC Takes to CBS Airwaves

Hundreds of thousands of Americans learned about the Media Research Center's activism thanks to MRC Chairman Brent Bozell's two-day stint as guest host of the nationally syndicated *Mary Matalin Show*.

On July 25, broadcasting to 32 states on over 60 radio stations on the CBS Radio network, Bozell interviewed Rep. **Lamar Smith** (R-Tex.), and Sen. **Joseph Lieberman** (D-Conn.) on their role in the MRC's campaign to restore the spirit of the "family hour" to prime time television.

Smith described the decline in programming standards during the first hour of prime time as a "cultur-

> ABC's John Stossel gave an insider's viewpoint on the press's tendency to distort the news.

al crisis," and advocated that the industry voluntarily reinstitute a safe viewing haven for family audiences.

The Texas Congressman continued, "We're not talking about censorship. We're not talking about the heavy hand of government on any network's shoulder. We're just frankly asking the networks to do what is in the best interest of America's children."

The following day, Bozell interviewed **John Stossel**, a correspondent from ABC's newsmagazine *20/20*. The reporter gave an insider's viewpoint on the press's tendency to distort the news: "We have an incentive in this business to make

the stories scarier, because if it's really scary, [reporters will think] 'I'm more likely to get on *Nightline*. I'm more likely to get more minutes of airtime. My story is more important. Therefore I am more important.'"

Bozell later interviewed *New York Post* film critic and author **Michael Medved**, who discussed the value system Hollywood is teaching America's children. Medved noted that Hollywood is more anti-religious than ever: "The Catholic Church...has become a main target...We've come a very long way from those days when all priests in movies were kindly, and had a sense of humor, and were played by Bing Crosby.

"Now if someone appears and is a priest, he is shown as a dangerous, demented guy," Medved concluded.

EXPOSE

Family Hour Friends on Capitol Hill

Several key public policy leaders have joined forces with the Media Research Center and our campaign to restore a voluntary family hour to prime time television. On July 18 Sen. Joseph Lieberman (D-Conn.) and Rep. Lamar Smith (R-Tex.) introduced a resolution in the U.S. Senate and the House of Representatives urging the networks to return to their practice of airing only family-oriented programs in the first hour of prime time.

At a Capitol Hill press conference Lieberman and Smith were joined by MRC Chairman Brent Bozell, and resolution co-sponsors Rep. Joseph Kennedy (D-Mass.) and Senators Kent Conrad (D-N.D.), Kay Bailey Hutchison (R-Tex.), and Sam Nunn

(D-Ga.), in making a case for the programming initiative.

"The television networks have been racing each other to the bottom of the cultural barrel...[They] bombard Americans with obscenities, adult situations, and gratuitous sexual innuendos," said Smith, adding, "Most people believe that television can be a positive influence on children. If you agree with that, then you should also believe that it can be a negative influence. We want to encourage the positive."

"We don't always have kind things to say about the television industry," Lieberman echoed, "but this is a case where for a long time the networks...did a public service by creating a safe haven for parents with young children. This is one re-

run that most American families desperately want to see again."

Bozell addressed the wide bi-partisan appeal of the resolution, which more than 70 members of the House and Senate publicly support: "When Rep. Bob Dornan finds common ground with Rep. Jim Moran; when Rep. Tom DeLay can link arms with Rep. Joe Kennedy; when Sen. Jesse Helms can agree with Sen. Paul Wellstone -- when dozens of liberals and conservatives, Republicans and Democrats, all come together for a cause, it's got to be a good one."

The Family Hour resolution is expected to be presented to Congress this fall following the August recess. Look for updates in upcoming issues of *Flash*.

PTC Promotes Family Shows for Emmys

The Parents Television Council is taking an insider approach to promoting family-friendly television.

Every year, just prior to the Emmy Awards, television networks, production companies, and the casts of the shows themselves lobby members of the Academy of Television Arts and Sciences for consideration for this prestigious nomination by advertising in trade publications, and hosting special screenings and other public events.

Borrowing a page from these industry insiders, the PTC recently promoted the nomination of three of the most pro-family dramas on prime time. *Dr. Quinn, Medicine Woman*; *Touched By an Angel*; and *Second Noah* were featured in a PTC-sponsored advertisement in the

June 17th *Daily Variety*; the three dramas were lauded as "family-friendly shows promoting positive values."

That evening the PTC co-sponsored a special screening of a two-part episode of *Dr. Quinn,*

Medicine Woman, a long-time staple of CBS's Saturday lineup. Over 300 attendees, including Hollywood insiders and the cast of *Dr. Quinn*, were present at the event, which was held at the Academy Plaza Theatre in North Hollywood.

PTC Executive Director Harry Medved joined *Dr. Quinn* star Jane Seymour, at the special screening of *Dr. Quinn, Medicine Woman.*

MRC Gets Wired

The Media Research Center has just signed on to Town Hall, an Internet service which specializes in website construction and cyberspace networking for the conservative movement.

The website (at http://www.mediaresearch.org) gives users a wealth of information on the newest projects now under way at the MRC. Visitors to our website can, with one click of the mouse, learn about the "decline of the family hour," read our Special Report on the subject, or receive a briefing on the impact we've had with our Family Hour campaign, our effort to restore family-friendly programming to the first hour of prime time.

For news aficionados, the home page also features updates on our Tell the Truth! campaign -- our extensive analysis of the media's performance during Campaign '96, as well as the MRC's presence at both party conventions, including excerpts from our daily newsletter, *Media Reality Check '96*, and other MRC Special Reports, all documenting distortions during this year's presidential campaign.

Several times a week the site is updated by our team of analysts, making the site the most comprehensive source for media analysis in cyberspace. Each time you visit our site you'll find new press releases, studies, Special Reports, all of our newsletters -- to include the back issues -- plus the latest outrageous quotes from the liberal media.

Visiting the website is also a fast and easy way to order (and receive your membership discount on) MRC merchandise and publications, change your address, or ask a question about your subscription.

Visit the MRC website today and see what's new!

Gay Group Blasts Bozell

The Motion Picture Association of America's President, Jack Valenti, was so impressed with the Parents Television Council's *Family Guide to Prime Time Television* that he distributed it to the industry executives who are currently formulating the television rating system.

But one radical group is taking exception to the MRC's role in shaping the cultural landscape. The Gay and Lesbian Alliance Against Defamation (GLAAD) has protested distributing the *Family Guide* at the closed-door session. In a letter to Valenti, released to the media, GLAAD's managing director William Waybourn labeled the *Family Guide* "extremist propaganda," adding that the "Media Research Center's Brent Bozell is a professional media terrorist who would wash the nation's screens of lesbian and gay images or of any diversity whatsoever."

Waybourn also commented that the *Guide* is "a biased ratings system, based on Bozell's hateful lies and his group's transparent political agenda." Waybourn concluded that the use of the *Family Guide* in the ratings talks "will be devastating, particularly at a time when the entertainment industry is just beginning to deal in an honest and forthright manner with the real diversity which is America – including gay men and lesbians."

See page 8 for details on how to order the PTC's *Family Guide to Prime Time Television*.

Scandals and the Press   By L. Brent Bozell III

On June 13, this page dropped a bombshell -- the firsthand account of a 26-year FBI veteran, Gary Aldrich, charging that top officials within the Clinton administration were raiding the personnel files of former Bush staff members. Two weeks later Regnery Publishing released "Unlimited Access," Aldrich's book blowing the whistle not just on Filegate, but also on the allegedly scandalous personal behavior of both the Clintons and the White House staff. This was too much for the 89% pro-Clinton media. It took only days for Aldrich's credibility to be reduced to ashes, for him to become, in the words of New York Times columnist Maureen Dowd, a "crud peddler."

It's worth taking a look at how the press has trashed Mr. Aldrich, if only to compare his treatment with the respectful attention granted to a far less credible peddler of left-wing conspiracy theories.

Administration Pressure

Initially there was intense media interest in the story, but the Clinton White House had other plans. Fred Barnes details in the July 22 issue of The Weekly Standard that, after "This Week with David Brinkley" booked Mr. Aldrich for its June 30 telecast, a phalanx of White House operatives lobbied ABC in an unprecedented demand that the segment be canceled. Though the Brinkley show kept Mr. Aldrich on the program, the entire interview was adversarial. Ignoring the charges Mr. Aldrich was raising, all three panelists pounced on him for refusing to reveal his sources.

> *Eleanor Clift on Gary Aldrich: "Listen, he talks about things that are totally ridiculous....He has no basis in fact.... This is right-wing fantasy!"*

Within an hour after the show aired, producers from "Dateline NBC" and CNN's "Larry King Live" canceled their planned interviews. A bevy of other network shows also bailed out.

Simultaneously, the Washington press corps opened fire on the talking-head circuit. "The book is ludicrous....it should've never been given credibility," snarled Time's Margaret Carlson on CNN's "Capital Gang." Her colleague, the Wall Street Journal's Al Hunt, said: "That book is so sleazy it makes you want to take a shower when you read it."

And then there's Eleanor Clift. On CNN's "Crossfire," the woman who denies any pro-Clinton bias, roundly denounced Aldrich. "Listen, he talks about things that are totally ridiculous .... He has no basis in fact .... This is right-wing fantasy!"

But the press corps has a different reaction to left-wing fantasies that impugn a Republican president. Back in the summer of 1980, the Reagan for President campaign warned of an "October Surprise," a back-room deal by the Carter administration to win release of American hostages held in Iran in time for the elections. After the elections, Reagan's enemies reversed the charges and accused the GOP of an "October Surprise" to keep hostages in captivity until after the voting.

There was nothing offered to substantiate the conspiracy theory, yet for the next 10 years the story refused to die. On April 15, 1991, it was back in the news.

The New York Times op-ed page published a lengthy manifesto from Gary Sick, a member of Jimmy Carter's National Security Council, formally accusing the Reagan campaign of carrying out the "October Surprise." Mr. Sick, like Gary Aldrich, used anonymous sources, including, he wrote, "a number of [whom] have been arrested or have served prison time for gun running, fraud, counterfeiting or drugs [and some] may be seeking publicity or revenge." The only sources Mr. Sick cited by name were Cyrus and Jamshid Hashemi, two brothers he described only as connected to the Iranian revolutionaries and involved in international arms sales.

The Times headline screamed "The Election Story of the Decade" and the same TV networks that dismissed Mr. Aldrich after one appearance aired 27 stories on the "October Surprise" between April 15 and Dec. 31, 1991. Mr. Sick's op-ed was followed the next night by a PBS "Frontline" expose, "The Election Held Hostage" -- starring none other than Mr. Sick himself. This psuedo-documentary cited another source, Richard Brenneke, who claimed to have been in Paris in 1980 when Reagan campaign manager (and later CIA Director) William Casey made the alleged deal with the Iranians.

Bush spokesman Marlin Fitzwater, like Clinton mouthpiece Michael McCurry, tried to establish a threshold of believability, labelling Mr. Sick "the Kitty Kelley of foreign policy" -- but the press would have none of it.

Columnist Mark Shields: "In his attack on Gary Sick, Fitzwater reveals more temper than judgement .... Gary Sick is an admirable and thoughtful former U.S. Navy captain." (May 11, 1991)

Carter State Department spokesman Hodding Carter, "Nightline": "Gary Sick has a reputation which he deserves for caution, for looking before he leaps, for thinking things through." (April 15, 1991)

Robert Koehler, Los Angeles Times: "Gary Sick, a highly respected former U.S. official..." (April 16, 1991)

Columnist Mike Royko: "He's an expert in foreign relations... and has a reputation for being an extremely intelligent, skeptical, systematic, probing thinker." (April 18, 1991)

Brian Duffy, U.S. News & World Report: "Gary Sick, a respected Middle East analyst..." (April 29, 1991)

Larry Martz, Newsweek: "Sick, a respected Columbia University professor..." (April 29, 1991)

So believable was this story that ABC's "Nightline" ran its own hour-long expose.

Continued on page 8...

MRC's *Impact*

The proof is in the press. The MRC's impact is far-reaching. Here's a list of some of the newspapers, and radio and television programs which have carried our articles, used our research, or covered our events recently:

MRC on Television

CNN's *Showbiz Today,*
  Crossfire
Race for the Presidency
  NET

WBAL NBC affiliate in
  Baltimore MD
CNBC's *The Charles*
  Grodin Show

Capitol Comment with
  Senator Kay Bailey
  Hutchison

MRC on Radio

National Public Radio
The Mary Matalin Show
  (Nationally Syndicated)
Janet Parshall's America
  (Nationally Syndicated)
Blanquita Cullum Show
  (Nationally Syndicated)

The Bob Grant Show
  (Nationally Syndicated)
Family News in Focus
  (Nationally Syndicated)
Jubilee Radio Network
KIFV Glendale CA
KPDQ Portland OR

Talk Radio News Service
WROM Rome GA
USA Radio Network
KVI Seattle WA
KOA Denver CO
WSB Atlanta GA
KNUZ Houston TX

MRC in Print

USA Today
Los Angeles Times
TV Guide (Front Cover)
Boston Globe
Associated Press
The Washington Post
New York Post
The Limbaugh Letter
National Review
Daily Variety
Hollywood Reporter
Investor's Business Daily
  (Front Page)
Insight
Conservative Chronicle
Kansas City Star
Courier-Journal Louis-
  ville KY
Silicon Valley Business
  Journal
Union Tribune San Diego
  CA

Tampa Tribune
In These Times Chicago IL
Electronic Media
Ledger-Enquirer
  Columbus OH
Kentucky Enquirer
Editor & Publisher
Human Events
Pueblo Chieftain
Las Vegas Review-Journal
Arizona Republic
Focus Point Minneapolis
  MN
Bangor Daily News
Entertainment Monitor
  Beverly Hills CA
Cincinnati Post
Orange County Register
Arkansas Democrat
  Gazette
Washington Times
Florida Times-Union

Sunday Tribune Review
  Greenburg PA
Sunday Oklahoman
Blade Toledo OH
MGW Newspaper
  Sacramento CA
Oakland Tribune
Akron Beacon Journal
Dallas Morning News
Asbury Park Press
Seattle Post Intelligencer
Atlanta Constitution
Post-Tribune Gary IN
Baltimore Sun
Rocky Register Star
  Rockford IL
Observer Dispatch
  Utica NY
Cincinnati Enquirer
Houston Chronicle
Sacramento Bee
Talk Daily

How to Identify, Expose & Correct Liberal Media Bias   165

The show's atmospherics included a dark set with no chairs, large pictures of Bush, Reagan, Casey, Khomeini and others, and Koppel dramatically walking us through "the fog of rumor" in search of truth.

There was only one problem. There was no truth to the story. The evidence was there for anyone to see, provided by the handful of journalists who actually bothered to investigate it.

In The New Republic on Nov. 18, 1991, Steven Emerson and Jesse Furman blew the whistle on the Hashemi brothers. Mr. Sick had not disclosed that they were illegal arms dealers, indicted for shipping tens of millions of dollars of military equipment to Iran. They claimed to have met with Casey in Madrid during October 1980, yet after their indictments they never brought this information to the attention of their attorneys or the government -- a surefire way to trigger lenient sentences. And the FBI had wiretaps of Cyrus Hashemi in his Manhattan offices on October 21, 1980 -- the day after he was sup-

posed to have been with Casey in Paris.

What of Mr. Brenneke? He was uncovered in the Village Voice by former ABC producer Frank Snepp, who found credit card receipts placing Brenneke in Portland, Ore., at the same time he claimed to be in Paris. So where did this whole conspiracy nonsense begin, anyway? The answer was provided by Newsweek's John Barry, who traced its origin to an article in the Dec. 2, 1980, Executive Intelligence Review, published by Lyndon LaRouche.

Even so, the Sick allegations triggered a congressional investigation. On Jan. 13, 1993, a bipartisan House task force released its report. The Reagan campaign was exonerated, but the report uncovered another "October Surprise"--an offer to Iran of $150 million in spare parts and $80 million in cash by the Carter White House in return for the hostages. The proposal was made by Warren Christopher, then deputy secretary of state, now secretary of state. When we asked if "Nightline" was going to cover the Christopher reve-

lation, a producer replied, "That's a headline, not a 'Nightline.'" What of the paper that sponsored Gary Sick? The New York Times ran nothing about Mr. Christopher's role. How many stories on the network news? Not a one.

Historic Hoax

Mr. Emerson, a former correspondent for U. S. News & World Report and now an occasional contributor to this page, said it best. The "October Surprise" theory is "probably one of the largest hoaxes and fabrications in modern American journalism.... None of [the sources] had any documentation whatsoever. So I still question why major American journalistic institutions accepted on face value the statements of these fabricated sources."

This same journalistic community is telling us today that it is Gary Aldrich who lacks a threshold of credibility.

Mr. Bozell is chairman of the Media Research Center.

You may or may not like the *MediaWatch*, *MediaNomics* or *Flash* design. After all, what is and is not an attractive design is a very subjective judgment. But look at the three newsletters to get an idea of how the MRC followed basic layout guidelines in creating a new design.

You have four resources to call upon in designing your newsletter:

● A professional design artist, such as the one you used for your corporation and/or foundation logo and newsletter logo.

● Your own knowledge of newsletter designs you like. Look at any newsletters to which you subscribe. Ask your colleagues to bring in any they get. Look them over to see what design ideas you like. Don't be afraid to mix and match. You might like the way the front page is designed on one and how the headlines are done in another. The goal is to identify design ideas you like.

● Desktop publishing. Major desktop publishing software comes with "pre-fab" formats you can load onto your computer. Once loaded into your computer system, they provide a framework you can leave untouched, or change all you want. Look back at the front page of *MediaWatch*. The vertical logo idea came directly from a sample newsletter design that came with Ventura brand layout software.

● A newsletter design seminar. Several companies, including Promotional Perspectives of Ann Arbor Michigan and the Institute for Continuing Education in Communications in Atlanta, regularly hold day-long seminars at hotels around the country. During these seminars, an expert explains the basics of graphic design, the terminology used (picas, points, scaling etc.) how to place pictures and the elements of good newsletter writing. They also hand out reprints of actual newsletters, pointing out the strengths and weaknesses of each. Even if you plan to use a professional designer, these seminars will give you a valuable overview of how to measure whether your design makes for an attractive, readable newsletter. Cost: $200 to $300.

You could rely solely on any one of these resources. Or, combine all four: Choose the pre-fab design you like best and use the desktop publishing software to integrate design ideas you find most attractive in newsletters you saw during a seminar. Get as far as you can, then bring your effort to a professional design artist. The designer can offer suggestions and work out any kinks you ran into.

One Color or Two? Another decision you'll have to make design-wise is color. Paper color and ink color. Your printer can provide you with a color palate showing the standard paper and ink colors available, the ones that won't cost extra to use. Before committing to a paper/ink color combination, see what it looks like. What you imagine red ink on gray paper will look like may not be how it really appears. If you can't find an existing newsletter with the combination you choose, see if your printer will print a few sheets for you.

A two-color newsletter, such as *MediaWatch*'s black and blue ink scheme, will cost about 25 percent more to print than a one color newsletter. So if money is tight, stay with one color. There's nothing wrong with that. *MediaWatch* was one color, blue, for five years.

Self-mailer vs. envelope. One last newsletter format decision. To save money, you could design your newsletter so it doesn't have to be mailed in an envelope. To do this, treat the bottom third of the back page as if it were the front of an envelope -- put your name and return address in the upper left corner and, if you decide to use an indicia for postage, place that in the upper right corner. When folded in thirds, the bottom third will be one of two facing out. You or the mailhouse will put the address label on it.

Self-mailers save money, and if you are handling the mailing yourself, will save you the time of inserting the newsletter into an envelope. On the downside, you'll have less space for articles, it may be damaged in the mail, stapling it closed will take time (and stapling is advised so it doesn't come apart in the mail) and you won't be able send anything with it.

Printer. To find a printer, ask local businessmen for references. Get the names of two or three printers, call them to make sure they print newsletters. Ask each to provide copies of newsletters they have printed. Sit down with a representative of each to go over the exact specifications of your newsletter -- paper weight, paper color and ink color. The printer should be able to provide samples of different paper colors in different weights. In the printing industry, paper thickness is measured by the weight of a roll of it. Newsletters are normally published with 50-pound paper. Whatever you do, feel a sample of the exact paper you plan to use. One paper manufacturer's 50-pound paper may not feel any more solid to you than another company's 40-pound paper.

When you've decided these details, get bids from each printer based upon the same specifications. If you plan to use a mailhouse, have each printer include those costs for the mailhouse they use.

Develop a mailing list

After you are up and running you can start a paid subscription effort. For now, you're just trying to put together a complimentary list. Start with all your financial supporters, names you gathered during talks to civic groups, and the talk show hosts, conservative columnists and editorial writers to whom you've been sending material.

Don't forget about contributors to other conservative groups in your area or state, such as an anti-tax group, gun owners club, coalition of parents concerned about sex education or a conservative religious organization. They may not yet contribute to your foundation, but if your newsletter impresses them, it will be a lot easier to turn them into financial supporters.

Hopefully, one or more activists in a few of these groups is part of your efforts and can provide a membership list. If not, explain to the head of each group that you only want to mail their members a free newsletter. If the group leaders see you as an ally, they may provide the list for free. If they see you as a competitor for money from their donors they'll be more reluctant. Assuming they are not willing to provide you their list on a complimentary basis, you can "rent" it. To learn how, see the section on direct mail marketing beginning on page 194.

You want those in the media to see your findings, so put as many of them on the list as possible. Go through your newspaper clips and write down the names of all reporters who cover politics. Check the masthead on the editorial pages to get the names of the top newspaper editors (Editor, Managing Editor, Assistant Managing Editor, etc.) and the Publisher.

For television and radio, scan through your database or analysis you've done on paper to see which reporters cover politics. Check the credits run at the end of television news to get the names of the producers and the News Director. At small radio stations the entire news staff will be on air, but in large cities the News Director probably won't ever be heard. So if you live in a big city, call to get his name.

Don't ignore lower level people. They do have influence and they do move up. The 24-year-old assistant producer working the weekend night shift may very well rise to weekday 6pm news producer within four or five years. So, put everyone you can on the mailing list. If the new 6pm news producer has been reading your newsletter for four or five years he's a lot more likely to be careful to include conservative views in stories than if he sees it for the first time two months after assuming his new position.

Gather the nine-digit zip code, often called "zip plus 4," as you put together your list. Most businesses include these with their address listings. At first the "zip plus 4" won't be of any use to you, but if and when you start using a mailhouse they will be critical for getting the maximum postage rate discount.

Using computer software. Database and word processing software can be used to store and print your list. Or, you can purchase software specifically designed for storing a list of names and addresses on a PC. Any chain computer store will have them in stock for $50 to $200. The instruction manuals for database and word processing software will explain how to enter names and addresses so that they can be printed on labels. A laser-jet printer will make this easy. Go to any office supply store and purchase mailing labels on 8-and-a-half-by-11 inch sheets. Put the label sheets in the paper tray, and if you've lined things up right in the software, three or four line addresses should print out on the labels. Peel them off and apply to your envelopes.

One hint: labels are supposed to be big enough to contain five lines, but that assumes everything works perfectly. If the printer pulls the label sheet through an eighth of an inch too low, all the labels will be off. Leave yourself a margin of error. Keep addresses to four lines. Example:

> Bob Smith, News Director
> WMRC-TV
> P.O. Box 12
> Anytown, USA 12345

> Not:
> Bob Smith
> News Director
> WMRC-TV
> P.O. Box 12
> Anytown, USA 12345

In fact, you don't need to list the titles at all. The newsletter will get there without it. But it might be useful to you to know Bob Smith's position at the television station. If you think that might be of interest, then put titles in your mailing list.

List maintenance and mailhouse companies. When your mailing list grows beyond a couple of thousand names, you'll want to use a list maintenance company and a mailhouse. You may want to jump to this step if your initial list runs into a few thousand names, or if you don't want to spend hours applying labels to envelopes. For a few cents per name, per month list maintenance companies maintain mailing lists for magazines and newsletters. Initially, however, they charge approximately 20 cents per name they input to their system. As you add names, the same initial input charge will apply.

They can print out what are commonly called "cheshire" mailing labels, which simply means they print 44 names and addresses on 11 by 17 inch sheets of paper. The sheets go to a "mailhouse," a company that folds and inserts a newsletter into a envelope, and then seals it, applies postage and a label. To attach the cheshire labels to the envelope, the mail house applies adhesive to the back of the sheet and then cuts the sheet to create 44 labels.

New technology offers another option. List maintenance companies can provide a computer tape of the list to the mail house. This allows for "ink jet" labeling. Actually, it's not a label at all. Instead, the mail house prints the name and address directly onto the envelope. Check your *Time* or *Newsweek*; they both use ink jetting. The big advantage over cheshire labels: As part of the ink jetting, the mail house can apply a bar code to the envelope -- the little eighth of an inch high vertical lines the Post Office uses to sort mail. For doing this, the Post Office will offer a postage discount.

Your printer should be able to refer you to a list maintenance company. Most printing companies which print magazines or newsletters have their own mail house or work closely with one. So, you shouldn't even have to deal at all with the mail house -- a printer should be able to print your newsletter and deliver it a mail house which will then mail it.

For cheshire labels, mail houses typically charge about two and a half cents per piece for their work, or $25 per 1,000 pieces. Often a minimum charge of about $100 will apply. Expect to pay a bit more for ink jet application. These prices should include most special sorting to take advantage of the postage discounts described in the next section.

Postal requirements

Other than salaries and rent, postage will be the foundation's biggest expense. Your newsletter will cost less than 15 cents to print, but at 29 cents for first class mail, twice that to mail. So learn how to take advantage of postage rate discounts.

First, you need to decide whether you want to use first, second or third class mail. As a practical matter, second class mail is not an initial

✔

EXPOSE

option. It's meant for newsletters, magazines and newspapers, but it comes with cumbersome requirements. At least half the issues being mailed must go to paying subscribers and you must be able to provide proof on demand (such as photocopies of cancelled checks) to the Post Office. Second class also requires the mail house to follow complicated (meaning expensive) mail sorting and minimum pieces per postal zone rules, so don't consider it until you have at least 5,000 paid subscribers.

That leaves first or third class mail. Third class is cheapest, but delivery can take up to six days in a metropolitan area; three weeks to go across the country. Studies have found that as much as ten percent never gets delivered. And if it's mis-addressed or the person has moved, third class mail is not returned or forwarded.

With third class, two ounces cost the same as one ounce. That means you could mail a one ounce newsletter (that's what an eight page newsletter weighs), plus an insert, such as a letter and return envelope for donations, for no additional postage cost.

Postage permits. Mailing first class will ensure quicker delivery, return of mis-addressed mail and forwarding to those who have moved. Of course, it costs more too. The Post Office is quite a bureaucracy: First and third class mailing permits each require separate application forms. The postal permit application fee costs $75 and a usage fee of the same amount must be renewed annually. To apply for a permit, call the Post Office to see which location handles permits for your zip code area.

As a foundation, you can apply for a special non-profit third class mail permit that will give you an additional discount. The IRS should have provided you with a letter stating that you are awaiting approval as a non-profit educational foundation. This should satisfy the Post Office, but they are toughening their standards. You may have to mail at regular third class rates, then when the IRS approval comes through apply for a refund of the difference between the regular and non-profit rates. The Post Office does not offer any special discount on first class mail for non-profit groups, but you can take advantage of pre-sort discounts just like any large mailer.

Discount requirements. Physically, to get the best possible mail rates you'll have to:

- Mail at least 200 pieces of mail.

- Bundle your newsletters by the first three digits of each zip code, with at least ten pieces going to each "zip three." In other words, if you're sending newsletters to zip codes 22312, 22314, 22316, 22003, 22042, 22043 and 22046, bundle all the 223 ones in one pile and the ones starting with 220 in another.

The exact price per piece on third class mail varies with the volume mailed and percentage that can be sorted by zip three, the full five digit zip or to the nine-digit zip code. If most of your mail goes to different zip codes, you'll pay more than if most of it goes to only a few zip codes. Ask the Post Office for a rate form. Roughly, for quantities under 10,000, regular third class mail costs 20 cents and non-profit about 12 cents. If you can get a couple hundred thousand subscribers, the non-profit rate drops to just 8 cents! Of course, a mail house operator is an expert at this kind of thing. Show him your list and he should be able to tell you the rate.

If you are handling the mailing yourself, you have two options for applying third class postage:

● Purchase special 3rd class stamps and apply them like you would any other stamp.

● Print an "indicia" directly on the envelope, or on the newsletter if you're not mailing it in an envelope. An indicia is a little square inside of which appears your foundation's name and third class mailing permit number.

Either way, you can't just go and drop the newsletters in the local mail box. You'll have to bring the mailing to the Post Office which issued the permit. You'll have to "bundle" the mail by zip code. If you have 125 pieces going to one five digit zip code, put them all together. If another eight "zip threes" have ten or more pieces going to each, put elastic bands around each set. A postal clerk will count the number of pieces and calculate the price. Be prepared to pay the full amount on the spot.

A mailhouse can take advantage of further discounts, refining the sorting to the nine digit zip code and even down to the carrier route.

For first class, following similar "zip three" bundling rules above, for instance, you can save four cents per piece -- mail first class for 25 cents instead of 29 cents. But you will have to obtain a first class bulk mail permit.

A discount beyond four cents will require you to use a mailhouse. With cheshire labels, the mailhouse can sort based upon the nine-digit zip code. If your mailhouse can do ink jet labeling, you can take advantage of bar coding -- the mailhouse can read the nine-digit zip and print the bar code directly on the envelope. This can knock another two cents off the rate per piece mailed.

EXPOSE

Of course, postal rates do change, so use all those listed in this book as general guidelines. In fact, late 1993 news stories reported the Clinton Administration was working to have the Post Office increase non-profit third class rates.

If you wish to keep your mailing operation in-house, but find applying stamps one-by-one a bit onerous, consider getting a postage meter. Pitney-Bowes and Hasler are the two major brands of meters. Look in the phone book for the local distributor. They are a major investment: about $3,000. Or, you can rent one.

One mistake to avoid. If you plan to handle the mailing yourself, don't forget to ask your printer to fold the newsletters — either in half to 5 and a half by 8 and a half inches, or down to #10 envelope size (that means folding an 8 and a half by 11 inch newsletter twice so it's 8 and a half by 3 and two thirds inches). You don't want to do that by hand.

Newsletter production

To produce a newsletter physically -- typesetting and layout -- you have two choices:

❶ Pay a design artist to handle each issue for you.

❷ Purchase a desktop publishing software package and do it all with your computer and printer.

The first option is the cheapest short term, but the most costly in the long-run since you'll have to pay every month forever. The second option will require an initial $10,000 investment, unless you know someone willing to let you borrow their desktop system, but will be less costly in the long run.

If you opt for using a design artist, you'll have to choose a compatible type of word processing software. Then you can give the designer computer discs of all your articles so he can load them into his computer system. For about $25 per page, the designer will layout each page and deliver them to you. Make corrections or changes directly on the pages, and send them back to the designer. You can go back and forth until you're satisfied. Making copy fit the page will be your biggest challenge. If an article is several paragraphs too long or short, you'll have to tell the design artist what to delete or add.

Desktop publishing

To avoid all this hassle, use a desktop publishing system. Using your own desktop layout system will give you total control over the final product and avoid the delays of going back and forth with a layout artist. Once you've written your articles, you want the printed issue to appear in mailboxes as fast as possible.

Just a decade ago only huge and expensive typesetting machines could adjust the space between each line so that the bottoms of all columns were even, produce "justified" text and high quality headlines. Look at any newspaper or magazine and you'll see that columns of text are even at the top and bottom of the page or article. It's also justified, meaning the space between letters and words is adjusted on each line so that the left and right sides are even. The text of this book is justified. After typesetting machines churned out the text of articles, newspaper layout artists still had to cut and paste the text onto big boards and add headlines across the top.

Now, a personal computer can do all that for you. That's what "desktop publishing" or "layout software" does -- let's you create and print out entire pages in final, ready to go to the printer form. "Wrap-around" text is another feature of desktop publishing. Wrap-around lets text automatically flow around a frame, such as for a picture, graph or cartoon, on a page. This paragraph wraps-around a frame. You'll see that the desktop publishing has automatically adjusted the text so that it remains even on the right side of this column.

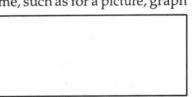

If the computers you are already using are Apple brand, then you should keep everything compatible and buy desktop publishing software made for Apple. If you have IBM or IBM compatible computers and want to be able to use the most popular software, then you have a choice -- Windows 3.1 or the newer Windows 95 system. If you don't know what Windows is, find someone who knows computers. This book can give you some basic guidelines and tips, but computer "How to" books for just one software package often run 300 plus pages.

✔ A Computer Knowledge Tip: One way to teach yourself about computers, besides actually sitting down and fooling around with one, is to start scanning through magazines. Go to any good newsstand and you'll see dozens of big thick computer magazines filled mainly with advertising. That computer equipment and software advertising, however, is very informative. Most ads tell you exactly what the product does, and how it's supposedly better than others. Between the ads, the magazines run new product reviews and "how to" advice columns by computer pros. Read these magazines for a few months and you'll gain an understanding of available products and computer capabilities.

Necessary hardware & software. The computer industry is quite dynamic, with new software and models of computers coming out weekly. So don't assume this book offers the final word on what to purchase. Use our computer tips as a general guide for the types of equipment and software you'll need. With that caveat in mind, for a complete desktop publishing system you'll need:

➤ A fast computer with a relatively large hard drive; ie: a 486 MHz or Pentium computer with at least a 400 megabyte hard drive. Computer speed is measured in megahertz. A Pentium 120 runs at 120 megahertz, wich is twice as fast as a Pentium 60. With Windows 3.1 be sure to get at least 8 megabytes of RAM, which stands for Random Access Memory. With Windows 95 you'll need 16 megabytes of RAM. Approximate computer cost: $2,000 to $3,000.

➤ A mouse. You'll use the keyboard for commands like "enter" and "save," but a mouse to interact directly with images on-screen. A mouse is a small hand operated unit. As you move it around a mouse pad, the cursor moves on screen. Cost: $100.

➤ Most importantly, a desktop publishing software package. The most popular are Corel's Ventura, Adobe's PageMaker and Quark's QuarkXpress. Microsoft makes a program called Publish. Asking a computer expert which is best is like asking an auto mechanic whether he prefers Ford or GM cars. Everybody has a personal opinion. It will be hard to find anyone who can offer a comparable analysis because most people have never even used more than one system.

In making your choice, know that all are well tested, well established systems manufactured by reputable companies. The MRC uses Ventura, but that doesn't mean it's any better or worse than the others. Base your choice on which one you or someone you know has used or knows how to use. That will save you dozens of hours of learning time.

If you and your colleagues have never used any of these software programs, be prepared to put in a lot of learning time. Once you learn the program, it will be easy to operate and well worth your time investment -- you'll be able to produce pages that look just as good as any newspaper or magazine.

Plan to spend several solid days to learn the basics. Then try working on your newsletter. Expect everything to take longer than you hoped. Believe us, you'll get stumped a few times. Have patience. After laying out two or three issues you'll be a layout whiz.

✔ Time and aggravation saving tip: Layout software instruction manuals aren't the best. Confusing instruction manuals are such a common complaint that a whole industry has sprung up of writers and publishers who put out "how to" books on virtually every major software program. Find a bookstore with a good collection of computer "how to" books and buy one for your software brand. It will be well worth the $20 or $30.

✔ You can also find someone to teach you how to use the desktop publishing software (and the supplemental software discussed on the next page). Every metropolitan area has companies and free-lancers who offer classes for all the major software programs. Ask someone you know at a local business who they may have used to teach their employees. Even if it was not for the same software you have, that instructor may teach classes for the one you bought or can refer you to someone who does. If you can't find anyone and you are overwhelmed, ask the manager at a local computer store for the name of a local instructor. Expect to pay upwards of $400 for a two or three day class; at least $25 an hour for someone to come to you office to provide one-on-one instruction.

Cost of layout software: $400.

➤ A high resolution monitor, preferably a color one. The bigger the screen, the easier it will be to see and read what you are laying out. A 17 inch monitor is most popular with desktop publishing users. Screen resolution is measured in the number of vertical and horizontal lines the screen will use to show images. The standard personal computer monochrome (one color) screen shows images at 640 by 480 lines. A standard color monitor shows 800 by 600 lines. You need a screen capable of 1280 by 1024 resolution. That costs some money. Estimated cost, depending on screen size: $1,000 to $1,500.

➤ A laser jet printer. Laser jet printers have long come standard with 300 dpi (300 dots per inch). The higher the dpi, the sharper the printed page. You'll need a top-of-the-line laser jet printer, not one of the cheaper models made for printing letters. The Hewlett Packard Series III was the industry standard in the early 1990s. In late 1993 Hewlett Packard started producing the Series 4, a 600 dpi printer and 600 dpi is now considered standard. Get the Series 4 or an equivalent. Among many, Canon, IBM, Texas Instruments, 3M and Mitsubishi all make laser jet printers. Be sure to tell the store or mail order house that you plan to use it for desktop publishing — that's so they install the necessary extra RAM in it. They normally come with one MB. You'll want two.

A 300 dpi printer will be adequate, but if you plan to do a lot of reverse printing (white letters in a solid background like the word Expose in the sideways chapter labels in this book) or print images with curves, a higher dpi will be desirable. The improved quality is stark and well worth the additional investment.

To get better than 300 dpi printing on a laser printer you may already own, add a special software package that is installed in both the printer and the computer. 800 dpi is the most popular upgrade from 300 dpi, but you can get dpi packages at higher levels as well. "WinPrint" is the brand name of a popular dpi upgrade package from LaserMaster Corporation.

For about $500 more than a dpi improvement package will cost, you can buy a new laser jet printer with 600 dpi built-in. That will provide adequate quality and sharpness. One warning: A color laser jet printer has no relation to a color newsletter. You must print-out your newsletter with black ink on a white page. You tell the printer which parts you want in blue or red or whatever. So spend the extra for a color printer only if you want to see how a certain color combination looks on a page.

A 600 dpi laser jet printer will run about $1,500 to $1,800. Software to generate a higher dpi will cost $800 to $1,000.

➤ A CD-ROM player. Now almost standard with newer computers, most software now comes on CD-ROM instead of on discs. Programs like Ventura and PageMaker include hundreds of fonts on their CD-ROM.

Those are the essential parts. In addition, you should consider the following:

➤ Drawing and Graphics programs. The layout software will let you design and typeset your newsletter, but you may need some additional software. If you plan to include graphs and charts in the newsletter, you'll need a graphics program. Harvard Graphics, and Lotus FreeLance are some widely available software packages. If you plan to draw images or original art, you'll need a drawing program, such as CorelDraw. Most mouses come with a basic software program. That should be adequate for simple things, like drawing a circle or signing a name that you want to appear. If you want to create complicated images, (such as a logo that combines a font with lines or graphics, or a unique combination of lettering over a background image), you'll need a drawing program.

Before purchasing any peripheral software, make sure it's compatible with the layout software you selected. If the box containing the software does not explicitly say it's compatible, assume it's not. To make absolutely sure, call the layout software company's 800 number. Graphics and Drawing programs cost about $500 to $800.

➤ A scanner allows you to "scan" images into your computer programs, such as the drawing or graphics packages described in the previous paragraph. These images can be later "imported" into your layout software so they will appear in your newsletter. Physically, a scanner is a two foot by three foot unit that's only a few inches thick. It works somewhat like a photocopier. You lay an image, say an editorial cartoon, onto a sheet of glass and close the top. The scanner will then transfer the image to your computer screen. Using the scanner software, you'll be able to change the cartoon's size or proportion. You can cut a portion of it off, or draw a box frame around it. When done, the cartoon can be moved onto a page of your newsletter.

If an occasional cartoon is the only graphical image you expect to put in the newsletter, then skip the scanner. Using the enlarge and reduce options on a photocopier will let you make the cartoon the right size to fit. Get a scanner only if you plan to carry lots of previously produced artwork, such as caricatures, cartoons, and drawings. Once scanned into your computer, you can move them from page to page and adjust their size proportionally. With a photocopier, a rectangular cartoon will always be rectangular no matter what size you make it. Scanner software lets you change a rectangular cartoon to a more square one. Cost of scanner and accompanying software: $1,000 to $1,500.

Where to buy computer equipment. To purchase all these items you have two options: A retail outlet or direct sale. The very competitive price cutting in the computer industry has driven out of business many of the retail chains that once sold most computers in America. Now, there are a few discount software outlets, such as Egghead, and larger retail outlets that sell both hardware and software, such as CompUSA, Computer City and Best Buy. But given the industry's volatility, these may be replaced by new stores by the time you read this. Whatever you do, don't go to a fancy computer store in a mall. They are very expensive and cater to naive parents out to buy a first computer for their child.

Direct sales, companies that sell directly to you via phone order, will offer lower prices and more options. Major companies like Gateway 2000 and Dell sell direct only. If you don't subscribe to a computer magazine, go to a newsstand and pick some up. They are packed with computer ads, complete with 800 numbers for ordering. The magazines include "reader service" numbers for each advertiser. Return the postcard, and the manufacturer's you list will send packets of information on the particular product.

All the major computer-makers have web sites. Check them for soecifications and prices before you go to a store or buy direct.

Once you obtain the computer, printer and software, it needs to be put together. Cables will need connecting and software will need loading into the computer. You don't want to attempt this on your own unless you know what you're doing. In fact, you should consult with someone who knows computers before buying a desktop system. The more knowledge you can bring to your decisions, the better ones you'll make.

Look in the business services section of the newspaper for a computer consultant. But be prepared to pay for their advice. You could also ask a local computer store owner for the names of local people who help set up and install computers. Alternatively, every office workplace has one or more people who, either as a full time job or as a task they handle in addition to their regular job, solve computer problems for their colleagues. Ask everyone you know to ask around at the office. If these computer people agree with your cause, they might be willing to help you for free. You could also ask them for the name of a good computer consultant contracted by their company.

A cheaper alternative? Desktop publishing is the best way to go because it's specifically made for typesetting and layout, and it's most likely to be compatible with graphics software programs. But there is a cheaper way to go that can still give you a professional looking newsletter. Currently available new versions of word processing software, such as WordPerfect, Microsoft Word and Lotus Word Pro, can produce justified text in various point sizes. If you already have one of these programs for general office use, then you can save money by not having to buy another software package. There are a lot of limitations compared to desktop publishing software, but many companies use it for simple looking products, such as an employee newsletter.

If you don't have much money and will be satisfied with a simple newsletter layout, a design that involves nothing more complicated than columns of text under headlines, then this is a viable option. If, however, you want a design that includes rules or reverse type or "bridges" that appear in the middle of text copy, that varies the space between lines of text so columns are even across the bottom of the page, then desktop publishing is probably a must.

We say probably because just as this book was going to press, one major word processing brand announced that its new updated version would include some desktop publishing features, such as the ability to have "wrap-around" text. Other word processing systems will probably soon follow, trying to make their product better suited to layout needs.

If you go the word processing route, you'll still need a laser-jet printer capable of printing the fonts included with the word processing software, a mouse, and while you won't need quite such a high resolution monitor, you'll need something better than the standard 600 by 800 resolution unit. Cost of word processing software: $600.

Creating your first issue

Once you've got your desktop publishing or simpler word processing system set up, it's time to actually produce a newsletter. By this point you should have chosen a logo and determined a design. What's left? Actual content! If you have all your employees or volunteers under one roof, they should all be using the same word processing software and operating system; ie: they are all using IBM compatible computers running Windows 95, with MS Word for word processing. If your newsletter article writers are using their own computers at home, then you'll want to have everyone compatible.

If you decide to use an IBM compatible computer, then your Apple owner should follow suit, and vice-versa. Windows can accept documents written on an Apple and vice-versa, but it takes some annoying additional steps. It's also possible to convert a document from one word processing system to another, say from MS Word to WordPerfect, but it takes several time consuming steps. You don't want to have to do that everytime. The best advice: Decide on a word processing brand, and have everyone use it.

Text in layout software is not actually entered into the software system. The layout software "reads" the text from the word processing software you use. In other words, you tell Pagemaker to put the

WordPerfect document named "Septpg1" in the space created for the page one article of your September issue. If you change the article in WordPerfect, it automatically changes in Pagemaker, and vice-versa.

Gather all your articles together on the computer and follow the layout software instructions to place the appropriate article on the proper page. In layout software parlance, you'll first create a "chapter" for each issue of your newsletter. The September issue will be a chapter, the October another and the November a third chapter, and so on. Each chapter includes the text files for your articles, the layout design commands, and any graphics in that issue, such as a table, logo or cartoon.

✔ One tip we can offer that many instruction manuals fail to mention: make all the word processing text single spaced with no indents. You'll set up the layout software to automatically indent every paragraph. If it's already indented, the layout software will indent it more so you'll have to go through and fix every paragraph.

Newsletter paste-up

Earlier we said that layout software lets you create pages ready to go to the printer. While that's largely true, you may not be quite ready to go. You can't just take pages out of the computer printer and give them to your commercial printer. You have two ways to provide the newsletter pages to the printer: 1) Put your newsletter on a computer disc and give it to your printer, or 2) Print out the pages and paste them up on boards that you will give to your printer.

Not all printing companies can handle the first option, but if yours can, this will be the easiest for you. The printer must have the same software as you. If you are using QuarkXpress, so must the printer. Basically, you save the newsletter "chapter" files onto a disk. Your commercial printer then "downloads," meaning transfers, the chapter into its computer system. The printer will create a negative film which is used to actually print copies of the newsletter.

If you have any graphic images that your computer software can't handle, or if you don't have a scanner for cartoons or other images, you'll have to go with the second option: Take pages from the desktop publishing system and paste them up yourself. This will allow you to lay in by hand cartoons, logos or other graphic images.

To do paste-up, go to a graphic art supply store and purchase three items:

● Layout boards. These are pieces of white cardboard covered by grid lines printed in a light shade of blue that will not be picked up by the printer. Get the 13 by 18 inch size that are made to accommodate two newsletter pages. Cost: About $1.00 per sheet.

● An "X-Acto" brand or similar knife.

● A hand held waxer, for about $35 to $45. You use a waxer to apply a thin sheet of wax to the back side the newsletter pages. The wax will make the pages stick to the boards, but let's you place and peel off a page several times as you adjust its position.

Creating "camera-ready" boards is your goal. "Camera-ready" is a commonly used printing term which means a board is ready to be "shot" with a camera by the commercial printer. The printer will use the negative created by this shot to determine where the ink goes on the paper.

One at a time, take each page from your printer, turn it up side down and set it on top of a larger piece of paper, or couple of similarly sized ones so that the desk or table top is covered. Then use the waxer to apply wax to the backside of each page. The paper underneath will protect the table or desk from getting covered with wax. Take the waxed page and lay it on the board. To minimize the chance of air bubbles, first press down the top left corner and then line up the top right corner so the page lies straight. While holding the page at the bottom so the rest of it is off the board, rub your hand back and forth across the page, slowly descending toward page bottom.

To see if the page is straight, hold the board up to a light. You should be able to see the light blue lines and compare them to your text. If the page isn't straight, peel it off and repeat the process. The pages should be placed to match how they are printed. With an eight page newsletter, put page 8 on the left side, page 1 on the right. On the next board, put page 2 on the left side, page 3 on the right, etc.

Once you have all pages waxed down, use the waxer to lay in any graphic images you have, such as a cartoon or logo.

Wax adhesion isn't too strong. As the boards get bent and shuffled the pages may start to peel back, so use a clear tape to secure the pages. A piece in the corners of each page will be plenty. Put at least one piece of tape on the side or corner of each cartoon, logo or graphic.

Screens and Colors. You can create shaded areas within the layout software, but a commercial printer can provide better quality. A shaded area is technically named a "screen." This paragraph is within a screened frame. The commercial printer uses a 100 percent ink concentration for text, ten percent for screens. So this frame is shaded with a "10 percent gray screen." Of course, a screen can be done in any color. (Look back at the reproductions of MRC newsletters. Each use screens on every page to break up the page or highlight a certain department.) All the MRC newsletters use black ink for text with another color for screens and some other elements, such as a the department head bars. In *MediaWatch* it's always blue, but with *Flash* the color changes with each issue.

To mark screened areas, put an eight and a half by 11 inch piece of paper on top of the newsletter page on the boards. Attach it to the board with a piece of tape just above the newsletter page. You'll be able to see the newsletter page through the cover sheet. Use a pen to mark the frames or boxes you want shaded. Put hash marks inside the frames.

If your newsletter will have more than one color, use the same method to mark color(s). Draw an arrow to each bar, line or frame you want in a color.

Photos. Unless you plan to have full color pictures in your newsletter, which is a very expensive proposition, obtain black and white photos. A color photo printed in black and white will often come out blurry. So get some black and white film and a 35mm camera. Local media outlets, especially TV stations, have publicity photos for the top reporters and anchors that they will provide for free. If you want to use a specific newspaper photo of a news event, call the local paper to ask about buying it for use. Depending upon their view of your operation, they may or may not cooperate. Expect to pay anywhere from $25 to $200 per photo. If it was an AP photo, or if you want to see a variety of photos of a particular event, contact Wide World Photo at 50 Rockefeller Plaza in New York City. They will send you several photos to look over. You use the one you want, and return all of them. Wide World charges $50 to $100 per photo used.

To put the photos in the newsletter, create a frame. If you want a color border around the photo, make sure the frame border is thick enough to show and is marked on the cover sheet. Attach the photos to the board. On the back or on an attached piece of paper, write the percentage reduction necessary to fit the appropriate frame. On the front side, use a photo pen to mark where you want the photo cropped.

Any quality photography store will have special pens made for writing on photos.

To determine the necessary percentage reduction or enlargement, also pick up a "proportional scale wheel" at the same photo store. (Your printer may also be able to supply you with both items.) The wheel lets you note the photo's current size and the size of the frame where you want it to fit, and then tells you the percent difference. If you have an eight inch wide photo and you want it to fit in a 4 and a quarter inch wide frame, the proportional scale wheel will tell you that will require a reduction to 53 percent of the original size.

Cropping means that you mark which portion of the photo you want to show. If a photo has a tree to the left of two people, you may want to show the people but not the tree. Mark that portion of the photo you want cropped out and it won't appear.

If you are sending the newsletter to the printer via disk, provide detailed instructions on where each photo should be placed.

Bluelines. By whichever manner you deliver the newsletter to the printer, ask for "bluelines" before they print the issue. A "blueline" shows you exactly what will be printed. This is especially important if you use photos or disk delivery. You want to make sure the printer did everything correctly. Whether the bluelines are faxed to you, delivered by courier, or you stop by the printing plant yourself, give your approval, or note any necessary changes, as quickly as possible. The printer can't print the newsletter until you give your OK.

Copyright & ISSN

In the box where you list your staff names and foundation address, also add a copyright notice. You don't want others to pass off your material as theirs or to use your material without attribution. Copyright law protects the owner of a written work. He decides who can reprint an article and what fee, if any, he wishes to be paid. In the case of a book, the author controls the copyright. In the case of a foundation or corporation-published newsletter, the foundation or corporation owns the copyright.

This is the standard copyright notice: "Copyright © 1994 by the [name of foundation]. Reproduction without written permission prohibited. However, excerpts may be quoted provided full credit is given to [name of newsletter]." This formulation will allow others to quote your newsletter -- something you want to happen, it's free publicity --

but they must write or call to ask your permission to reprint an entire article. As a practical matter, you certainly don't mind if a church or Chamber of Commerce newsletter editor wishes to run one of your articles, but it should only be done after you've given permission.

If you run this notice, you are obligated to file a formal application for copyright with the Library of Congress. Call (202) 707-9100 to request several copies of "Short Form SE." It isn't complicated to fill out.

One more catch: It costs money to copyright. Return the Short Form SE along with two copies of the newsletter and a check made out to the "Registrar of Copyrights" for $20. Every time a new issue arrives from the printer you must fill out another Short Form SE and return it with two copies and a $20.00 check. Don't ever forget. Your copyright protection is dependent upon these forms being properly filed. You have up to 90 days from publication date to file. About two or three months after each filing you should receive a copy of the Short Form SE with the official Library of Congress "Certification of Registration" seal printed in one corner. Put these in a safe place.

The Library of Congress also issues ISSN numbers, the International Standard Serials Number. Libraries and computer database systems identify all serial publications (newsletters and magazines) based on this number. It doesn't cost anything, and will make it a lot easier for researchers to find your newsletters, and more likely that library periodicals departments will carry it. To obtain an application form, write: Library of Congress, National Serials Data Program, Washington D.C. 20540. Once you have been issued an ISSN, it should appear in every issue of the newsletter. List it in your "publication box," the area where the copyright notice, foundation address and subscription price appear.

Running Copyrighted Material. Just as your newsletter is copyrighted, so is material you may want to run in your newsletter, such as editorial cartoons and newspaper columns. You must get permission from the copyright owner and pay any required fees. In general, newspapers and syndicates assess a fee based on the size of the publication.

To get permission, call or write the copyright owner. For a column you saw in the newspaper, contact that paper. If it's a nationally syndicated columnist, ask for the name and number or address of the syndicate. The same goes for editorial cartoons. In general, the smaller you are the less you'll pay. A large metropolitan newspaper might pay

$500 for what a free church newsletter can reprint for no fee. So, tell the copyright owner how many paid subscribers you have. You should never have to pay more than $100.00 and many local newspapers won't want any fee for reprinting one of their columns or news stories.

Once you get permission, you must note the copyright ownership at the end of the article. For a column by a local columnist appearing in the Smithtown *Daily Herald*: "Copyright © 1993 by Smithtown *Daily Herald*. Reprinted with permission." For a syndicated column by, say, Mona Charen: "Copyright © 1993 by Creators Syndicate." Editorial cartoonists always include a copyright statement right in the cartoon. Look closely and you'll see it near their signature. But you still must get permission and pay any required fee.

Cartoon tips:

✔ Many syndicates require a standard flat $100 fee for reprint rights. If you find that you want to run cartoons from the same cartoonist every month, it might be cheaper to sign a contract with the syndicate. Often, for $7.00 or $8.00 per week a syndicate will mail you every cartoon of the particular cartoonist and you won't have to pay anything additional when you run one. Another advantage: You'll have original quality cartoons, instead of ones just cut out of the newspaper.

✔ A local cartoonist who is not syndicated will most likely love the extra exposure an appearance in your newsletter will generate. Talk to the cartoonist about a standing agreement whereby you don't have to call each time to ask permission, but will send a check for $10 to $20 each time for reprint rights.

✔ If newspapers in your area don't run a lot of conservative cartoons, consider subscribing to the *Conservative Chronicle*. (See page 254 of Appendix 1 for price and address.) This tabloid newspaper runs dozens of syndicated columns and cartoons every week.

Newsletter marketing

In addition to the brochure and web site described in the foundation marketing and promotion section, newsletters are traditionally sold by four means: Through display ads in magazines, through appearances and paid ads on talk shows, through flyers sent with mailings sent by other groups (conservative ones in this case) and through direct mail.

Display ads

Look in any newspaper or magazine. The ads you see selling everything from women's dresses to TV sets are called "display" (or "space") ads since they display the product, as contrasted with "classified" ads. When selling a newsletter, a display ad allows you to achieve two goals: Sell subscriptions while also publicizing your foundation.

A reduced-size reprint of a Media Research Center display ad for a magazine page appears on the next page. The first MRC ad sold only *MediaWatch*, but as the MRC grew we added other publications to our ads. You should do the same as you grow. The more items you have to sell, the better the chance a reader will find at least one appealing.

Your display ad must look attractive, so even if you have a desktop publishing system, go to a professional designer. Saving money on design won't do you any good if the ad you put together yourself doesn't generate any orders. Remember, people didn't buy the newspaper or magazine to read your ad, so you need to draw them into it. An ad crammed with writing won't appeal to anybody. And if no one reads it, you won't get any orders.

Before producing an ad, call the publications where you think you might want to place an ad and ask about size requirements. Most magazines are 8 and a half by 11 inches, but many don't want a full page ad to be any bigger than 7 and a half by 10 inches. The maximum measurements of other size ads (half page, third page etc.) will vary by magazine. The same goes for newspapers.

Newspapers and magazines will want to get a "camera-ready" ad from you. The first step in printing is to have a picture taken of a page. This negative, like any photo negative, shows black where no ink goes and clear space where the ink will go. So in a page of text, the whole negative will be black except for all the type, which will be clear. So a camera-ready ad is simply one the publication can send to their printer as is, it doesn't need any additional typesetting or graphics work. Using your layout software system, you can create camera-ready art as can any professional designer.

MediaWatch, a monthly newsletter that reviews news coverage of political and current events by the television networks, newspapers and news weeklies. "Newsbites" provide ongoing examples of bias and the "Janet Cooke Award" examines the month's most distorted story. Plus: In-depth studies and analysis.

TV, etc., a monthly newsletter that investigates the liberal issue agenda permeating prime time television, current cinematic fare and record releases and catalogues the off-screen political activities of the Hollywood Left.

Notable Quotables, a bi-weekly compilation of the most outrageous and humorous examples of bias from the media. At year-end the Linda Ellerbee Awards present the best quotes of the year.

MediaNomics, a monthly newsletter that examines national news coverage of business and economic issues and Hollywood's economic message.

And That's the Way it Isn't: A Reference Guide to Media Bias provides 350 pages of summaries, excerpts and reprints of 45 studies that demonstrate the media's liberal bias. A one-stop resource containing all the facts and figures, examples and quotes proving the media's bias.

Why aren't liberals in the media smiling anymore?

Because their days of unchecked bias are over. The Media Research Center is reading and listening to what they write and say.

When columnists, elected officials and other opinion leaders want examples of liberal bias, they turn to our publications.

So should you.

The Media Research Center's newsletters and books provide all the proof you'll ever need to demonstrate the news media's liberal bias. And the bias in Hollywood.

You can use the newsletters and books to win arguments with your friends and colleagues. Learn *what* shows to avoid, *which* reporters slant the news, *how* they do it and *why* they do it.

EXPOSE

Some basic tips to follow:

✔ Put a short, but catchy, headline across the top. Keep wording in the ad as short as possible so that in a matter of seconds people can learn what you are selling. Include reduced sized pictures of your newsletters and any other publications.

✔ Put your address within the borders of the response coupon. If someone cuts it out and puts it aside, you don't want them to have to go back later to look for the address somewhere else in your ad. If you wish to accept credit card orders, talk to you bank about setting up a Visa and/or MasterCard account. You'll have to show that you are a legitimate business and meet some financial requirements. The bank will deduct a certain percentage from each sale before depositing the money in your account.

Where to Place. When placing the ad, your goal should be to break even at a minimum. If an ad costs $500 to place in a publication, you want to generate at least $500 in orders, plus enough to cover order fulfillment -- the cost of printing and mailing 12 issues. You'll learn by trial and error in which publications your ad does and does not work.

Some general tips:

✔ The longer an ad is "active," the better. An ad in a daily newspaper will only be seen once by readers. The same ad in a monthly magazine will probably be seen several times as readers pick up the magazine throughout the month. It is very difficult, some would even argue impossible, to sell subscriptions through newspaper ads.

✔ Publishers of smaller magazines and newspapers who have a hard time selling ad space might consider selling space on a "per inquiry" basis. In this arrangement, you pay the publication a pre-determined amount for each order you receive. If your newsletter costs $32 per year, you could split the revenue 50-50 -- pay $16 for each order you receive. But don't count "Bill Me" orders until they pay because many who use this option won't pay up. In the MRC's experience, only about one-fourth will end up paying.

✔ Look for publications read by conservatives. If your region of the country does not have a conservative-leaning publication, you'll have to consider more general interest publications. Most cities or states have a city or regional magazine, such as *Los Angeles, Atlanta, Chicago Monthly*, and *Boston*. Even if only a small percentage of their readers are conservative, the ad will be "active" for a month so conservative readers will have plenty of opportunity to respond.

While ads in daily newspapers usually don't do as well as a magazine ad, at smaller newspapers the ad rates may not be very expensive and with a weekly the ad will be active for seven days. Try placing a quarter page ad; in a broadsheet newspaper that will be the same as a full magazine page (7 by 10 inches), on or near the op-ed page. If the ad costs $200 and your newsletter costs $32, you'll need about eight paid responses to cover the placement and fulfillment costs.

✔ Place an ad code in the corner of the coupon so you can track ad responses from each publication. Even if you think you can recognize the publication by looking at the back of the coupon, many people will send you a photocopy of the ad. Without a code you'll have no idea from where it came. An ad code can be any combination of letters and numbers you choose, but there's no need for any more than four or five digits. Most commonly, advertisers use an abbreviation of the publication's name followed by a date. For many years, the MRC code for ads in *The American Spectator* was "AS" followed by a letter. "ASA" for the first ad placed, "ASB" for an ad placed a couple of months later followed by "ASC" etc. Later, we made it even simpler: "AS103" for an ad in the October 1993 issue. The code for our ad in the September 6, 1993 *National Review*: NR993.

Talk show appearances

Whenever you are interviewed on a talk show, take advantage of the free opportunity to sell your newsletter. Talk show hosts will bring you on to discuss the media, but almost all realize that you want to sell your newsletter. As long as you aren't obnoxious about it, they won't mind if you tell listeners how to subscribe. At some point during your appearance say something like "Bob, can I tell people how to get ahold of our newsletter?" Chances are, talk show host "Bob" will allow it. But don't wait too long. Some stations run news on the hour, but end the talk show at :57 past to run a couple of minutes of ads.

Some pointers: Tell the host or producer before you go on that you wish to mention how people can subscribe. Often, that will prompt the host to ask at some point, "So, Jane, how can our listeners get a copy of your newsletter?" But don't count on this question. Many a well intentioned host will get so wrapped up in the conversation or in trying to squeeze on another call that he'll forget.

If you have a Web site, tell the address. If you have a phone line set up, give it out, not a mailing address. Do you have a pen and piece of paper in your hands while listening to the radio? Probably not. Most people listen to the radio while doing everything from cooking dinner to driving their car. People can remember a phone number a lot easier than an address. Try to get a phone number for your foundation that's easy to memorize, such as 235-6000 or 235-2424. Or, work with the phone company to get one based on the letters assigned to each digit; ie the MRC has 2427 for the last four digits -- 2427 matches BIAS. You could see if the digits matching words like NEWS or MEDIA (with M being the 6 in an exchange like 346) are available. The phone company will charge you a bit extra for a special number, but it will be worth it.

At night and on weekends, use an answering machine. In your message, tell the cost of your newsletter and provide your address so people can send you a check. State your address at least twice so people can get it down. Or, you could offer to send a complimentary copy of your newsletter to anyone who leaves their name and address on the tape. You'll have to decide ahead of time which way to go. Don't say call 235-6000 for a free copy and then have callers get a message saying "for thirty-two dollars you can receive *Nebraskans for a Balanced Media Report*."

The MRC took a bit of a different approach: we set up an easy to memorize phone number with an answering machine separate from our regular phone number. The MRC did it to provide a toll-free 800 number for calls from around the country. If you are receiving calls just from a metropolitan area, an 800 number probably won't be needed to encourage calls.

If you offer to send a complimentary copy, send it along with an order form and return envelope (either a stamped envelope with your address or a Business Reply Envelope; see page 196 for more on BREs.) If the person does not order, follow up a month later with a letter, order form and return envelope. The letter can be a form letter that explains how the recipient received a complimentary copy a month ago, gives an overview of the newsletter's features and includes a couple of endorsement quotes.

If someone initially pays for a subscription, or returns the order form after getting a complimentary copy, send him a thank you letter. This letter can go with the newsletter you send. Pass along to your finance director the names of all those who responded to your radio appearance even if they don't subscribe. By responding, they showed an interest in media bias, so they are all potential subscribers or donors for the future.

Radio advertising

If you listen to Rush Limbaugh's radio show you've heard ads for *The American Spectator* and *Conservative Chronicle*. Both have used very successfully radio advertising to attract subscribers. Both have also lost money advertising because it's a very risky proposition, especially when you are selling a product and not just promoting your organization. As with display ads, your goal is to at least break even. After all production, placement and fulfillment costs are factored the total should be matched or exceeded by gross revenue generated by the ad.

At the local level, radio advertising offers the ability to reach a targeted audience for relatively low ad time and production cost. A one-minute radio ad will cost anywhere from $10 to $200 depending upon the time of day and market size. On the production side, a radio ad requires no more than a professional announcer to narrate a script. Most radio stations have an in-house announcer and, as an inducement to advertisers, offer his services for little or no cost.

Buy advertising time during shows most listened to by conservatives, such as a political talk show. If a particular host is popular with conservatives, ask him to narrate your ad. He'll probably want a "talent fee" for this service, but if he adds credibility the extra money will be well worth it.

Advertising works through repetition. To test your ad, at a minimum you'll have to run it once per hour during a three or four-hour show for two weeks. With 30 or 40 ads at, say $25 per, you'll need to invest upwards of $1,000 just for ad time. In a large city, ads may cost $100 per even at night. So this could be a very expensive mistake if your ad doesn't work. But if it does work, buy more ad time on that show and test the ad during other shows.

The ad should include an easy-to-remember phone number that the narrator mentions two or three times. This can be the same number you obtained for your talk show appearances, but since you don't want to lose any buyers, make sure you have enough lines to handle incoming calls. One answering machine on one phone line won't be adequate if the ad works. Get at least three lines working off the same number. If the ad really does well and you start running it on several stations throughout the day, contract with a "service bureau," a company that answers 800 calls for a fee. A radio station sales department should be able to refer you to one.

Broadcast television ads are just too expensive to consider until you are well established and have a lot of money you can afford to lose. A professional looking TV ad will cost at least $5,000 to produce and ad time usually costs ten times more than radio.

A cable television ad will cost just as much to produce, but local ads will cost no more than radio for time, maybe even less. Local cable operators can place three minutes of ads per hour on cable channels, including CNN and the Family Channel, but not all do. If a cable operator in your area does sell this ad time, find out what it costs per minute. You may be able to run six ads per day on CNN for just $5.00 per appearance.

Turn on your television late at night or just listen to local ads on the radio and sometimes you'll see or hear commercials that are simply atrocious. They were produced by people who didn't understand the business of advertising -- and it showed. Don't make the same mistake. If you decide to go the paid advertising route, learn the business. Better yet, if you can afford to advertise, you can afford professional help as your consultant. It will be well worth it.

"Ride-along mailings"

Talk to the leaders of all conservative groups in your state or region. If they have a newsletter or occasionally mail an update package to their members, ask if they will let you place an ad for your newsletters in their mailing. As an inducement to let you "ride along" with their mailing, offer to pay part of the postage cost. If your insert will add to the postage cost, pay the additional increment, plus a little extra. It could be well worth it. You will be getting a subscription appeal into the hands of politically active conservatives, your most likely customers.

The subscription appeal can be nothing more than a photocopy of your display ad. Or, you can write and design a special letter and return form targeted to the concerns of the particular group.

Later, when you have several hundred or thousand subscribers, you can offer an exchange. The tax group puts your appeal in their mailing, you put their appeal in the envelope along with your newsletter. Neither group pays for anything more than printing the subscription appeal.

One caution: You don't want to be seen as overtly political by journalists. So include "ride-along" mailings only with newsletters going to paid subscribers, not your complimentary list of media names. Besides, other conservative groups want to reach your paying subscribers, not members of the media.

Direct mail

Direct mail is just a fancy name for what most people call "junk mail." But don't knock it. That junk mail can raise funds for your operation. Virtually every newsletter and magazine acquires most of its subscribers through a direct mail appeal. You can also do general fundraising for your foundation through direct mail.

Creating a successful direct mail package is a skill. Don't try doing it yourself. Many a conservative group has lost fortunes because a direct mail letter bombed. Direct mail is a risky undertaking, so follow the advise of someone with experience in the field.

Here's a thumbnail sketch of how the direct mail process works:

A "list broker" can make recommendations about which lists you should consider "renting." An experienced broker will be able to tell you how other conservative groups fared using the lists you are considering. A broker can also "rent" names from national conservative magazines for zip codes in your area or state. "Renting" means that they pay a certain amount per name (usually $90 to $120 per thousand names) for the right to mail something to that list.

Political groups and publications regularly rent out their donor or subscriber lists, almost always on the condition that they approve of the letter's content. (If you subscribe or contribute to a few conservative groups, that's why you get so many direct mail letters.) With a local or state group that hasn't rented its list, a price can be negotiated that's acceptable to both parties.

List brokers are often affiliated with a direct mail company, so if you find one you've often found the other. Their job is to obtain lists, collect the rental fee and provide the direct mail firm with labels or a computer tape of the list in the desired format.

A direct mail company produces a "package" (at a minimum a letter, order form, return envelope). Direct mail company price policies vary, but usually they charge a per piece fee of five to seven cents for each package mailed. Some companies will agree to a one-time flat fee ranging from $1,000 to $2,500. You will, of course, have to pay for postage and printing.

To test the list, the package is sent to a random segment of it, typically 5,000 names from a list with a total universe of 20,000 or more names. If the letter is successful, then you can "roll out" to another segment or to the rest of the list. In the direct mail industry, 25,000 names is typical for the second mailing. If, however, you've successfully mailed to 5,000 names from the "Americans for Lower Taxes" list and the total universe of available names is 40,000, go ahead and mail to the remaining 35,000 names. "Successful" means that the money received from orders covers the entire cost of the mailing, including direct mail company fees, list rental, postage and printing. This will be achieved with anything from a two to ten percent response rate.

BRM's and BRE's. As a foundation, you qualify for non-profit, third class postage rates (see postage on page 171), so your letters can be mailed for 12 cents or less per piece. To receive responses, you should set up a "BRM" account with the Post Office. BRM stands for Business Reply Mail. The Post Office will give you the artwork for a Business Reply Envelope (BRE), the kind of envelope that says "No postage necessary if mailed in the United States" and "Postage will be paid by addressee."

A BRE included with your direct mail package will make it easier, and thus more likely, that a recipient will respond. With a BRE, you pay the regular first class rate, plus a postal processing fee for each response received. To be clear, the beauty of a BRE is that you pay only for those returned to you. To receive the BRE's, the Post Office will want you to establish a Post Office box. You will be required to pay a nominal box fee and you must deposit funds into your BRE account. Incoming mail returns will be charged against your account.

If you have a local list maintenance company for your newsletter list, they can probably handle a lot of this. You must set up the BRM/BRE account, but they can pick up you mail, deposit checks into a special bank account, and give you a weekly report on the amount received in contributions or the number or orders. They can also automatically add subscribers to your mailing list. (Of course, you will need to sit down with them to set up a subscription fulfillment system so subscribers get renewal notices.)

Or, when you've found a good direct mail company which creates successful packages, you can rely on them to handle the BRE collection process. (But you'll still need a list maintenance company to fulfill subscription orders.) To find good direct mail companies, talk to the finance chairmen for conservative politicians. Ask for the name of who handled the campaign's direct mail, and more importantly, how well it worked. To determine which company can sell your newsletter, challenge three or four companies to agree to a comparison test. Have them rent some mailing lists and then mail their letter to a segment of each. Make sure all BRE's go to your BRE P.O. Box so you can compare the results to see who does best.

Even if one company outshines the others during the testing phase, continue testing with the other firms. It's always good to have competition to help keep costs down and results up.

Foundation fundraising through direct mail. As a group battling the liberal media, your cause will appeal to many conservatives. Some people like to subscribe to publications, others will never subscribe but are happy to donate money to a cause in which they believe. Your direct mail subscription letters will do best by using subscriber lists. Use conservative political campaign and group donor lists for your fundraising packages. Such a letter is not aimed to obtain subscribers, but donations to your foundation. The letter should describe the battle you are fighting to identify, expose and correct the media bias and ask for help to accomplish your mission. In short, send subscription appeals to subscribers; donation appeals to donors.

Whether a subscription or fundraising package, include endorsement quotes from politicians and members of the media. These can be made part of the letter, or listed on a separate sheet that's part of the package. A good direct mail company will figure out how to best showcase these endorsements, but it's up to you to provide them with these quotes. You may wish to approach a well-known politician or talk show host about signing your letter. For a new organization, a well-known signer can help boost your response rate by providing credibility to your appeal. Your direct mail company can help you determine who would work best for your appeal.

There are a variety of other issues for a direct mail expert to consider, such as: length of letter; whether or not to include a survey in the package (surveys often increase the response rate); whether to use "tease" copy on the outside of the carrier envelope; which font style to select for the letter; whether to include a P.S.; etc. These may appear to be minor considerations, but each can have an impact on your response rate.

One final word of caution. Listen to the direct mail experts. They have much more experience at direct mail and marketing than you. Many direct mail principles go against common sense, such as single sentence paragraphs. But they generate the best response. Your direct mail consultants have the benefit of years of testing for many different clients. Let their instincts guide them. As you test one company against another you will have the ultimate power to select the most successful firm to "roll out" to the best lists.

CHAPTER
THREE

CORRECT

As C-SPAN President Brian Lamb once noted, "In dealing with the media, conservatives are their own worst enemies. Suspicious of the liberal press, they often avoid it, fearing that they will be misquoted or taken out of context. Conservatives ought to realize that a newspaper or TV station is nothing but a business. Publishers and station owners know that if they consistently fail to present a widely-held point of view, a substantial part of the community will eventually turn away from them."

How should conservatives deal with the media? How can they use it to correct liberal bias? How do conservatives get their message heard when the hostile liberal press is the same press they must use to communicate with the public? They should learn methods that effectively communicate an idea or view: The methods of modern public relations.

Public relations has rules and practices which have been accepted by both the groups who are promoting themselves and the press. In this chapter, you will learn these rules and standard practices. By following them, the job of promoting your findings on liberal bias and the conservative view on a particular issue will be successful; and the press will respect your organization for its professional manner.

Methods for correcting bias range from gentle persuasion to economic warfare. This chapter covers your overall communications strategy and the tools you'll need to carry out your public relations duties effectively.

■ You'll learn how to promote your message by making contacts with reporters and then helping them learn and understand conservative views.

■ To accomplish this, you'll read tips and rules for creating news using one-on-one press contact, press releases and news conferences.

■ Then, this chapter will describe how to correct bias through seminars to bring together local media figures, concerned citizens and political leaders. You'll also learn how to use your contacts to help get media internships for students and jobs for conservative college graduates.

■ Finally, if all else fails, you'll be acquainted with the basics of how to use advertiser pressure to encourage a media outlet to change.

Throughout all your dealings with the press, keep in mind your two ultimate goals: correcting media bias and promoting conservative views to the media. All your actions should further these aims.

You may be the only one concentrating on bias in your local area. Therefore, you have a unique opportunity to be the expert on media bias, the person or persons the press will turn to as the authority. Through your studies, newsletter, press releases, and seminars you'll make liberal media bias an issue in your community.

Your second goal is to promote conservative alternatives to your local media outlets. When you get to know reporters, you'll be able to bring them the conservative point of view by sending along articles on different issues and by promoting conservative spokesmen for interviews. And you'll teach conservative groups and businessmen how to get coverage of their views and reactions to policies.

✔ CORRECT

Section One:
How Exposing Bias Can Help Correct Bias

Several of the skills you learned in the Expose chapter can also be used to correct bias. These include:

- Feeding information to an ombudsman
- Getting on radio talk shows
- Distributing your newsletter to members of the media and political leaders

❶ In the last chapter you learned what an ombudsman is and what he does. If a local paper or broadcast outlet has one, he or she can be a good contact to effect change. The ombudsman not only writes a column, but has influence within the newspaper or TV station. He may write internal memos formulating ethics policies and guidelines for the outlet.

Send the ombudsman all your releases, invite him to all your press conferences. Make sure he gets your newsletter and ask the Media Research Center to put him on the distribution list for *MediaWatch* and *Notable Quotables*. Try to develop a relationship with him or her. This relationship will be based less on selling a story or release to him, than on discussing journalistic issues and possible ways to correct bias.

If a newspaper does not have an ombudsman, advocate one. Assuming you've made contact with reporters and editors at the newspaper, urge them to raise the idea with their bosses. If you know the Editor or Publisher, then recommend this to them directly. Explain how an ombudsman will increase the paper's credibility and show the community that it cares about accuracy and fairness.

The ombudsman ranks around the country are made up of former reporters, editors and columnists, current reporters or editors on leave for a year or two, and journalism professors. Be ready to suggest names of those you think could fit the bill.

❷ In chapter two you learned how to expose media bias through calls and guest appearances on radio talk shows. You were also told how to provide information to talk show hosts. Later in this chapter you'll learn how to make media contacts and feed conservative viewpoints to reporters who are not necessarily conservative. Combining all these activities will help correct media bias.

Once you've come to know some local journalists, encourage them to accept a talk show host's invitation for them to debate you on the air. Such an appearance will let you and/or the host present the media bias case to a reporter or editor. And it will allow callers to express their views and criticisms directly to an actual journalist. Through these debates, the media will better understand your concerns; will hear specific examples; and, hopefully, in some small way realize media bias is at least an occasional problem that they need to correct.

❸ In the last chapter you learned how to create a newsletter to expose bias to members of the political and media community. A newsletter can also help correct bias. So, if you've begun one, don't think of it as a project you move beyond as you work to correct bias. It's integral to your correction efforts. It's what gives your group the visibility and credibility needed to be a player in the media and political world.

Why? First, because every month members of the media will see your analysis. That means the colleagues of those you quote or cite will see it too. Concern for what their colleagues will think is a very effective means of correction. To explain: A reporter may not really care that conservatives found his story biased. But he is concerned that his boss or colleagues might believe he violated basic rules of fairness and balance. Embarrass a reporter once, and he may very well be more careful not to repeat the same biased reporting technique. A television network news executive has told the MRC that he reads our newsletters and then passes along to his reporters any articles mentioning their stories.

Second, your newsletter will be seen by politicians and other community officials. They regularly talk to members of the media at parties, fundraisers, charity events, and over lunch at the restaurant near the county courthouse. Have a conservative state representative tell a reporter that he read about the reporter's slanted story in your newsletter, and you'll have an impact. That reporter will realize your newsletter is taken seriously by opinion leaders.

You will not change reporting overnight. But if your actions cause even a few reporters to make sure their story is balanced -- by making that phone call to get the conservative perspective -- then your newsletter will have helped correct media bias. (This is another reason to keep political rhetoric to a minimum in your newsletter while maximizing the space provided for quotes from news stories. The more opinion leaders and members of the media see your newsletter as a credible, serious critique of the local media, the greater the impact it will have.)

✔

CORRECT

Section Two:
How to Work With Reporters

One of the major reasons conservatives get far less press coverage than liberals is that liberals do a better job of creating news. Nearly every day, liberal organizations release studies, hold marches or rallies, make announcements, and otherwise promote their views. Yes, liberal reporters are naturally drawn to cover liberal events. But there's another factor at work. The media, needing material to fill the columns of newspapers and the minutes of news broadcasts, dutifully report these liberal activities.

There are two kinds of news you want to create:

● News about liberal bias in the media

● News promoting the conservative perspective on current issues

As a general rule, conservatives must work much harder than liberals to get coverage. The media know the liberal perspective. They have heard the liberal argument throughout college and journalism school. No doubt they continue to hear the "politically correct" side from their friends and colleagues in the newsrooms. On the other hand, they are often ignorant of the conservative perspective on issues and unaware of the experts available to provide it.

Conservatives must puncture the liberal bubble and get their arguments and views into newspapers, radio, and TV. They have to be creative to get their point across and imaginative in their presentation of themselves and their views when dealing with the media. Creating news hinges on your ability to become a credible, informed source for the media. It's safe to assume most reporters are liberal, but when dealing with them you should not hide your ideology. They are biased and so are you.

You can be a conservative and still be effective with the media -- even with very liberal reporters who may despise your ideology. These same reporters may also respect your honesty and positions on issues because of the professional relationship you have established with them. This credibility is earned, but if lost, will be impossible to restore. You can earn credibility by following a few simple, common-sense rules when dealing with the media.

Here are some tips for success that you should follow as you implement the ideas in this chapter.

✔ **Be honest.** In your dealings with the media be open and direct. If you don't know an answer, own up to it. Never take credit for anything you didn't do. Conversely, never say you did not do something that you did. Remember, it's the media's job to be thorough and get all the facts; if they find you have not been completely open, your story or assertion will be suspect.

✔ **Be informed.** Know your subject thoroughly. Have facts to back up your story. Offer background material for the reporter to use in the piece. Offer your expertise as a source for the media. If you can't answer a question, promise to find an answer.

✔ **Be concise.** Be able to state your case succinctly. Never offer too much information, or rattle on. The piece may be cut if the reporter feels there is too much to cover in a press release or if he thinks he cannot get a simple answer out of you in an interview. The strongest case is made when the facts about media bias speak for themselves.

✔ **Be available.** To make news, you must be available to answer questions and provide information. Cooperate with the media's needs. Try to accommodate their schedule. If you are not around to answer phone calls or do an interview, reporters will stop calling. If a radio or TV station producer wants you to come to their studio for an interview, drive there. If they want you to come to a hotel where they already have a film crew in 30 minutes, agree to it. No matter how quickly they need you, be available. They'll appreciate the cooperation and may even feel they owe you a favor for filling a hole in their broadcast at the last minute.

Once you have gotten the interest of the media, don't deny them the ability to follow up. If you need time to gather your facts, say so, but don't brush them off. Remember, you are the one who encouraged contact.

Realize how liberals in the media view conservatives. There are some doctrinaire liberals in the media who may view conservatives as a bunch of oafish, hateful, religious nuts. There are also many more liberal reporters who may not agree with you, but will make an attempt at fairness or balance and will treat you with respect. Keep in mind these two separate camps of liberal reporters. However they treat you, surprise them by being thoughtful, down-to-earth, with a sense of humor. These traits will help enormously when dealing with the press.

There are also things you should never do when dealing with the media:

✔ **Don't ever misrepresent the facts**. Be careful not to exaggerate or overstate any fact. Once you have misrepresented yourself to the media, they will never trust you again.

✔ **Don't become angry.** Even if you have good reason to be, never show anger toward a reporter or interviewer. Anger is a sign to a reporter that he has touched a sore spot -- and many will keep pressing that spot to see what will happen. Also be careful not to become flustered and lose your train of thought or switch your story. The media see this as a sign that something is not quite right with your story or that you are unsure of yourself and your information. They will pounce like piranhas.

✔ **Don't ever go back on your word**. If you promised to do an interview or get information to a reporter, editor, or commentator, be sure to do it as promised. The media work on deadlines -- if you forget to get back to them, they may cut you out of their story entirely. If you don't show up for an interview, you can pretty much forget about that particular contact using you in the future.

✔ **Don't push a dead issue.** If a media representative tells you he is not interested in one of your ideas or releases, let it drop. If a publication is reviewing an article you submitted and won't know for a few days whether or not they will use it, don't pester them. It is good to be aggressive and make sure they don't forget about you, but there is a fine line between being aggressive and being a pest. Take care not to cross that line.

CORRECT

Develop a media contact list

To contact the media, it is crucial that you develop a target list of reporters, editors, producers, assignment editors and news directors in your area. This list should contain both names and addresses of the contact, as well as the fax number for the newsroom. You may already have taken the time to learn about each media outlet in your area when you developed your newsletter mailing list. Even if you haven't, as an attentive news consumer you're probably fairly familiar with the key staff at each newspaper, radio station and television outlet. Note which reporters cover which "beat," such as city hall, education, the state legislature, and the media. Put every reporter who covers any political or government affairs beat on the list.

If you are not familiar with who covers which beat, jot down the names of all the media outlets in your region including print media (daily and weekly newspapers, local magazines, etc.), radio stations, and television stations. Using your local phone book, get the phone numbers of each newsroom. Call each outlet to get the name of the appropriate contact, the address and the fax number. For print media ask for the name of the editor and reporter covering your issue. For radio get the name of the news editor, and the names of all the radio talk show producers and hosts at the station. For television get the name of the assignment/news editor, and the producers of the evening and morning news programs.

Even if you think you know the names of key reporters, make sure you have those who make the assignments -- at TV stations, the "assignment desk" decides which potential news story will get a reporter and/or film crew. So learn the name of the assignment editor and put him on your contact list. In TV news, a field reporter is not always necessary; an anchor can read a brief news item. But without videotape to talk over, there's no TV story. For radio stations, include the news director. At newspapers, whoever makes the assignments. If you don't know, hopefully someone you've met at the newspaper can let you know. In general, at smaller newspapers it's the editor; at larger ones, it's probably someone with the title of "city editor," or for political stories, the "political editor."

Many larger outlets will have several fax numbers, maybe two for the newsroom, one for the editorial writers, and another for the sports department, not to mention the advertising department. So be sure to specify that you want the one for the newsroom. Most won't have any problem giving it to you once you explain that you wish to send them press releases. Keep this need in mind as you make personal contact with reporters: they can tell you the best number to use, such as the one closest to their desk. As you put together your media contact list don't overlook the conservative print and electronic media in your community, such as a local conservative talk show host and/producer and the conservative newspaper columnist. Include all those with whom you've already developed a relationship, those to whom you've sent material, appeared on their talk show or provided information for a story. These people already know you and, hopefully, respect you. So they will be most receptive to your public relations efforts.

Keeping your media contact list current is critical. You must regularly update your list with the names of all those you get to know as time passes.

Computerizing your media contact list

To maintain a media list, you have a couple of options. You could modify your computer database system, described in the last chapter, to include names, outlets, telephone and fax numbers, deadlines and beat area. But since you have a computer, you might want to purchase some software that includes a computerized Rolodex™ type card file system. Such software isn't very expensive costing anywhere from $50 to $300 depending upon the complexity and features offered and are available at any well-stocked computer software store.

Decide which way to store the information: alphabetically by name, all the names under the outlet for which they work, or by "beat." Whichever way you feel is easiest for your purposes, the key is being able to find the appropriate names to contact about a particular story. You don't want to burden a city hall reporter with news about the Governor or state legislature. That's why you must identify the "beat" of each reporter or producer. Always identify the television assignment editor or radio station news director, since they should get all of your releases. So if you organized your list by beat, make the assignment editor is always included.

If you go with a computer database or Rolodex™ type software, you can sort names by all three criteria. You could use the same database software you are using for news analysis and set up a separate file with fields for each area -- a field for the name, a field for the outlet and three or four fields for beat areas since many reporters cover more than one beat. For assignment editors and general assignment reporters you can put "all" or "everything" in the beat field.

If you are using a database software system to maintain your complimentary mailing list, then these fields could be added for all members of the media community. Of course, you won't print these fields when you run off the mailing list.

Once done, you will have constructed your media contact list of reporters and editors who will receive your media advisories, media availabilities and press releases and be invited to your press conferences. But even before you implement these various ways to communicate with the media you should start establishing personal relationships with members of the local media community.

Contacting reporters

Establishing a relationship with local reporters is the most effective way to correct liberal media bias. They should know there are people who think there is a liberal tilt to the media, and aren't very happy about it. In the next section you'll learn about communicating with the media through media advisories and press releases, but you should first use your contact list to develop a personal working relationship with individual members of the media. That will encourage them to turn to you as an information source and as a reference to steer them toward conservative experts.

Look over your media contact list. Pick out the names of reporters who have called you in the past, reporters who you think are conservative or who you think are the most biased to the left, the top editors at the local newspaper and high-ranking television producers. In short, those you think are most open to your views, most in need of hearing them, or who hold decision making positions. You obviously can't meet them all at once and many won't want to meet with you. So, start with a list and work your way through it.

To make the initial contact send an introductory letter on your organizational letterhead. This acts as an ice-breaker, introducing yourself so they will at least be familiar with you when you phone. Your letter should describe your background, why your group was created, and your goals. All this should be said in two pages or less.

Follow up with a phone call. Give your name and mention the letter. Explain you are concerned about correcting what your group perceives to be bias in news on the national and local level. Mention the newsletter you have started. Assuming they are on your complimentary mailing list, they'll make the connection between the newsletter and you.

Suggest you meet, perhaps to have lunch. Stress that the lunch is about you getting to know them -- that you want to learn their views on the local media's strengths and weaknesses -- not to air your beefs about media bias.

When you do meet the reporter, producer, editor or news director get to know what he does in his job. Ask about his background, beliefs, and approach to reporting news. Be prepared to answer the same questions. And if your meeting is over lunch, try to pick up the check. Some news organizations have ethics rules which prohibit reporters from accepting a free lunch, but offer anyway.

See if he is receptive to receiving copies of articles from you which present the conservative perspective on topics of interest to him. Explain that you know conservative policy experts and activists in the community, and would be glad to direct the journalist to them. All he has to do is call. If it's a radio or television reporter, ask if he's had any problems using any local conservative spokesmen. TV and radio reporters and producers need sources that speak in short, catchy soundbites that encapsulate an argument. Explain that you understand his needs and can recommend spokesmen who can speak in soundbites. It is a skill.

If the member of the media is receptive to receiving material from you, help him plug in to the conservative movement by passing along a column every now and then when you think it may interest the reporter. Give him articles from conservative publications such as *National Review*, *Conservative Chronicle*, and *The American Spectator*. Do the same with syndicated columnists. (See page 254 in Appendix 1 for a list of conservative publications, their addresses and subscription prices.)

Tie those articles in with local issues. For example, show him the connection between a Paul Craig Roberts column on regulatory excess and the local builder who is in trouble for running afoul of Americans with Disabilities Act regulations. Or give him a Don Feder or Mona Charen column on condoms in schools if that is a hot local issue. If the minimum wage increases, give him articles on how the minimum wage causes unemployment, and try to find some people actually laid off in your area for the journalist to interview. You are not trying to launch a crusade to turn reporters into conservatives. Your goal is to help the reporter understand the conservative take on different issues.

CORRECT

Don't overdo it. Send a pile of clips three times a week and the reporter will soon see you as more of an annoying pest than a helpful, information source. Remember the maxim: Less is sometimes more. One good article sent at a reasonable interval will have a lot more impact than an envelope stuffed with articles the reporter will never have time to read. Always make sure your information matches one of his fields of interest.

Even if you don't come across any articles of interest to a particular reporter, keep in touch. Send an occasional letter with story suggestions or to renew your offer to serve as a referral for conservative experts.

As we noted earlier, not every journalist will be interested in meeting with you. That's fine. You want to establish personal contacts. Start with one and build more over time. Each contact will lead to others. If you impress a television reporter during your lunch, he may suggest to his boss -- the evening news producer or News Director -- that he get together with you.

More will accept your invitation than you might expect. Some, because they are quietly conservative and agree with your concerns. Others out of sheer curiosity. Others still, on the opposite end of the spectrum, will want to convince you of how wrong you are.

From the very beginning of your relationship with reporters and producers, it's important to make sure you define yourself, your organization, and your goals to them. Define yourself your way, or a hostile reporter might well do it for you.

Section Three:
Getting Attention

Beyond one-on-one personal contact, there are several effective means for you to widely disseminate your views to the media community and thereby reach the public. In this section you'll learn how to:

- Write and distribute press releases, press advisories and press availabilities. You'll see actual examples of five kinds of releases
- Organize a press conference, a way to publicize a study or comment on an event which will allow you to interact with reporters

But before you can engage these communication methods, you must know media deadlines and how, like it or not, they will impact whether or not your release or press conference is covered. You must also understand how to measure newsworthiness.

When to contact reporters/deadlines

The ideal time to distribute a communication to the media is first thing in the morning. If your release or advisory can wait until the morning, hold off and send your communication out between 8:00 and 10:00 am. The media must make decisions all day long about which breaking events to cover. A late afternoon explosion at a downtown hotel will definitely get covered, but almost all outlets decide in the morning which non-breaking stories are worth assigning a reporter or producer to cover.

An outlet has only so many reporters or producers. You are competing with the school committee meeting, water department briefing on new sewer lines, a state representative's unveiling of a gun control bill and the high school academic achievement awards ceremony. Give yourself an even chance by being on the table when the assignment editor or top editors meet to make coverage decisions during their morning meeting.

Learning deadlines will enable you to tailor your communication to the reporter's schedule, thus maximizing the chance for coverage. Television, radio and newspapers operate differently. Most TV news operations have a 2pm cut off for news (other than, of course, for a major fire, crime, or hot breaking issue) for that night's early evening newscast.

Most local stations have a late evening newscast as well. Much of this is regurgitated news from the earlier newscast. However, some of it is news based on breaking events. If events unfold that meet the early news deadline your spokesman should be prepared for an interview. When this occurs, it is often better simply to call the news editor or producer and make your spokesman available for comment on the late-breaking story.

If you are planning an evening event such as a dinner, and want the late evening newscasts to cover it, get the newsworthy aspects out of the way early, preferably by 8:30 pm. So have your big-name speakers give their addresses first. This gives the reporters, producers and editors time to go back to the studio and edit the piece for the late evening newscast.

In general, deadlines are less important for radio news because they have hourly broadcasts throughout the day. Still, don't wait until late in the day. Unless it's an all-news station, radio reporters only have three or four minutes an hour to deliver the news, but they like to mix in different stories each hour. The earlier in the day they get a news item, the better the chance they'll work it into an hourly newscast. If they get it late in the day, they may not use it and by the next morning it will be considered old news.

Morning newspapers have deadlines around 4pm. Evening papers may not come out until 1pm, but they are printed in the late morning. So other than covering a nighttime school board meeting or running an early morning AP story about an international development, their deadline is the same.

Weekly newspaper deadlines vary according to what day they are published. A paper printed each Wednesday morning will want all articles written by Tuesday morning. But since reporters for a weekly paper usually have to write several stories, don't wait until the last minute. They'll appreciate having stories to write on Wednesday, Thursday or Friday, when they are less rushed.

Newsworthiness

You must understand what is newsworthy and what is not newsworthy. News is new or unique information on issues or events which may directly affect or interest the public. Something is newsworthy if it involves one, two or even all these characteristics:

- if it is a significant event
- if people are talking about it
- if there is an element of conflict to it
- if it involves prominent people
- if it seems to be worth covering in the eyes of the reporters and editors of the media outlet

Too many groups waste a lot of time and effort trying to get attention, but end up getting none because their releases and conferences are not newsworthy. When you have an idea for a press release or conference, check it against the list of newsworthy characteristics. If it fits, run with it. Watch other groups, both liberal and conservative. See how they make news, see what works for them. Pretty soon you'll have a good feel for what is newsworthy.

When thinking about press releases and press conferences, it's crucial to your success to remember the deadlines for different media as listed on your contact list. Knowing the deadlines reporters must meet will help you decide when it is a good time to put out a press release or hold a media event. It will increase the chances your news will make it into the newscast or newspaper.

Also, you must be aware that a reporter is often under enormous pressure to get the story filed on time. Unless you have an angle on a "hot" story of the day, it is better to wait until the next morning to contact the reporter. If you have an angle on a breaking story, however, be concise and to the point. Let them know you are aware that they are probably on deadline, but that you have some additional information for them. Reporters are under incredible pressure from editors to get the story in for editing. If you are close to deadline time make sure you have something you sincerely feel they can use for their story.

✔

CORRECT

Press releases

Press releases should be issued when your organization wishes to make a point about a current issue, or when you intend to break/create news by releasing new information.

Press releases should be written from the perspective of a reporter, or similar to a news story in your local newspaper. They should include quotes by your spokesman, and provide detailed facts to support your comments and position. Press releases should not be longer than a page and a half. Releases are also an excellent tool for informing a broad number of media contacts about your position on a key issue. The first objective of a press release is to get media attention; the second is to serve as an update and reminder for the media contact.

The key to writing a good press release is to keep this fact in mind: reporters can be lazy. We don't mean that as an insult. Reporters are human. Sometimes, they want to get as much done with as little work as possible. Or sometimes they are working on a variety of stories and don't have time to focus specifically on every detail -- so you must make their job easy. Maybe that's why they so often accept the latest propaganda from left-wing interest groups in Washington -- that apples treated with Alar cause cancer, for example -- without bothering to check the facts. The Left creates interesting news stories which reporters snap up.

When he was asked why he didn't report on a ten-year government study that found acid rain caused no discernible damage to lakes and forests, *Washington Post* environmental reporter Michael Weisskopf responded: "This is such a dynamic city, with so many pressure groups pushing their point of view, you don't have to do investigative reporting to find these reports. If they are truly important, they are promoted and put forward." So, Weisskopf relied on his liberal sources.

Reporters tend to be uninterested in conservative views. They don't look for stories that support the conservative perspective, and when they stumble across such stories they treat them with skepticism. So conservatives must work especially hard to make their stories interesting.

In writing a press release, your goal is to do a reporter's job for him. You want to write the release just like a news article, so the reporter can use it "as is" without significant changes. This is your chance to effect the story -- and try to get the reporter to tell it the way you want. He probably won't simply reprint your release, but an effective and concise summary of your points make the story easier to write.

Of course, the reporter assigned to the story will usually call a spokesman for the opposition for his reaction and put that response in the story, probably after the first or second paragraph. Anticipate any critics (or what in your release may be criticized) and attempt to refute them in your release. If you expect them to deny bias, include a number of examples to prove otherwise. Nobody expects your press release to present both sides. But the reporter will use a lot more of your phrasing and "spin" if the release is more professional.

Writing a Press Release

There are some well-tested rules to writing press releases. First, it should include the five W's: who, what, when, where, and why. Questions to ask yourself as you write the release:

➤ Who is doing the action? Who are the main players?

➤ What is it that you are doing? What will result from this action? What was your motivation?

➤ When will/did this activity take place? When will/did it conclude?

➤ Where will/did this action take place?

➤ Why will/did this happen? Why is it important?

List the date of release, a contact person and a phone number at the top of the release. Lead off with a concise and interesting headline. The headline should give the reader a glimpse of what the release is about, but doesn't give away too much -- you want the reporter to read deeper into the release.

A good opening sentence is especially important. You want to grab the reporter or editor's attention, and keep it so he will read on through the release. State the purpose by crafting a clear, engaging summary in the first paragraph. If a reporter cannot get the point by reading the headline and the first two or three lines, he may not read any more.

Keep it short. A press release should almost never exceed one single-spaced page (double-spaced between paragraphs). Any more and you may lose the reporter's attention. Whatever the length, remember to put the most important information first. Each succeeding paragraph declines in order of importance, so put your most important point up front.

Here are some tips for setting the tone in a press release:

✔ **Don't get carried away.** Be very careful when criticizing your opponents. Criticism must be *both* (1) true with proof to back up your charge and (2) within the bounds of fair play. If you lie, or even if you exaggerate, you will pay a stiff price; no one will believe you. If you go overboard -- for example, making a historical comparison of your adversaries to Hitler or Stalin or Pol Pot -- you will invite ridicule upon yourself and persuade no one.

✔ Always end your release with a quotable line -- a reference to history or pop culture or a clever turn of phrase that (you hope) people will be repeating tomorrow: "President Reagan answered: 'Go ahead, make my day,'" "This will be the mother of all confirmation battles," "Where's the beef?"

✔ After the last line of your release, skip two lines, insert "-30-" or "###" in the center of the line. This signifies to the reader that the release is complete at this point.

As a media monitoring group, there are three basic types of press releases you can issue. Here are descriptions of each along with corresponding examples of MRC releases:

➤ **Comment on a current news event by summarizing how coverage was biased.** Tying your release to an event will increase your chances of getting into the press. This requires good timing. Anticipate what events are coming up. If the state budget is being released or the local school board is voting on a controversial new curriculum, plan on putting out a release about biased press coverage on these subjects. By creative timing of the release -- tying it to an event -- you increase your chances of being part of the coverage of that event.

On the other hand, there is also an opportunity to comment on an event after it happens, especially if it was controversial. The days after an event are a good time for reflection; it is when many columnists craft their opinions of the event. You could be part of this discussion if you put out a release.

The next two pages show an actual MRC press release issued a week or so after the 1992 Los Angeles riots. To show reporters how the riots received biased coverage, the MRC release included several examples of biased quotes.

MEDIA RESEARCH CENTER

FOR IMMEDIATE RELEASE
MAY 7, 1992

FOR MORE INFORMATION CONTACT
MEG GILKESON AT (703) 683-5004

MEDIA REACT TO KING VERDICT: QUOTES EXPOSE LIBERAL MEDIA'S TOLERANT JUSTIFICATION OF CHAOS AND MURDER, SAYS MRC'S BOZELL

Alexandria, VA -- L. Brent Bozell III, Chairman of the Media Research Center and Publisher of **Notable Quotables**, today released a compilation of quotes which "proves an outrageous liberal media agenda in their coverage of the Rodney King verdict."

"Media coverage of the verdict and the ensuing riots virtually absolved the L.A. terrorists of any wrong–doing. The press continues to justify as 'racially correct' three days of chaos and mayhem which held an entire city hostage. Pious newsmen of the media establishment just can't accept the fact that a jury could subvert the 'guilty' verdict promoted, predicted, and expected by networks and newspapers around the country.

"Take, for example, *Philadelphia Inquirer* reporter Alexis Moore's justification of the violence on C-Span's **Journalists' Roundtable**: 'When you have no hope and when you've been told for years that you're supposed to believe in the system and the system turns around and delivers a verdict that on the face of it is just wrong, then you cannot but expect people to say well that if the justice system doesn't work and I don't have any hope for the future then I'm going to take it into my own hands.'

"Or Hugh Downs on ABC's *20/20* the night of May 1: 'We should avoid focusing exclusively on the rage and inappropriate behavior of oppressed and frustrated people who started these riots.'

"The media irresponsibly and dishonestly blame Republican campaign ads for the violence instead of focusing on the premeditated and destructive intent of a lawless mob. *Time* special correspondent Michael Kramer wrote in the May 11 issue: 'It would help, too, if the man who sanctioned the infamous Willie Horton ad during his 1988 run for the White House would admit his complicity in developing the images and code words that encourage whites to demonize blacks.'"

Bozell continued, "The press is so out of touch with mainstream America that they can't accept the reality of the verdict. Instead, the media callously blame conservatives for inciting racial unrest in American cities. John Chancellor charged on the April 30 *NBC Nightly News* that 'Politicians have fanned these flames with code words about "welfare queens," "equal opportunity," and "quotas." Language designed to turn whites against blacks. With two–party politics that favored the rich and hurt everyone else.'

---

113 South West Street • Second Floor • Alexandria, Virginia 22314 • (703) 683-9733

✔ CORRECT

"Bryant Gumbel whined on the May 1 *Today* show: 'Taking their cues from Washington, most Americans over the past dozen years have chosen to ignore the issue of civil rights, and the growing signs of racial division....The rage that is spilling into the streets of L.A. may have been sparked by the Rodney King verdict, but it's fueled by the frustration and anger that accompanies the feelings of inequity and despair.'"

Bozell concluded, "The media are so sure of their own infallibility that journalists simply can't comprehend this rejection of their version of the facts. In order to save face, the media are forced to justify the plundering of Los Angeles by concentrating only on what they perceive as "justice." But they've missed the point. The American press is too close-minded to see the riots as the violent pounding of the last nail in the coffin of the Great Society programs -- programs that have subjugated and oppressed the poor of this country for too long."

The Media Research Center is a non-profit, educational foundation which documents bias in the news and entertainment industries. For more information or to arrange an interview with an MRC spokesman, please contact Meg Gilkeson at (703) 683-5004.

To obtain a copy of the Rodney King

Notable Quotables *via fax, please*

contact Meg Gilkeson at (703) 683-

5004.

➤ **Challenge reporters to improve coverage.** You can do this by either: a) before an event occurs, such as an abortion march or State House hearings on the sales tax increase proposal, cite past biased media coverage of the topic and state that you hope the media coverage will be better this time around; or b) after an event has occurred, summarize how coverage was biased and challenge reporters to do a better job in the future.

With the first angle, try to release your statement up to two days before the major event. But a release the morning of the event is also good. If it is major news, be aware it will be a hectic time for the reporters. By releasing it a bit early, you won't get trampled in the coverage.

This MRC press release on the next page commented on the biased media coverage of the April 1993 gay march on Washington. In pointing out the differences in what was broadcast in the media and what actually occurred, it challenged reporters to realize their errors and correct them in future stories.

✔ CORRECT

For Immediate Release
June 1, 1993

Bringing political balance to the media

For More Information Contact:
Meg Gilkeson, (703) 683–5004

Bozell Challenges Media to Cover Gay Agenda In Full

Washington, DC -- L. Brent Bozell III, Chairman of the Media Research Center, today challenged the media to "do a better job when covering the homosexual rights movement and the gay agenda," at a national news conference releasing the latest video from the Oregon based group, The Report.

"The Gay March on Washington was the march that no one saw. Americans watching television the weekend of April 25, 1993 certainly couldn't have seen on the network evening news shows what has been captured on this video. The more egregious error, though, is that Americans didn't hear the whole story from the news media," Bozell explained.

"Media Research Center analysis of coverage supports the statements in this video and I applaud The Report for informing the public when our national media failed to do so.

"Media reports tended to emphasize the mainstream elements of the march and marchers, calling it time and again a civil rights march. The more radical demands of the organizers' platform were ignored by those in the media, who chose to report only that, 'Organizers had a long list of demands. The top three: civil rights protection, an end to the ban on gays in the military, and more funding for AIDS research,'" Bozell observed.

"No one mentioned that the platform also included, 'The redefinition of sexual re-assignment surgeries as medical, not cosmetic, treatment,' and in schools, a 'culturally inclusive Lesbian, Gay, Bisexual and Transgender Studies program...at all levels of education,' and a host of other action items contrary to the values of average citizens."

Bozell concluded, "Americans watch the news because they seek information on which they will base decisions and opinions regarding important issues facing their country and their communities. The news media have an important responsibility to provide balanced reports on issues and events.

"As we can see from this tape, the media failed Americans the weekend of April 25. The Media Research Center congratulates The Report on their diligence and dedication to setting the record straight on this important issue. It's time Americans got the whole story and made up their own minds."

The Media Research Center is a non-profit educational foundation which documents bias in the news and entertainment industries. To arrange an interview with Mr. Bozell or a spokesman, please contact Meg Gilkeson at (703) 683–5004.

Publishers of *Media Watch, TV, etc,* and *Notable Quotables*

113 South West St., 2nd Floor ■ Alexandria, Virginia 22314 ■ (703) 683-9733 Fax (703) 683-9736

➤ **A press release on a study you have done.** These releases are much more pro-active. They give you credibility in that you are breaking news to the media contact by informing him/her of an exclusive study or report your organization has completed. In the Expose chapter you learned how to complete several kinds of studies. You could do a study counting how many times the media have called for increased spending on education. Include statistics in your study because the media love to use them. When done, summarize it in a press release.

If you have a newsletter, run an article detailing the study results. Have the press release announce the results of a study appearing "in the August issue of...." Make sure you end with an offer to fax a copy of the newsletter article to any reporter who calls.

A release summarizing the findings of a MRC study on political donations from media company foundations is reprinted on the next two pages.

✔

CORRECT

MEDIA RESEARCH CENTER

FOR IMMEDIATE RELEASE   FOR INFORMATION CONTACT:
MARCH 16, 1990   GREG MUELLER (703) 683-9733

MEDIAWATCH PUBLISHER SAYS MEDIA COMPANIES AND FOUNDATIONS FUND LEFT WING CAUSES; CITES NEW STUDY

WASHINGTON, DC - L. Brent Bozell III, Chairman of the Media
Research Center (MRC) and Publisher of **MediaWatch**, today released
a **MediaWatch** study showing that media companies and media-related
foundations give "90 percent of political grant money to left-wing
groups."

"Both this study and our study last year unequivocally prove
that media companies contribute overwhelmingly to left-wing groups
and causes. It disproves the myth that these companies are
ideologically conservative. This year's study investigates
contributions to political organizations from the Gannett
Foundation, the Knight Foundation, the Hearst Foundations, the
Boston Globe Foundation, and the Chicago Tribune Foundation. We
found that of $2,204,930 million donated, 90 percent ($1,978,593)
went to left-wing groups. Only $225,500 was allocated to
conservative groups, most of which came from the Hearst
Foundations. It gave $205,000 to conservatives and $541,400 to
liberals. The Knight Foundation and the Boston Globe Foundation
did not give a penny to conservative groups," Bozell said.

The recent **MediaWatch** study will be published in the upcoming
issue. Media analysts examined annual reports and foundation
records at the Foundation Center to discover how much grant money

111 South Columbus Street • Alexandria, Virginia 22314 • 703/683-9733

was allocated to political groups by media companies from 1982-89.

Last year's study investigated political grants awarded by the Times Mirror Foundation, The New York Times Foundation, the Philip L. Graham Foundation, the General Electric Foundation, and the Capítol Cities Foundation. Out of the $1.75 million worth of political grants the MRC identified last year 90 percent, or $1.579 million, went to left-wing organizations.

Bozell said that the "studies display a trend on the part of media companies and foundations. In both cases, 90 percent of the money went to liberal groups. In both cases, money went to organizations such as the National Organization of Women's Legal Defense and Education Foundation, the ACLU Foundation, Planned Parenthood, the NAACP, etc.

"Combining the totals of both studies, we found that out of $3.95 million donated, liberals received $3.55 million while conservatives received $407,500. These numbers are quite overwhelming and incredibly slanted in favor of the Left. Moreover, it proves that the media industry is controlled by liberal ideologues who appropriate large sums of grant money to their liberal activist friends," Bozell concluded.

For a complete copy of the study, contact Greg Mueller at the number listed above.

-30-

✔ CORRECT

➤ **Media availabilities and media advisories.** Shorter than press releases, media availabilities and media advisories should be used to alert reporters to a specific fact. Media availabilities should be distributed when an issue is breaking in which a pattern of media bias is developing. They inform the contact that your organization's spokesman is available to comment and offer analysis on the bias in reporting that has occurred pertaining to the issue at hand. To encourage television and radio producers to cover the topic of interest to you, title the availability release a "Segment Idea." Media availabilities or segment ideas should be short -- no more than half a page. Below, we've reprinted an MRC segment idea.

MEDIA
RESEARCH
CENTER

FOR IMMEDIATE RELEASE   FOR MORE INFORMATION CONTACT:
OCTOBER 20, 1992   MEG GILKESON, (703) 683-5004

SEGMENT IDEA

**IMPACT MEDIA COVERAGE OF CANDIDATES HAS ON
THE 1992 PRESIDENTIAL ELECTION**

SUBJECT: Assuming a tight race, will biased media coverage provide Bill Clinton with the margin of victory in November? Has the press jumped to the foregone conclusion that Clinton will win the election? What impact does this have on voters?

WHO: L. Brent Bozell III, Chairman of the Media Research Center and Publisher of *MediaWatch* or Tim Graham, Associate Editor of *MediaWatch*.

POSITION: Media coverage of the campaign dramatically impacts voters' decisions in an election year. In a close race for the Presidency or any office, media bias in favor of one candidate can affect both voter turn-out and choice. The media does a disservice to the public when it presents only one side of an issue or only one view of a candidate, leaving Americans with little valid, relevant information on which to base important decisions.

CONTACT: Meg Gilkeson, (703) 683-5004.

Media advisories are used to alert the media to events you are planning: press conferences, seminars, special events, etc. These are completely informational, serving to alert the media to the date, time, and purpose of your organization's event. Media advisories should be concise – no more than three quarters of a page.

An advisory alerting reporters to the time, date, location and speakers at a MRC roast of Oliver North appears on the next page.

THE ★★★★ OLIVER NORTH Roast

FOR IMMEDIATE RELEASE
MARCH 21, 1990

FOR INFORMATION CONTACT:
CREATIVE RESPONSE CONCEPTS
GREG MUELLER, (703) 683-5004

MEDIA ADVISORY

WASHINGTON, DC - "The Oliver North Roast," sponsored by the Media Research Center, will be held on Wednesday, March 21 at 7:30 p.m. in the Independence Ball Room of the Grand Hyatt Washington Hotel, 1000 H St., NW, Washington, D.C.

Members of the media interested in covering the event should contact Greg Mueller at the above number to reserve press credentials.

Attending media should report to the Latrobe Room - Level 3B - between 6:00 and 7:10 p.m. to pick up reserved credentials and additional information. Sandwiches and beverages will be served in the Latrobe Room from 6:00 to 7:00 p.m. The media will be escorted to the Independence Ball Room at 7:10 p.m.

Syndicated Radio Political Commentator Rush Limbaugh will emcee the event. The roasters include: CBN founder and former G.O.P. Presidential candidate Dr. Pat Robertson, Congressmen Henry Hyde, Robert Dornan, Phil Crane, and Chris Cox. Celebrities Bob Hope and Robert Conrad will roast via audio and videotape. The American Spectators' R. Emmett Tyrrell will introduce the final speaker -- Lt. Col. Oliver North.

-30-

Media Research Center
111 South Columbus Street • Alexandria, Virginia 22314

Distributing a press release, availability & advisory

All press releases, advisories and availabilities should be faxed, on well-designed letterhead, to the reporters, editors and columnists on your media contact list. You could send releases by mail, but it doesn't have the same impact. Releases sent by the mail don't have the urgency as releases that spit out of the fax machine. They also don't seem as important. So almost everything you do should be faxed.

A 1993 survey of newspaper business section editors by *Editor & Publisher* magazine asked "By which method...do you prefer to receive critical information?" The number one response: by fax. Business editors surely reflect the preferences of editors of other sections as well.

What you'll need:

● **Letterhead**. Make sure you have professional-looking letterhead for your official organizational releases. It should be a clear, attractive design which identifies your group to the reporter. This should all be evident from a quick scan, or else your release may end up in the bottom of a paper pile on a reporter's desk, or even worse, in the trash.

The design could be a modified version of your regular letterhead with your logo, address and phone number. Add to it large printed words saying "Press Release" or "News from...." so it can be easily identified as a press release.

Define yourself quickly to those who are unfamiliar with your organization by putting a "mission statement" on the letterhead. This is a short, one sentence statement describing the aim of your organization. The Media Research Center's is "Bringing political balance to the media." It appears under the MRC logo on the newsletters and on our letterhead. Think up one of your own and put it on your letterhead.

● **A fax system and/or fax software for your computer.** Fax machines range in price between $300 and $1,200 depending upon their features and quality. You may want to dedicate one phone line for the fax if you're planning on receiving or sending a lot of faxes. But to minimize cost, it could share your present line with your telephone. It may become a bit clumsy if someone sends an unexpected fax to you, and you pick up the phone thinking it is a call.

To avoid this situation, there are switches that attach to the fax machine which recognize the tones and automatically route the call to your fax. Conversely, it recognizes a call is not a fax and routes it to your telephone. This device sells for less than $100 at a computer store. Some new fax machine models come with this feature already built-in.

A better idea: Get software that will enable your computer to send faxes. A "board," a piece of plastic covered with diodes and wires, will have to be installed in your computer. The board and accompanying software costs about $200. Get someone who knows what he is doing to handle the installation. One slip of the screwdriver inside the computer and you won't have a working computer any more.

This "computer fax" software can hold dozens of names and numbers on a fax list and dial these numbers automatically, redialing numbers that are initially busy. That's a lot easier to do than standing over a regular fax machine, dialing each number one by one and then hand-feeding your fax page by page. This software will also let you receive faxes -- the computer will send them to your printer. Some software packages running in the $300 range combine a Rolodex™ type system with fax software.

One complication with this option: You'll have to spend the money for a dedicated phone. Once you push "go" so it starts dialing your fax list, it will tie up your phone line until it's gotten through to every number.

Call-outs

After you fax the press release, it is time to begin call-outs to your contact list. Ideally, you should send the communication out first thing in the morning. Then, allow one hour for the media contact to receive and digest the information sent. After an hour, begin call-outs to confirm receipt of the communication. If you reach the contact, utilize this opportunity to expand upon your organization's position, and encourage an interview with your spokesman. If the media contact has not received the communication it will prompt him to go look for it. Call back within an hour to make sure he/she received the communication. If not, fax it again.

It is important to use this contact as an opportunity to sell the reporter or editor your release by briefly reiterating why it is important and newsworthy. Whatever you do, learn to take a hint. If the recipient is trying to gently say he's not interested, take the hint and say goodbye. That reporter may be excited by a press release you put out at another time, so don't get him mad at you.

If your release isn't published, don't get angry. Perhaps a more important story took precedence. Perhaps a higher-up editor overruled the editor or reporter you talked to. Perhaps your story wasn't really newsworthy. People often think their story is the most important one of the day or the week; often they are wrong.

Never assume a reporter or editor is biased over a single failure to publish anything about your release. If there really is bias, you will see a pattern of unfairness over a period of time. If you believe you were treated unfairly and can prove it, confront the reporter or editor in a firm but friendly manner. (If your critiques are routinely ignored, you can show that the media outlets you're criticizing can dish it out, but can't take it. There's nothing more ironic than a reporter or editor responding with "No comment.")

Radio actualities

A special type of press release tailored to the needs of radio is called a radio actuality. This is a recorded newsworthy statement, about thirty seconds in length, fed over the phone to a radio station. If you want to use actualities, call each station beforehand. Radio stations have different policies regarding actualities. Not all stations accept them, preferring live interviews with a reporter.

Assuming at least one local station accepts actualities, whenever you write a press release record a matching actuality that summarizes your point in two or three sentences. Same goes for press availabilities: Don't wait for a station to call you; call them with your opinion on coverage of a topical event.

The equipment needed to feed a radio actuality over the phone is not expensive and it's available at any Radio Shack or similar electronics hobbyist store. The very least you'll need is a cassette tape recorder, alligator clips, and, of course, a telephone. To record the actuality, give a brief, concise statement on one topic into the tape recorder as if you were answering a question from a reporter. Test out different messages to see which is best. It must sound like part of a natural conversation, not like you are reading off a script.

To transmit the actuality, hook one end of the cable/alligator clips into the tape recorder and the alligator clips onto the metal in the telephone receiver's mouthpiece. Call the station, tell them you are ready to play your actuality. For a clear-sounding statement, turn the treble up and the bass down on your tape recorder. Then count backwards from three and play the recorded statement into the telephone. Check with the station to make sure the actuality was recorded clearly before hanging up.

✔

CORRECT

Press conference

Scheduling. When you plan a press conference make sure that you avoid conflicts. If your news event isn't high priority on a busy news day, chances are you will have a very small turnout. You don't want to schedule your press conference at the same time as two or three others. Ideally, you want to have the only media event scheduled at the time you select.

Your local Associated Press bureau manages a "Daybook," which serves as the media's calendar of events for that day. If you are scheduling an event, call the daybook and ask them if this is a busy day before you schedule the event. If they are uncooperative, speak to one of your more friendly media contacts. Ask them to check to see what's going on that day. This will help further develop your relationship with him. It also shows that you are trying to make his job easier by avoiding potential conflicts.

Media events should be held at a location close to where your media contacts work. The best days to hold a news conference are Tuesday, Wednesday or Thursday. This doesn't mean you can't have an event on a Monday or Friday, but Tuesday, Wednesday and Thursday are better days for getting coverage for press conferences. Monday is less than ideal because you'll have to put out your press advisory the previous Friday and some reporters may forget about it or weekend events may make your event seem less compelling. Friday is bad because reporters who work the weekend will often take Friday off; and the Saturday newspaper has the smallest "news hole." It's the day with the least space for news stories.

If, however, your event must be held on a Monday or Friday to remain timely, hold it then anyway. Indeed, if the state legislature passes the school funding bill Thursday night, you don't want to wait until the following Thursday to release your analysis of how the debate was covered. Do it on Friday so you can be included in Sunday newspaper stories on reactions to the legislature's funding formula.

Press conferences should take place between 10:00am and 2:00pm. Any later than 2:00pm and you get to close to deadline. Anything earlier than 10:00 may be too early, unless you are arranging a breakfast event.

Location. Press conferences can be held inside or outside, but having them inside is less complicated and you don't have to worry about the weather. There will be times to hold an event outdoors. For example, outside a television station or other media outlet whose biases you may be protesting. Or, you may want to hold an event outside the town hall, police station or State House if those backdrops match the subject of your press conference.

It's important to get permission to hold the conference in a public place. Check if you need a city permit, or just verbal permission from the property owner or manager. It would be very embarrassing to have the police come over during your press conference and order you to vacate the premises. If you are holding your event outside, it is important that you rent an outdoor sound system, and a podium. If you are holding an inside event, make sure to have a mike with a podium.

For an inside press conference consider a major hotel. Reporters will be familiar with the location, it will have the necessary electrical requirements for television lights, and hotel staffs will know how to properly set up a podium, chairs, and refreshments for you. All large or chain hotels have meeting rooms which can be reserved; some may require a small fee or a deposit. Call the catering office to reserve a room.

Put the podium up front, and a theater-style arrangement of chairs with an aisle. Make sure you have enough seats for the number of reporters you expect. You can arrange seating for outdoor events, but the media usually tend to stand. It's best to set up the podium, and allow the media to gather around you for the outdoor event.

Whether indoors or out, place your logo so it can be seen in newspaper photos or television video. A two foot square version can be placed on the from of the podium. Or, you could print it on a large banner that could be hung on the wall behind the podium.

Inviting reporters. Once you've booked the room and the day, it is time to alert the media to your event. The initial step to holding a press conference is to put out a media advisory. As mentioned on page 228, this is a special kind of news release issued to alert the media to an upcoming event which they may wish to attend. A media advisory is similar to a press release: on letterhead and distributed to your media contact list by fax.

The release should be clearly labeled "Media Advisory" or "News Conference." It should be short, no more than three paragraphs. The body should have no quotes, but answer who, what, when, where, and why so the press will become interested and find their way to the conference. But you don't want to give too many facts away or the media won't have to attend your event. You may want to put a headline

CORRECT

on your advisory to tease the media's interest. For example, if you are protesting a local station's coverage of an issue your headline could read: NEBRASKANS FOR A BALANCED MEDIA TO PROTEST WMRC'S COVERAGE OF _____; GROUP TO HOLD NEWS CONFERENCE OUTSIDE WMRC STUDIOS. This makes the event much more spicy for the media.

Below there's an example of a media advisory for a joint Catholic Campaign for America/MRC news conference on coverage of the Pope's visit to Denver in the summer of 1993.

Catholic Campaign for America

816 Connecticut Avenue NW • Suite 800 • Washington, DC 20006
Tel. (202) 833-4999 • FAX (202) 833-5569

FOR IMMEDIATE RELEASE:
AUGUST 23, 1993:

FOR INFORMATION CONTACT:
MICHELLE POWERS OR MEG GILKESON
(703)683-5004

MEDIA BIASED AGAINST CATHOLICS DURING PAPAL VISIT

MEDIA CRITIC, CATHOLIC AND CHRISTIAN LEADERS TO HOLD JOINT NEWS CONFERENCE

Board of Directors

Frank J. Lynch, Chairman
Richard V. Allen
William J. Bennett
Mary Ellen Bork
The Hon. Hugh L. Carey
Thomas G. Ferguson
Most Rev. Rene H. Gracida
William R. Sasso
Frank Shakespeare
Robert Van Dine

Thomas V. Wykes, Jr.
Executive Director

Michael Schwartz
Communications Counsel

ALEXANDRIA, VA -- The Media Research Center (MRC), Catholic Campaign for America (CCA) and the Christian Coalition will hold a joint news conference at 10:00am on Wednesday August 25, in the Murrow room of the National Press Club to release data documenting the national media's anti-Catholic bigotry in their coverage of the Pope's visit.

L. Brent Bozell III, Chairman of the MRC, will discuss a study his organization conducted based on the coverage of Catholics and Church issues during Pope John Paul II visit to the United States. He will also show a video of collected television news clips supporting his charge of media bias against the Pope. Thomas V. Wykes, Jr., Executive Director of CCA, will offer commentary and discuss plans to combat media bias against Catholics. Ralph Reed, Executive Director of the Christian Coalition, or a representative from the organization will also be available to discuss their experience with media bias against Christian Americans.

NEWS CONFERENCE ON MEDIA BIAS
WEDNESDAY, AUGUST 25, 1993
10:00 AM
NATIONAL PRESS CLUB - MURROW ROOM
CONTACT: MICHELLE POWERS OR MEG GILKESON (703) 683-5004

The media advisory should be sent two days before the press conference. Like a press release, you want to make two sets of follow-up calls. The first is to make sure they received the advisory, and answer any questions. During this call, ask if the person has any special requirements. A radio reporter, for instance, may need to file his story from a telephone in a quiet room. If so, talk to the hotel staff about a location the reporter can use for a few minutes.

The second to remind them of the event and see if they plan to attend. Once again, follow-up calls are important, demonstrating that you consider your advisory important and giving you a chance to reiterate why your press conference will be newsworthy. If you are holding a late morning or early afternoon event, you may choose to fax the advisory again the morning of the event.

Conducting the press conference

Have a sign-in sheet with space for each attendee to fill in his name, outlet, phone and fax number. Not all will sign in, so have one of your colleagues ask each journalist to sign it. After the press conference concludes, make sure late-comers see it. Later, go through it to see if it includes anyone not already on your contact list. If so, add them. Use the sign-in sheet as a guide for whom to invite to lunch to get better acquainted. Whether or not they do a story on your press conference, they were interested enough to show up. That makes them the journalists with whom you want to develop a relationship.

Distribute a press packet to the media before the conference begins because the material may be forgotten in the rush to leave when the conference is over. Print your logo on some folders with pockets to hold your information. These packets should include:

● Your statement, what you will read from the podium. This will allow reporters to follow along and mark the sections they wish to quote or soundbite.

● A sheet providing some background information on your organization, including your goals.

● Sheets with a brief biography for each speaker.

● Photocopies of recent press clippings mentioning your group.

● The latest issues of your newsletter.

Start on time, going for no more than thirty minutes, including the question and answer period. Your opening statement should be about two to three double-spaced pages and should take no longer to read than four or five minutes. It should outline all your points clearly and succinctly and be written so that broadcast reporters can identify understandable soundbites. If you have specific examples of bias, quote one but explain that you have many more. You can cite others in response to questions from the reporters.

Prepare thoroughly by practicing your statement and drawing up a list of possible questions that might be asked. With a little thought, you will be able to anticipate almost all the questions asked. When answering questions, remember to keep your mind on your message, the reason for calling the press conference.

Try not to get side-tracked into other issues while answering the questions, thereby muddying your message. If distracting questions are asked, give a short answer, and return to your main message. This is very important because knowledge of your subject will affect how reporters view you. If you seem an expert and well-versed in what you want to say, they'll respect you and accept you as an expert in your field.

Post press conference follow-up. Some reporters who said they planned to attend won't make it. The fact that they agreed to attend shows the subject interested them. They may have been prevented from coming by a last-minute news event or assignment, or maybe they just plain forgot. Don't ever get mad at these reporters. They may still be able to do a story. So get them the press packet as soon as possible. Drop it off at the reception desk where they work, making sure their name is clearly marked on it. Call an hour or so later to be sure they received it. If the reporter's office is far away or in an inconvenient location, at least fax your statement to him.

Finally, remain available for the rest of the day. As reporters sit down to write their stories they may think of questions, become confused about something you said, or wish to get your reaction to a comment from a liberal who disparaged your study. Stay by your phone. You don't want a story killed by an editor because the reporter couldn't nail down a fact or get you to comment on a particular point.

Section Four:
Teaching Conservatives How to Use the Media

Teaching conservatives in your community how to publicize their views will help get more conservative views into the news. You are already doing this with the media bias topic through your new organization and newsletter. But you can also network with other conservatives, help them get press and draw attention to the conservative message. Share with other conservatives what you've learned from this book and through hands-on experience.

Learn who the good local conservative spokesmen are on particular issues. Take down their telephone number, tell them you'll steer reporters to them on their issue of interest. They'll probably offer to do the same for you. This is all part of your goal to promote conservative views to the media. But always remember to be careful about who you refer. Make sure they can talk in soundbites for TV or radio and can express their thoughts clearly and succinctly for a newspaper reporter.

If there is no recognized spokesman on a particular issue, say a wacky new multicultural curriculum, create one. There's probably someone who is interested in the issue, a concerned parent or teacher, and you can turn him into a spokesperson. Give him articles by conservatives you have clipped on multiculturalism. Familiarize him with the arguments. Then begin referring the media to your new spokesperson. Or, a conservative professor at a local college may already be a multiculturalism expert, but reporters don't know about him. So, all you have to do is start referring reporters to him and you will have created another conservative source for the media.

Encourage these conservatives to make their own media contacts and include them in some of your media events if possible. One of the most important objectives for conservatives is to work together, form our own informal communication networks, and help each other become more effective.

You may also want to include conservative elected officials in your network. Invite your Congressman, local state representative, or even a well-known local businessman who wants to get involved to your press conferences or events. Many of these people attract reporters so they can lend you some press attention and credibility. If you hold a press conference to release a study showing that reporting tilted against the term limit ballot question, ask the leaders of the term limit fight to attend. They may be the only ones reporters end up quoting in news stories, but they will increase the likelihood that your study will be covered.

It is important to note that you personally can act as a referral source for reporters, steering them to conservative spokesmen, and suggesting stories. But your media bias organization should remain committed to its one and only goal: identifying and publicizing media bias. The group should not be taking part in press conferences on taxes, unless of course there is an instance of media bias for you to talk about.

Teach conservatives how to emphasize what is newsworthy, which is not necessarily the same as the conservative message. For example, a single businessman who opposes an increase in the meter fee for parking spaces near his downtown store may not be considered newsworthy. It's just another businessman opposed to a fee or tax increase. There is nothing novel to it.

Talk to the leaders of the Chamber of Commerce about putting out a press release or organizing a press conference of all the major merchants. If they aren't interested, advise the businessman to form an ad-hoc group of local store owners. Tell him to talk about the economic impact on the community, how it will drive potential customers to the mall outside of town, thus forcing the downtown stores to lay off employees. Ideally, you'd get a local university professor or polling firm to conduct a survey which would, hopefully, show that the meter increase would make most shoppers more likely to shop elsewhere.

As a conservative, an added attraction to this story is that the poll and the opposition of businessmen demonstrates the conservative point that taxes/regulations can affect business negatively. You should suggest that the business group emphasize that it could cost the city more in less tax revenue or lost business income in the long run. When you put out a press release, you are trying to "sell" a news story to a journalist who is probably a liberal, but who is nevertheless interested in (what he considers) real news. They may dislike a story with just a conservative message, but very few reporters are so liberal that they are uninterested in a good story.

Getting media jobs for conservatives

Use your media contacts to help get media jobs for conservatives. You probably know some young conservatives who are attending high school or college or who have recently graduated from a university.

Just like any employer, media outlets are always looking for good, hard working employees. Help them fill their needs. The media contacts you've made may not be in charge of hiring, but they can certainly recommend people to those who are responsible. Your goal should be to get internships and full-time jobs for qualified conservatives.

Internships. Most newspapers and radio and television stations have an intern program. A larger outlet may offer a stipend or hourly wage for interns. Obtaining one of these internships is usually very competitive with a formal application process. A smaller station or newspaper may not be able to afford to pay interns, but will gladly provide an internship opportunity to anyone interested enough to inquire. Of course, they can only take on so many interns at a time.

Determine the internship situation at all your local media outlets, including the names of those who make the decision and whether high school students, or just college students, are accepted. Let all your colleagues know about the opportunities and ask them to inform conservative students of the opportunities. Contact the conservative clubs at your local universities. Don't forget about local students away at college but who will be home for the summer.

Professional journalists are always more impressed with students who show enthusiasm for being a journalist, so encourage students to join the staff of the college newspaper, radio station or if it has one, the college television station. Or, if their college has an alternative conservative newspaper, encourage them to volunteer to help produce it. (See Appendix 1 for information on the Madison Center and Leadership Institute, which both offer seminars for students interested in producing a conservative paper.)

If some or all local outlets can't afford to pay interns, consider sponsoring one or two. Talk to businessmen or your foundation donors about putting up the money. If a bright young student needs to make money during the school year or summer, don't make him choose the supermarket grocery bagging or pizza delivery job. Let an internship be a possibility. At the end of his time with the media outlet he'll have earned media experience and made many contacts. When he graduates from college, he'll have made connections that he can use to obtain a media job.

Think of it this way: That investment you made in an intern two years ago may mean that a newspaper or television station now has a conservative reporter or producer on staff in a position to influence news content. Isn't that worth the investment in a young person?

Full-time jobs. Start passing along the resumes of college graduates to your media contacts. Few media outlets deliberately hire liberals. Almost all try to hire the best people they come across, but since liberals seem drawn to journalism while conservatives favor other fields, their hiring skews left. Give them a chance to change things. Don't portray those you recommend as conservatives dedicated to promoting right wing views. That will only scare off potential employers. Emphasize how they are smart, eager college graduates interested in a journalism career. They just happen to be conservative, just as liberal journalists just happen to be liberal.

If an outlet fails to hire one person you recommend, don't automatically make accusations of bias against conservatives. There may have been a more qualified or experienced applicant. If after a few years you find that a specific media outlet repeatedly fails to hire otherwise qualified conservatives, then raise the issue with the Editor, Publisher or News Director.

And if that doesn't change the situation, put the outlet on the defense by writing about it in your newsletter. Pressure from liberal groups has been successful in getting media outlets to set hiring goals for women and certain minorities. As a conservative, you don't believe in quotas, but if embarrassing a media outlet leads them to hire conservatives, then take advantage of the opportunity. On the other hand, if a newspaper, radio station or television operation stands out for trying to balance out the newsroom by hiring conservatives, praise them.

Section Five:
Organizing Seminars and Debates

Another way to bring attention to your cause is by holding a seminar on liberal bias in the media. Why hold a seminar? It's a good opportunity to make contacts with people you and your organization want to work with in the community like businessmen, politicians, and journalists. You may also bring out potential supporters and donors who are interested in media bias and would like to get involved. It can also be newsworthy, especially if you have prominent officials addressing a significant number of attendees from your community.

A seminar with you as the organizer and moderator would also increase your foundation's recognition in the community, and increase your organization's visibility in local politics. This is a circular process where the more important and influential you appear, the more you will truly become influential.

Your seminar or conference will also show the invited journalists who and how many people are concerned about media bias. Bias will become a bigger issue as you push it to the top of the local agenda. The journalists will also get to hear from regular people -- readers, listeners and viewers – about bias.

You'll also be establishing two-way communication. Once an editor or news director sees that your group is serious and reasonable, he will be more likely to read your next press release, send a reporter to your next news conference, and read the next edition of your newsletter. In short, a conference is another way to establish your organization's credibility with the media.

At first, you may not have the time or money to organize a major event. And you might have some trouble getting enough panelists. So, start by having a journalist address a group over a catered lunch, followed by a question and answer session. Hotels can best provide a big room with a meal, all for a pre-determined price.

Topics and participants. After a successful first luncheon, graduate to a larger conference running all day, or for an afternoon or morning with a number of speakers and discussion sessions. There could be panels discussing different topics like "The Media and Environmental Issues" or "Bias in Political Reporting" or "The Media and the Myth of

Heterosexual AIDS." After a major controversial event that may have generated charges of bias from various interest groups, such as a prolonged legislative debate over state aid for schools, put together a panel to discuss media coverage. Such a panel could include a conservative legislator, talk show host, newspaper editor or reporter and/or a broadcast producer or reporter. You could even balance the panel with a liberal politician or teacher's union representative. Such a balanced panel would encourage participation from members of the media and though it would give a platform to your political opponents, as moderator you would still control the direction of the discussion.

Try to set up a debate between a conservative radio talk show host or columnist and a liberal journalist, talk show host or columnist on media bias. The Conservative Political Action Conference features an annual debate between ABC News' Sam Donaldson and conservative columnist Robert Novak about liberal bias in the media. It's always the best attended event on the schedule. Construct a similar debate using local participants.

A journalism professor, politician or conservative commentator could debate a liberal in the media. Most people would be honored to participate on such a panel, so it shouldn't be too hard to get conservative participants. But beware -- it will be hard to get a liberal to join a panel if he thinks he's walking into a lion's den. If you can line up a credible, well-known conservative, liberal columnists or editors may be more willing to take part. They may not want to pass up a chance to debate a conservative columnist or Congressman.

Also use your contacts: maybe ask a local media figure, someone who you have established a relationship with, to convince a liberal to take part in a debate. Have the conservative stress how it may be fun. If you get at least some well-known people to serve on these panels, and know sparks may fly during the discussions or debates, it will make it easier to sell the conference to the media as newsworthy.

Where to hold. Your conference can be held at a local hotel or nearby college that has a conference room. There might be a fee for the room. Don't forget to arrange for tables, a podium and microphones to be provided.

How to publicize. Promote the seminar the same way you'd promote a press conference. Send media advisories to your media contact list announcing the conference. Do your two follow-up phone calls, always pushing the newsworthy angle of the conference. Have media kits ready, with the latest edition of your newsletter, a schedule of events, and short biographies of the panelists and speakers. If any of the panelists plan to make a brief opening statement, try to get some of those typed up ahead of time and include them in the press kit. Just as with press conferences, you want to make it as easy as possible for the reporters to write articles or local TV news outlets to do pieces on your conference. Check to make sure all the reporters' needs are met.

Don't forget to monitor how the conference is covered in the media. Learn from how it "plays." If you don't think it got enough attention, maybe you didn't push it enough. It's possible you sold an angle that wasn't exactly newsworthy. Learn from your mistakes and do better next time.

CORRECT ✔

Section Six:
Using Advertiser Pressure

Boycotts are the last move to be made when protesting bias. It is a burn-your-bridges action when you have received only hostile responses from officials of the newspaper, radio station, or TV station. If all else has failed, and there is no hope for future agreement, you may want to launch a boycott.

For a boycott to have a chance of success, there must be a large and dedicated group of people willing to take part. Many may not be willing for business or personal reasons. For instance, there may be one local newspaper. A businessman who advertises in the biased newspaper might feel he has no where else to go with his advertising dollars or a politician may not want to join in, feeling he shouldn't anger one of his communication lines to the public. These real complications must be anticipated and weighed by those contemplating a boycott.

Don't attempt a boycott if you don't have some support in the community. You must have the full support of friends and associates and they must be prepared to take part in the boycott. You're staking your reputation on this boycott. If it is not successful, you'll be seen as powerless.

In this section you'll learn:

● The steps to take before launching a boycott, steps that may effect the results you want without ever implementing a boycott

● Who you must convince to be part of your advertiser boycott to make it work

● How to develop a press strategy to maximize publicity

● Picketing businesses which don't pull their advertising from a biased media outlet

Steps before a boycott. Before seriously considering a boycott, first exhaust other avenues of pressure you can bring on the offending media outlet. Talk to some local sympathetic businessmen who advertise on the biased station or in the biased publication. Discuss your concerns with them and stress how they can help, how they can make a difference. Have them call the advertising director and complain about the coverage.

If the advertising director offers no help or is powerless to push for change, have them go up the chain of command. Ask for a meeting with the editor or news director. The more advertisers involved the better. Get several to draft a group letter to the person responsible for the financial health of the company -- the newspaper publisher, or radio or television station general manager.

In small towns, local businessmen may know the publisher of the newspaper or owner of the radio station. They may belong to the same country club or civic organization. Try to convince the local businessman to intercede with the owner to correct the biased reporting. Have them suggest a group meeting among the publisher, editor, businessmen, and yourself. Bring examples of the offending bias, discuss why it is wrong. Show the publisher or editor that you have a reasonable goal: improving the coverage of the conservative take on issues/eliminating the liberal bias. Remain positive, stressing you know they can improve. You'll almost always get better results this way. But if a media outlet absolutely refuses to mend its ways, has refused to meet with your organization, and totally ignores you, consider moving to the actual boycott.

Implementing a boycott. Even the threat of a well-organized boycott can be very effective. Fearful of protests by homosexuals, HBO whitewashed its movie version of *And the Band Played On*. The Randy Shilts book on the history of the AIDS epidemic contained criticism of the gay community's promiscuous sex and drug use, which were contributing factors to the spread of AIDS. These scenes were left out of the movie. HBO also allowed 17 AIDS and gay groups to screen the movie for their approval, lest they were antagonized by the final product.

There are two types of boycotts:

➤ **Subscription boycott.** Nothing gets the attention of a newspaper like large numbers of people canceling their subscriptions. Not only do newspapers lose the revenue from subscriptions, but -- because they base their advertising rates on the number of readers -- they lose advertising revenue as well.

➤ Advertiser boycott. Another type of boycott goes to advertisers directly. They stop placing ads with the offending publication or station. Whereas subscription boycotts apply only to newspapers, advertiser boycotts hit both print and broadcast media. Most newspapers get a large portion of their revenue from advertising, and radio and TV stations get virtually all their revenue from advertising. So pressure from advertisers can be very effective, especially so in smaller markets. If a large advertiser refuses to pull his ads, then you can bring pressure on him by organizing a boycott of his stores or service.

Many of the papers and radio stations in small towns rely heavily on the advertising money from small shop owners and local businessmen. They may not have many advertisers, so if one business pulls its ads from the paper or radio station, the outlet may be losing 1 to 2 percent of its advertising. You can bet they'll be interested in what they can do to get back those ad dollars. For these reasons, organizing an advertiser boycott in a small market may be particularly effective. But as mentioned earlier, it may be difficult to recruit advertisers in the fight: you may have to push some of them into it.

Organizing a boycott, step one. The first step in organizing a boycott is to identify the sector of the public most affected by the bias -- church groups if the bias is against religion, business groups if the bias is against free enterprise, etc. Contact key leaders among those groups and recruit them to your effort. You'll need these people to help pull the boycott off.

Review your tapes of the TV or radio station broadcasts to determine the names of local advertisers on the station. For a newspaper or magazine, flip through the pages for a few days and write down the names of all regular advertisers. Call and set up a meeting with the advertisers. Bring a businessman who has already agreed to join the boycott to the meeting. A fellow businessman may be more persuasive than you. At the meetings, layout the reasons for the boycott, bring examples of the offending pieces (transcripts of radio or TV stories, or photocopies of newspaper articles), and list your goals while pointing out how reasonable they are. Leave your materials with the business owners, telling them you will be back in two to three days for a decision.

Step Two. Next, hold a press conference to announce the boycott. An advertiser boycott is a high-profile undertaking so you want as much news coverage as possible. Get as many advertisers as possible who have agreed to join your boycott to attend. As with any press conference, you'll need to send out a media advisory to the names on your media contact list. In your advisory, you want to spell out your reasons for the boycott, who will be taking part in it, and the specific goals of the boycott. Emphasize that you want balanced coverage of the topic in question, not a rightward tilt. Then pass along the usual directions to and time of the press conference.

Before the conference, make your follow-up calls to the journalists who received your advisory. Play up the newsworthiness of the conference. While some in the press may be happy to cover a competing outlet in controversy others will be uneasy about attending. After all you are attacking another media outlet. Sell the conflict angle to them: your small group against the powerful town newspaper or TV station. Repeat your goals, and point out how reasonable they are.

Make sure you have appointed one spokesman, maybe yourself, to make the statement at the press conference. The spokesman should be familiar with the examples of bias that led to the boycott and the measures to be taken during the boycott. He should also anticipate all the questions that will come from the media, and rehearse answers to them. It's important to keep the same spokesman for the whole boycott. Replacing the spokesman, for whatever reason, would give the press reason to speculate, however untrue it may be, on the possible failure of the boycott.

Press conference. As usual, if you plan to hold your press conference in a public place, check with the local police department if you need to get permits. Also set up a podium, a sound system, and a mult box so the press can plug their microphones directly into the sound system. Have your organizational logo hanging on the podium or wall behind you, so it will get into the camera shots.

At the press conference, put together a packet you can distribute to the press consisting of the text of your statement, examples of bias that caused you to boycott, a chronology of your contacts with the media outlet and their hostile responses. In your statement, you'll want to repeat your reasons for the boycott, your goal, and what you will do to reach your goal. Make sure you announce some sort of action -- a picket of the outlet or that you will be contacting advertisers to withhold their advertising dollars from the outlet.

If your boycott is toothless, the media will know it and that's the end of coverage of the boycott. That's why you should be prepared to announce some accomplishments at the press conference -- such as how many subscriptions you have already caused to be cancelled or the names of specific merchants who have decided to pull their advertising. Pass out copies of the letters each merchant sent to the media outlet explaining why he has joined the advertising boycott. Make sure all the conservatives in the local media, such as columnists and talk show hosts, get a press kit.

After the announcement, check back with advertisers who had yet to decide whether to join to see if they've made a decision. If one agrees to pull his advertising from the station until it reforms, thank him. Then tell him you'll encourage your supporters to do business with him. Praise him in your newsletter. Use his agreement to take part in the boycott as an example with the smaller advertisers. Hopefully, once they see the big advertiser boycotting, they'll be more agreeable to take part. And make sure to alert all the reporters who attended your press conference (as well as your conservative friends in the media) about the latest addition to your boycott effort.

Organizing a picket line. If the business owner refuses to pull his advertising, tell him you'll have to consider picketing and boycotting his store. Whether you do or not will depend upon the dynamics of your boycott efforts. You only want to boycott the stores frequented by your supporters so that its lost business will have an impact. It may take a while for the picketing and boycott to have its effect. But if you stay with it, it could be quite successful. A picket line in front of the offending media outlet is also very good way to generate publicity.

When organizing a picket, first check with the police to get the necessary permits. Then gather a group, go out once a week for one or two hours in front of the business, newspaper, or broadcast station. Picket during heavy traffic hours for high visibility, alerting the media to your appearance. Send out a media advisory with the details a few days ahead of the picket. Make the usual follow-up calls selling the picket for its conflict value. Picketing in front of the media outlet will provide a nice video backdrop which will help attract television coverage.

Have your spokesman at the picket site to answer any media questions. Your picket signs should show simple, catchy phrases that convey the reasonableness of your goals. Phrases like: "All We Ask for Is the Truth" or "We Want Balance Not Bias" and "No More Bias From Channel 4." After you are done, pack up and announce your intentions to return in a few days or the next week.

Remember, you are picketing to bring attention to your cause, embarrass the business owner into pulling his advertising, and to convince other business owners that you are serious and they should join up to avoid a similar fate. You are not picketing to interfere with people walking into the business. Don't block the door or shout at the customers. This tactic is bound to bring bad press and turn off some potential supporters, not to mention get you arrested. Such a strategy is acceptable to some who are dealing with life-or-death issues like abortion, but would be seen as overkill when you are protesting media bias.

Eventually, a boycott will work. People do not like getting continual bad press. There are plenty of examples of boycott success: In Dallas, Dr. Richard Neill has had great success with an advertiser boycott against the syndicated TV talk show *Donahue*. The American Family Association successfully got Southland Corporation, parent company of 7-11 convenience stores, to stop selling *Playboy* and *Penthouse* magazines at their stores after a three year effort of picketing, bad press, and a letter-writing campaign to Southland's chairman of the board.

Conservative Resources

The Expose and Correct chapters discussed how you should provide conservative arguments and data to talk show hosts, ombudsmen, reporters and editors. In addition, you may need to find the best argument and statistics to use in calls to talk shows, letters to the editor and meetings with members of the media. There are many conservative magazines and research foundations which can help provide the information you need.

This appendix includes a list of:

- Conservative magazines and newspapers
- Guide books to conservative resources
- Conservative research and policy groups

Conservative magazines and newspapers:

These are the leading national conservative publications. Most will provide a complimentary sample copy if you send them a written request.

◆ *The American Spectator*
2020 N. 14th Street, Suite 750
Arlington, VA 22201
http://www.spectator.org

frequency: monthly
one-year subscription: $35

◆ *Chronicles*
The Rockford Institute
934 North Main Street
Rockford, IL 61103-7061

frequency: monthly
one-year subscription: $24

◆ *Commentary*
165 East 56th Street
New York, NY 10022

frequency: monthly
one-year subscription: $39

◆ *Conservative Chronicle*
P.O. Box 37077
Boone, IA 50441

frequency: weekly (a compilation of syndicated conservative
    columns)
one-year subscription: $45

◆ *Human Events*
422 First Street SE
Washington, D.C. 20003

frequency: weekly
one-year subscription: $49.95

◆ *National Review*
  150 East 35th Street
  New York, NY 10016

  http://www.nationalreview.com

  frequency: biweekly
  one-year subscription: $57

◆ *Policy Review*
  The Heritage Foundation
  214 Massachusetts Avenue NE
  Washington, D.C. 20002-4999

  http://www.heritage.org

  frequency: bi-monthly
  one-year subscription: $27

◆ *The Public Interest*
  1112 16th Street NW, Suite 530
  Washington, D.C. 20036

  frequency: quarterly
  one-year subscription: $25

◆ *Reason*
  3415 S. Sepulveda Boulevard, Suite 400
  Los Angeles, CA 90034

  frequency: monthly
  one-year subscription: $26

  http://www.reasonmag.com

◆ *Weekly Standard*
  1150 17th St. NW, Suite 505
  Washington, D.C. 20036

  frequency: weekly
  one-year subscription: $79.96

Guides to conservative organizations and resources:

In addition to the guidebooks below, these two Web sites offer conservative policy information and links to conservative groups:

◆ Town Hall: *http://www.townhall.com*
◆ The Right Side of the Web: *http://www.rtside.com/rtside/*

◆ *The Annual Guide to Public Policy Experts*
Heritage Foundation   (http://www.heritage.org)
214 Massachusetts Ave. NE
Washington, D.C. 20002
(202) 546-4400

Softcover 420-page listing of conservative experts in 12 broad categories and 77 sub-categories. Each name also listed alphabetically and by region of the country. $14.95, plus $3.50 shipping and handling.

◆ *The National Review Politically Incorrect Reference Guide*
National Review   (http://www.nationalreview.com)
150 East 35th Street
New York, NY 10016
(212) 679-7330

Softcover 320-page guide to conservative sources arranged under hundreds of topics and divided into two sections, "Books and Articles" and "Organizations." $19.95, plus $3.00 shipping and handling.

◆ *The Right Guide*
Economics America, Inc.
612 Church Street
Ann Arbor, MI 48104
(313) 995-0865

A hardcover 444-page comprehensive guide to conservative organizations. Features include indexes of keywords and subjects, a profile section with a detailed abstract of over 500 organizations, and a features section with more expansive information on over 30 groups. $49.95, including shipping and handling.

Conservative foundations and policy groups

The following list includes the best-known conservative organizations, but it is by no means a complete list. (See the previous page for guides to conservative groups and resources.) Contact these organizations to obtain studies, position papers or other help on conservative issues within their interest areas. For a small donation, most will add you to their newsletter mailing list and alert you to new research papers. Some run as membership organizations, providing various benefits depending upon the level of your annual contribution.

If you have a specific question or want to learn the conservative arguments on a particular issue, call during daytime hours and explain what you need. Many have Web sites packed with valuable information, or at least a guide to their projects and publications.

◆ Accuracy in Media
4455 Connecticut Ave. NW, Suite 330
Washington, DC 20008
Phone: (202) 364-4401
Fax: (202) 364-4098
http://www.aim.org

Area of interest: document and expose liberal media bias
Research/publications: monthly newsletter *AIM Report*

◆ American Defense Institute
1055 N. Fairfax Street, Suite 200
Alexandria, VA 22314
Phone: (703) 519-7000
Fax: (703) 519-8627

Area of interest: maintenance of a strong national defense
Research/publications: monthly newsletter *ADI Briefing*

◆ American Enterprise Institute for Public Policy Research
1150 17th Street NW
Washington, DC 20036
Phone: (202) 862-5800

Fax: (202) 862-7177

http://www.aei.org

Areas of interest: limited government, private enterprise, national defense
Research/publications: bimonthly magazine *The American Enterprise*

◆ American Family Association
P.O. Drawer 2440
Tupelo, Mississippi 38803
Phone: (601) 844-5036
Fax: (601) 844-9176

http://www.gocin.com

Area of interest: Christian organization emphasizing the Biblical ethic of decency in American society, focusing primarily on TV and other media
Research/publications: monthly *AFA Journal*

◆ Americans for Tax Reform
1320 18th St. NW, Suite 200
Washington, D.C. 20036

http://www.atr.org

Areas of interest: Advocate anti-tax pledge by presidential candidates. Work for a flat tax.

Research/publications: monthly *American Tax Reformer* and *Tax Reform News*

◆ Capital Research Center
727 15th St. NW, Suite 800
Washington, D.C. 20005

http://www.capitalresearch.org

Areas of interest: Tracking the agenda and funding sources of "public interest" and advocacy groups

Research/publications: monthly newsletters *Organization Trends, Foundation Watch* and *Culture Watch*. Also, publish annually the book *Patterns of Corporate Philanthropy*

◆ Cato Institute
1000 Massachusetts Avenue NW

Washington, D.C. 20001
Phone: (202) 842-0200
Fax: (202) 842-3490

http://www.cato.org

Areas of interest: free enterprise, individual rights
Research/publications: *Cato Policy Report* newsletter, *Cato Journal* and *Regulation* magazines in addition to regular Policy Analysis reports, studies and books

◆ Center for Security Policy
1250 24th Street NW, Suite 350
Washington, DC 20037
Phone: (202) 466-0515
Fax: (202) 466-0518

http://www.security.policy.org

Area of interest: national security
Research/publications: papers, press releases

◆ Center for the Study of Popular Culture
P.O. Box 67398
Los Angeles, CA 90067
Phone: (310) 843-3699
Fax: (310) 843-3692

http://www.cspc.org

Areas of interest: study of popular culture and television, especially PBS; track political correctness in culture and academia
Research/publications: *Comint*, a quarterly journal about public media and *Heterodoxy*, a monthly tabloid

◆ Christian Action Network
P.O. Box 606
Forest, VA 24551
Phone: (804) 385-5156
Fax: (804) 385-0115

Area of interest: pro-family Christian values
Research/publications: monthly newsletter *Family Alert*

◆ Christian Coalition
1801-L Sara Drive

Chesapeake, VA 23320
Phone: (804) 424-2630
Fax: (804) 424-9068

http://www.cc.org

Area of interest: restoring American greatness through a return
   to moral strength
Research/publications: the *Christian American* newspaper
   and *Religious Rights Watch* newsletter

◆ Citizens Against Government Waste
1301 Connecticut Ave. NW, Suite 400
Washington, D.C. 20036
Phone (202)467-5300
Fax: (202) 467-4253

http://www.govt-waste.org

Areas of interest: promoting the elimination of government
   waste
Research/publications: *Government Waste Watch*, a quarterly
   newspaper

◆ Citizens for a Sound Economy
1250 H Street NW, Suite 700
Washington, DC 20005
Phone: (202) 783-3870
Fax: (202) 783-4687

http://www.cse.org

Areas of interest: trade, privatization, and fiscal policy
Research/publications: policy papers *Issue Alert* and *Capitol
   Comment*, monthly special reports, quarterly *CSE Reports*

◆ Competitive Enterprise Institute
1001 Connecticut Avenue NW, Suite 1250
Washington, DC 20036
Phone: (202) 331-1010
Fax: (202) 331-0640

http://www.cei.org

Areas of interest: deregulation, free trade, antitrust law, free-
   market environmentalism, tax reform
Research/publications: monthly newsletter *CEI Update*, quarterly *Washington Anti-Trust Report* as well as reports
   and an index of congressional voting records

◆ Concerned Women for America
370 L'Enfant Promenade SW, Suite 800
Washington, DC 20024
Phone: (202) 488-7000
Fax: (202) 488-0806
http://www.cwfa.org

Areas of interest: protecting the family and preserving traditional values
Research/publications: Concerned Women for America newsletter, *Family Voice* magazine

◆ Eagle Forum Education and Legal Defense Fund
P.O. Box 618
Alton, IL 62002
Phone: (618) 462-5415
Fax: (618) 462-8909
http://www.eagleforum.org

Area of interest: family, feminism, taxes, education, defense
Research/publications: books and periodic reports

◆ Family Research Council
700 13th Street NW, Suite 500
Washington, DC 20005
Phone: (202) 393-2100
Fax: (202) 393-2134
www.frc.org

Areas of interest: traditional family values, social policy
Research/publications: newsletters *Washington Watch* and *Family Policy* as well as press releases

◆ Federalist Society
1700 K St. NW, Suite 901
Washington, D.C. 20006
http://www.fed-soc.org

Areas of interest: dedicated to bringing conservative and libertarian ideas into law schools and the organized bar

Research/publications: quarterly journal and monthly newsletter

◆ Focus on the Family
Bank Building
Explorer Drive
Colorado Springs, CO 80995
Phone: (719) 531-3400
Fax: (719) 548-4670

Area of interest: the stability of the family in society
Research/publications: *Focus on the Family* magazine, news-
letters *Focus on the Family Physician, Parental Guidance,
Citizen*, and *Teachers in Focus*

◆ Foundation for Research on Economics and the Environment
945 Technology Blvd., Suite 101F
Bozeman, MT 59715
Phone: (406) 585-1776
Fax: (406)585-3000

http://www.free-eco.org

Area of interest: to foster free and responsible people in their
relations with the environment
Research/publications: newsletter *FREE Perspectives*

◆ Free Congress Foundation
717 2nd Street NE
Washington, DC 20002
Phone: (202) 546-3000
Fax: (202) 543-8425

http://www.fcref.org

Area of interest: empowering citizens to advance values of
private property, free enterprise, and limited government
Research/publications: *Policy Insights* and *Essays on Our Times*

◆ Freedom Alliance
45472 Holiday Drive, Suite 10
Sterling, VA 20166
Phone: (703) 709-6620
Fax: (703) 709-6615

Area of interest: educational foundation concerned with family, defense and free enterprise issues
Research/publications: monthly newsletter *The Free American*

◆ Heritage Foundation
214 Massachusetts Avenue NE
Washington, DC 20002
Phone: (202) 546-4400
Fax: (202) 546-8328

http://www.heritage.org

Area of interest: research institute devoted to free enterprise,
limited government, liberty, and strong national defense
Research/publications: quarterly magazine *Policy Review,*
newsletter *The SDI Report,* as well as books, frequent Backgrounder and other research reports, and briefing audio
tapes

◆ High Frontier
2800 Shirlington Road, #405A
Arlington, VA 22206
Phone: (703) 671-4111
Fax: (703) 931-6432

Areas of interest: promotion of strategic defense issues, space,
and commercialization of space
Research/publications: monthly newsletter *Newswatch*

◆ Hudson Institute
Herman Kahn Center
5395 Emerson Way
P.O. Box 26-919
Indianapolis, IN 46226
Phone: (317) 545-1000
Fax: (317) 545-9636

http://www.hudson.org

Areas of interest: education, health care, welfare, national se-
curity
Research/publications: newsletters *Hudson Opinion* and
Hudson Communique, as well as articles, papers, and books

◆ The Leadership Institute
1101 N. Highland St.
Arlington, VA 22201
Phone: (703) 247-2000
Fax: (703) 247-2001

http://www.lead-inst.org

Areas of interest: training conservative activists, helps start student newspapers, helps prepare for the foreign service exam, helps with jobs and internships on Capitol Hill
Research/publications: quarterly *Building Leadership*

◆ Madison Center for Educational Affairs
1015 18th Street NW, Suite 200
Washington, DC 20036
Phone: (202)835-3870
Fax: (202)775-0857

Area of interest: aids conservative students in publishing alternative newspapers through its Collegiate Network and the European Journalism Network; preparing students for careers in journalism

Research/publications: *Diversity & Division* (quarterly), *Precis* (quarterly), *The Common Sense Guide to American Colleges* (annual)

◆ Media Research Center
113 South West St., Second floor
Alexandria, VA 22314
Phone: (703) 683-9733
Fax: (703) 683-9736
http://www.mediaresearch.org

Area of interest: Bringing balance to the media by documenting and distributing evidence of the media's liberal bias
Research/publications. Four newsletters: *MediaWatch*, a monthly which reviews news coverage of political and current events; *Notable Quotables*, a bi-weekly compilation of the latest outrageous quotes in the liberal media; *Media-Nomics*, a monthly which examines national news coverage of busness and economic issues; *Flash*, a monthly report to MRC members. Also, the books *And That's the Way It Isn't*, a collection of 45 studies proving the media's liberal tilt; and *Pattern of Deception: The Media's Role in the Clinton Presidency*

◆ National Center for Policy Analysis
12655 N. Central Expressway Suite 720
Dallas, TX 75243
Phone: (972) 386-6272

Fax: (972) 386-0924

http://www.public-policy.org

Areas of interest: health care, social security, fiscal policy, and environmental issues

Research/publications: monthly newsletter *Executive Alert*, opinion pieces, frequent "backgrounder" policy reports, and co-publication of books

◆ National Center for Public Policy Research
300 Eye Street NE, Suite 3
Washington, DC 20002
Phone: (202) 543-1286
Fax: (202) 543-4779

http://www.nationalcenter.inter.net

Area of interest: promotion of grassroots conservative activism

Research/publications: newsletter *National Policy Watch*, Technology Series (manuals), National Policy Analysis (papers), Memorandums, Talking Points, Factfiles, others

◆ National Rifle Association of America
11250 Waples Mill Rd.
Fairfax, VA 22030
Phone: (703) 267-1000
Fax: (703) 267-3957

http://www.nra.org

Areas of interest: combatting gun control, firearm training, promotion of hunting safety

Research/publications: *American Rifleman*, *American Hunter* and *The Badge* magazines, other publications and films

◆ National Right to Life Committee
419 7th Street NW, Suite 500
Washington, DC 20004
Phone: (202) 626-8800
Fax: (202) 737-9189

http://www.nrlc.org

Area of interest: abortion, infanticide, and euthanasia

Research/publications: biweekly *National Right to Life News*, books, pamphlets, brochures, tapes and videos

◆ National Right to Work Committee
8001 Braddock Road, Suite 600
Springfield, VA 22160
Phone: (703) 321-9820
Fax: (703) 321-7342

http://www.nrtw.org

Area of interest: promoting the idea that all employees have
the right not to be compelled to join a union
Research/publications: quarterly *Insider Report*, monthly
Right to Work Newsletter

◆ National Taxpayers Union
108 North Alfred St.
Alexandria, VA 22314
Phone: (703) 683-5700
Fax: (703) 683-5722

http://www.ntu.org

Area of interest: lower taxes, less government spending, taxpayer rights
Research/publications: *Dollars and Sense, Tax Savings Report*,
brochures, monographs, and newsletters

◆ Pacific Legal Foundation
2151 River Plaza Drive, Suite 305
Sacramento, CA 95833
Phone: (916) 641-8888
Fax: (916) 920-3444

Area of interest: public interest law in defense of individual
and economic freedoms

◆ Political Economy Research Center
502 S. 19th Avenue, Suite 211
Bozeman, MT 59718
Phone: (406) 587-9591
Fax: (406) 586-7555

http://www.perc.org

Area of interest: applying free market economics to environ-
mental and natural resource issues
Research/publications: newsletters *PERC Reports, PERC
Viewpoints*

◆ U.S. Term Limits
1511 K Street NW #540
Washington, DC 20005
Phone: (202) 393-6440
Fax: (202) 393-6434

Area of interest: making Congress responsible for the laws they
pass through term limits
Research/publications: bi-monthly newsletters *Outlook* and
No Uncertain Terms

◆ Young America's Foundation
110 Elden Street
Herndon, VA 20170
Phone: (703) 318-9608
Fax: (703) 318-9122

http://www.yaf.org

Area of interest: strengthening conservative activism on cam-
pus through lectures, texts, conferences and scholarships
Research/publications: quarterly *Libertas*, monthly *Campus
Leader* and *Continuity*

News Media Addresses

To find the correct address to use when writing letters to reporters, editors, producers and executives of major news media outlets, use this appendix. Staff positions at media outlets are constantly changing, so we've not listed any names. Many media outlets now have Web sites and e-mail addresses that you can use to share your comments. Usually, newspapers list these somewhere on the editorial page.

This appendix lists the mail and Web site addresses for:

■ Major news magazines and their Washington bureaus

■ Washington bureaus of major newspaper chains

■ Wire services

■ The broadcast networks, CNN and MSNBC

Major News Magazines

Newsweek
251 West 57th St.
New York, NY 10019

Washington bureau:
1750 Pennsylvania Ave. NW, Suite 1220
Washington, D.C. 20006

Newsweek has an area on America Online

Time
Time & Life Building
Rockefeller Center
New York, NY 10020

http://allpolitics.com

http://time.com

Time also has an area on CompuServe

Washington bureau:
1050 Connecticut Ave. NW, Suite 850
Washington, D.C. 20036

U.S. News & World Report
2400 N St. NW
Washington, D.C. 20037

http://www.usnews.com

Major Newspapers

Arizona Republic
200 E. Van Buren Street
Phoenix, AZ 85004

http://www.azcentral.com

Washington bureau:
1000 National Press Building
Washington, D.C. 20045

Atlanta Journal-Constitution
72 Marietta Street, NW
Atlanta, GA 30303

http://www.ajc.com

Washington bureau:
see Cox Newspapers in next section

Baltimore *Sun*
501 N. Calvert Street
Baltimore, MD 21278

http://www.sunspot.net

Washington bureau:
1627 K Street NW, Suite 1100
Washington, D.C. 20006

The Boston Globe
P.O. Box 2378
Boston, MA 02107

http://www.boston.com/globe

Washington bureau:
1130 Connecticut Avenue NW
Washington, D.C. 20036

The Boston Herald
One Herald Square
Boston, MA 02106

Washington bureau:
865 National Press Building
Washington, D.C. 20045

The Charlotte Observer
600 S. Tryon Street
Charlotte, NC 28202

http://www.charlotte.com

Washington bureau: See Knight-Ridder in next section

Chicago Sun-Times
401 N. Wabash Avenue
Chicago, IL 60611

http://www.suntimes.com

Washington bureau:
1112 National Press Building
Washington, D.C. 20045

Chicago Tribune
435 N. Michigan Avenue
Chicago, IL 60611

http://www.chicago.tribune.com

Washington bureau:
1325 G St. NW, Suite 200
Washington, D.C. 20005

Cleveland *Plain Dealer*
1801 Superior Avenue
Cleveland, Ohio 44114

http://www.rockhall.com

Washington bureau:
930 National Press Building
Washington, D.C. 20045

Daily Oklahoman
P.O. Box 25125
Oklahoma City, OK 73125

http://www.oklahoman.net

Washington bureau:
914 National Press Building
Washington, D.C. 20045

Dallas Morning News
P.O. Box 655237
Dallas, TX 75265

http://www.dallasnews.com

Washington bureau:
1012 National Press Building
Washington, D.C. 20045

Denver Post
1560 Broadway
Denver, CO 80202

http://www.denverpost.com

Washington bureau:
1270 National Press Building
Washington, D.C. 20045

Des Moines Register
715 Locust Street
P.O. Box 957
Des Moines, IA 50304

Washington bureau:
1300 I St. NW, Suite 1010 E
Washington, D.C. 20005

Detroit Free Press
321 W. Lafayette Boulevard
Detroit, MI 48231

http://www.freep.com

Washington bureau:
700 National Press Building
Washington, D.C. 20045

Detroit News
615 Lafayette Boulevard
Detroit, MI 48226

http://detnews.com

Washington bureau:
1148 National Press Building
Washington, D.C. 20045

Fort Worth *Star Telegram*
P.O. Box 1870
Fort Worth, TX 76101

http://www.startext.net

Washington bureau:
  1705 DeSales Street NW, Suite 400
  Washington, D.C. 20036

Houston Chronicle
801 Texas Ave.
Houston, TX 77002

www.chron.com

Washington bureau:
  1341 G Street NW, Suite 201
  Washington, D.C. 20005

Los Angeles Times
Times Mirror Square
Los Angeles, CA 90053

http://www.latimes.com

Washington bureau:
  1875 I Street NW, Suite 1100
  Washington, D.C. 20006

Miami Herald
1 Herald Plaza
Miami, FL 33101

http://www.herald.com

Washington bureau:
  see Knight-Ridder Newspapers in next section

The Milwaukee Journal
P.O. Box 661
Milwaukee, WI 53201

http://www.onwisc.com

Washington bureau:
  940 National Press Building
  Washington, D.C. 20045

Minneapolis *Star Tribune*
425 Portland Avenue
Minneapolis, MN 55488

http://www.startribune.com

Washington bureau:
1627 I Street NW
Washington, D.C. 20006

Newsday
235 Pinelawn Rd.
Melville, NY 11747

http://www.newsday.com

Washington bureau:
1730 Pennsylvania Avenue NW, Suite 850
Washington, D.C. 20006

The New York Times
229 West 43rd Street
New York, New York 10036

http://www.nytimes.com

Washington bureau:
1627 I Street NW, Suite 700
Washington, D.C. 20006

The Oregonian
1320 S.W. Broadway
Portland, OR 97201

http://www.oregonian.com

Washington bureau:
see Newhouse Newspapers

The Philadelphia Inquirer
400 N. Broad Street
Philadelphia, PA 19101

http://www.phillynews.com

Washington bureau:
see Knight-Ridder Newspapers

Pittsburgh Post-Gazette
  34 Boulevard of the Allies
  Pittsburgh, PA 15222

  Washington bureau:
    955 National Press Building
    Washington, D.C. 20045

Rocky Mountain News
  400 W. Colfax Avenue
  Denver, CO 80204

  http://www.denver-cmn.com

  Washington bureau:
    See Scripps Howard

St. Louis Post-Dispatch
  900 N. Tucker Boulevard
  St. Louis, MO 63101

  http://www.stlnet.com

  Washington bureau:
    1701 Pennsylvania Ave. NW, Suite 550
    Washington, D.C. 20006

San Diego Union-Tribune
  350 Camino de la Reina
  San Diego, CA 92108

  http://www.uniontrib.com

  Washington bureau:
    See Copley News Service

San Francisco Chronicle
  901 Mission Street
  San Francisco, CA 94103

  http://www.sfgate.com

  Washington bureau:
    1085 National Press Building
    Washington, D.C. 20045

San Francisco Examiner
  110 Fifth Street

San Francisco, CA 94103

http://www.sfgate.com/examiner

Washington bureau:
  see Hearst News Service in next section

San Jose Mercury News
  750 Ridder Park Drive
  San Jose, CA 95190

http://www.sjmercury.com

Washington bureau:
  see Knight-Ridder Newspapers in next section

Seattle Post-Intelligencer
  P.O. Box 1909
  Seattle, WA 98111

http://www.seattle-pi.com

Washington bureau:
  see Hearst News Service

Seattle Times
  P.O. Box 70
  Seattle, WA 98111

http://www.seattletimes.com

Washington bureau: Robert Nelson, Bureau Chief
  245 2nd Street NE
  Washington, D.C. 20002

USA Today
  1000 Wilson Boulevard
  Arlington, VA 22229

http://www.usatoday.com

The Wall Street Journal
  200 Liberty St.
  New York, New York 10281

http://wsj.com

Washington bureau:
1025 Connecticut Ave. NW, Suite 800
Washington, D.C. 20036

The Washington Post
1150 15th Street NW
Washington, D.C. 20071
http://www.washingtonpost.com

The Washington Times
3600 New York Ave. NE
Washington, D.C. 20002
http://www.washtimes.com
http://www.washtimes-weekly.com

Washington Bureaus

If you see an article with a Washington dateline written by a news service or Washington bureau of a newspaper chain, use this list to find the best address for corresponding with the reporter.

Copley News Service
1100 National Press Building
Washington, D.C. 20045

Cox Newspapers
2000 Pennsylvania Avenue NW, Suite 10,000
Washington, D.C. 20006

Gannett News Service
1000 Wilson Boulevard
Arlington, VA 22229

Hearst News Service
1701 Pennsylvania Avenue NW, Suite 610
Washington, D.C. 20006

Knight-Ridder Newspapers
700 National Press Building
Washington, D.C. 20045

Newhouse News Service
1101 Connecticut Avenue NW, Suite 300
Washington, D.C. 20036

Scripps Howard News Service
1090 Vermont Avenue NW, Suite 1000
Washington, D.C. 20005

Wire Services

Associated Press
50 Rockefeller Plaza
New York, New York 10020

Washington bureau
2021 K Street NW, Room 600
Washington, D.C. 20006

Knight-Ridder/Tribune Information Services
790 National Press Building
Washington, D.C. 20045

Los Angeles Times-Washington Post News Service
1150 15th Street NW
Washington, D.C. 20071

New York Times News Service
229 W. 43rd Street, Room 943
New York, NY 10036

Washington bureau:
1627 I St. NW
Washington, D.C. 20006

Reuters Information Services
1700 Broadway, 31st Floor
New York, New York 10019

Washington bureau:
1333 H Street NW, Suite 410
Washington, D.C. 20005

United Press International
1400 I Street NW, Suite 800
Washington, D.C. 20005

Television Network News and Public Affairs

ABC News
47 West 66th Street
New York, New York 10023
http://www.politicsnow.com

Washington bureau:
1717 DeSales Street NW
Washington, D.C. 20036

ABC News Radio
125 West End Avenue
New York, New York 10023
http://www.abcradionet.com

CBS News
524 West 57th Street
New York, New York 10019
www.cbsnews.com

Washington bureau:
2020 M Street NW
Washington, DC 20036

Cable News Network
P.O. Box 105366
One CNN Center
Atlanta, Georgia 30348
http://allpolitics.com
http://cnn.com

Washington bureau:
820 First Street NE, Suite 1100
Washington, DC 20002

New York bureau for CNN and CNNfn:
5 Penn Plaza, 20th Floor
New York, New York 10001

C-SPAN
400 North Capitol St. NW, Suite 650
Washington, D.C. 20001
http://www.c-span.org

Fox News/Fox News Channel
1211 Avenue of the Americas
New York, New York 10036
http://www.foxnews.com

Washington bureau:
400 North Capitol St. NW, Suite 550
Washington, D.C. 20001

MSNBC and CNBC
2200 Fletcher Ave.
Ft. Lee, NJ 20267
http://www.msnbc.com

NBC News
30 Rockefeller Plaza
New York, New York 10112
http://www.msnbc.com

Washington bureau for NBC News and MSNBC:
4001 Nebraska Avenue NW
Washington, D.C. 20016

Washington bureau for CNBC:
  1825 K St. NW, Suite 900
  Washington, D.C. 20006

NBC Radio News/Westwood One
  1755 South Jefferson Davis Hwy, Suite 1200
  Arlington, VA 22202

National Public Radio
  635 Massachusetts Ave. NW
  Washington, D.C. 20001
  http://www.npr.org

PBS
  1320 Braddock Place
  Alexandria, VA 22314
  http://www.pbs.org

NewsHour with Jim Lehrer:
  WETA-TV
  3620 South 27th St.
  Arlington, VA 22206

How to Identify: Answers to "Your turn" section.

So, in what ways were the stories on pages 57 to 59 biased? This is how the MRC analyzed them.

Story A. First, bias by spin as the piece matches the Democratic spin that the rich got away with murder in the '80s, instead of the conservative spin that while tax rates were reduced on the rich they actually ended up paying more taxes.

Second, bias by selection of sources. All three of Threlkeld's "man on the street" interviewees favored higher taxes on the rich. The only politician featured was a liberal Democrat, U.S. Representative Barbara Boxer, since elected to the Senate. And the experts were also pro-tax: Carol Cox's group campaigns for higher taxes. Kevin Phillips, who CBS cleverly (though accurately) labeled a "Republican political analyst," does not in any way provide balance to the story. In fact, his Reaganomics-bashing book *The Politics of Rich and Poor* was hot among Democrats at the time. So the story is completely one-sided in its sources.

Third, bias by omission. Here's where you may need an economic expert to point out what's slanted. We consulted Christopher Frenze, a staff economist on Capitol Hill with the Joint Economic Committee. Threlkeld did not attribute his statistics to any source, but they matched a March 1990 Congressional Budget Office (CBO) report titled "Tax Progressivity and Income Distribution." We found Threlkeld didn't even report the CBO figures honestly. While he said the bottom ten percent's taxes went up 28 percent from 1980-90 (as noted on page 30 of the report), he skipped over the next column in the CBO table: the bottom ten percent's tax share went *down* 15 percent from 1985-90. Threlkeld had juggled the numbers to make Reaganomics look bad.

Story B. Bias by selection of sources should have jumped out at you. To comment on a report from a liberal group dedicated to increasing government spending on food, James turned to? Two recipients and a member of the Hunger Coalition, which commissioned the study. She offered no soundbites from anyone with a different perspective.

Second, by failing to properly describe the Hunger Coalition as liberal, she committed bias by labeling. Indeed, anchor Stone Phillips was even more misleading, giving the study increased credibility by attributing it to UCLA without mentioning the Hunger Coalition. Furthermore, James also failed to properly identify the liberal nature of the Tufts University study claiming "12 million children are going to bed hungry." What's wrong with this isn't obvious at first, but it shows how you must sometimes do a little investigation of your own to track down facts left out. James was actually referring to the left-wing Center on Hunger, Poverty and Nutrition Policy at Tufts University.

By filing a story based solely upon a study issued by a liberal group, NBC showed bias by story selection. (If NBC also had aired a similarly one-sided story from the conservative position around the same time, then this would not reflect bias by story selection. But they didn't.) Finally, by relaying the liberal statistics as if they were indisputable, James exhibited bias by commission. She did not offer a soundbite from a conservative expert or even cite government figures compiled in a conservative study which would have shown how hunger is much less of a problem than the liberal activists contend.

About the Author

Brent H. Baker has served as Executive Director of the Media Research Center (MRC) since its founding in 1987. He is the Editor of the MRC's *MediaWatch* and *Notable Quotables* newsletters. *MediaWatch* is an eight-page monthly dedicated to documenting liberal bias in reporting, especially the TV networks. The two-page *Notable Quotables* is a bi-weekly compilation of quotes from the liberal media which reflect biased reporting. In 1996 Baker created *Media Research Center CyberAlert*, an e-mail service highlighting the latest bias.

At the end of each year, Baker coordinates production of "The Annual Awards for the Year's Worst Reporting," a collection of the best *Notable Quotables* from the previous year. The most biased quotes in 16 award categories are selected by a panel of 50 members of the media and media observers. In 1996 he edited *Media Reality Check '96*, a daily newsletter, fax and e-mail analyzing Republican and Democratic convention coverage. During the 1992 Democratic and Republican conventions, Baker edited *MediaWatch ConventionWatch*, a daily newsletter analyzing network coverage of the party conventions.

Baker was co-editor of *And That's the Way It Isn't: A Reference Guide to Media Bias*, a 1990 book containing excerpts, reprints and summaries of 45 studies documenting the media's liberal bias during the 1980s.

Before helping found the MRC, he was Editor of *Newswatch*, a newsletter published by the National Conservative Foundation. During college he edited a conservative student newspaper.

Baker's articles analyzing media coverage of current and political events have appeared in numerous newspapers, including the Colorado Springs *Gazette Telegraph*, *Union Leader* (Manchester, N.H.), *The Orange County Register*, *Wheeling Intelligencer*, *Panama City News Herald*, Cleveland *Plain Dealer* and *Human Events*. In addition, Baker has written pieces for *USA Today* magazine, *National Review*, *Journalism Quarterly* and *Vista*, the Hispanic Sunday newspaper supplement.

In 1985 Baker, who lived in Wellesley, Massachusetts before attending college, received a Bachelor of Arts degree with special honors in political science from George Washington University in Washington, D.C.

MRC Books

Pattern of Deception: The Media's Role in the Clinton Presidency, assembles a mountain of evidence proving how the liberal media, especially the television networks, have promoted the Clinton agenda, both during his campaign and his presidency.

And That's The Way It Isn't: A Reference Guide to Media Bias, now in its seventh printing, provides over 350 pages of summaries, excerpts and reprints of 45 studies that demonstrate the media's liberal bias. A one-stop resource containing all the facts and figures, examples and quotes proving the media's bias.

Out of Focus: Network Television and the American Economy "does for TV viewers what Consumer Reports does for car buyers," according to National Review. An in-depth analysis of how both news and entertainment shows undermine the free enterprise system.

MRC's Press Picks, includes over 700 recommended print, radio, and broadcast media professionals that are committed to fair and balanced journalism. Available in print, and on disk.

MRC PUBLICATIONS

MediaWatch, a monthly newsletter that reviews news coverage of political and current events by the television networks, newspapers, and news weeklies. Also, "Newsbites" provide ongoing examples of bias, and the "Janet Cooke Award" examines the month's most distorted story. Plus: in-depth studies and analysis.

MediaNomics, a monthly newsletter mailed along with *MediaWatch*, that examines national news coverage of business and economic issues and Hollywood's economic message. The "Issue Analysis" section reveals long-term trends in financial reporting and a back page essay explains how reporters could better cover the economy.

Notable Quotables, a bi-weekly compilation of the most outrageous and sometimes humorous examples of bias from the media. A year-end awards issue presents the best quotes of the year as determined by a distinguished panel of judges.

The Family Guide to Prime Time Television, is published annually, and is the most comprehensive study of the year's prime time fare. *The Family Guide* provides information on what shows may contain subject matter that is either offensive or inappropriate for children, and what shows promote family-friendly themes.

MRC PUBLICATION ORDER FORM

❑ *MediaWatch/MediaNomics* ($40 for 12 monthly issues)
❑ *Notable Quotables* ($24 for 26 bi-monthly issues)
❑ All three newsletters for one year ($50). Save $14!

❑ *Pattern of Deception* ($16.95)
❑ *And That's The Way It Isn't* ($14.95)
❑ *Out of Focus* ($19.95)
❑ *MRC's Press Picks* ($7.95)
❑ *The Family Guide to Prime Time Television* ($9.95)

Name _____

Address _____

_____

Phone _____

Method of Payment:

❑Check   ❑Visa   ❑MasterCard

Card Number _____

Expiration Date _____

Make check payable to Media Research Center

Media Research Center
Publications Department
113 South West Street, 2nd Floor
Alexandria, VA 22314